STENDHAL:

Notes on a Novelist

STENDHAL:

Notes on a Novelist

ROBERT M. ADAMS

MINERVA PRESS

Minerva Press edition published in 1968
by arrangement with Farrar, Straus & Giroux, Inc.

Publication of this book has been made possible by a grant
from the Hull Memorial Publication Fund of Cornell University.

Funk & Wagnalls, A *Division of* Reader's Digest Books, Inc.

Printed in the United States of America

For *J* knows who and *M* knows why

La vie est courte, et le temps perdu à bâiller ne se retrouve plus.
                                                    —Stendhal

Contents

Preface:

First Principles and Acknowledgments

For all that has been written about him, it is curious how little
has been done to estimate the literary stature of Henri Beyle,
who liked to call himself the Baron Stendhal. Curious, for he
is a spectacular example of a man ill esteemed by his contemporaries, who has enjoyed an impressive revival of fortunes over
the past fifty years. One would think it might be interesting to
explore the reasons for this change in status, by way of estimating its probable permanence. His literary reputation is, in a dim
way, splendid—that is, it is the fashion to refer to him as one
of the masters; and the conner of contemporary criticism will
find a good deal of this casual, knowing reference to Stendhal
on the periphery of other considerations. But he will find almost
nothing in English, and very little in French, to support the
central judgment. There are biographies and biographical studies
galore. With the fresh flood of Beyle-materials which started
to come in about 1890 (the *Journals* were first published in

1888, *Henry Brulard* in 1890, and *Souvenirs of Egotism* in 1892), came a whole series of studies, appreciations, editions, introductions, and reconsiderations. Above all, the discovery of these vast autobiographical materials—cryptic, detailed, and elaborate, as they were—invited the operations of biographical pickers and gleaners, in a vast vacuum-cleaner operation, the like of which has been seen only in the somewhat similar case of James Boswell. Half the fascination of this game lay in the fact that Beyle as autobiographer turned out to be satisfyingly inaccurate; there was not only a mean pleasure in correcting him but a kindlier sort of pleasure in estimating the drift and tendency of his errors. They served, more often than not, to satisfy a special dramatic flair; and many talents were fruitfully occupied for a long time in discovering Beyle's creative errors and assessing the habit of mind which they revealed. Another satisfying activity was the discovery of a multitude of detailed insights in which Beyle did or did not anticipate the observations of Freud and Marx.

It is no part of my present intention to deprecate these activities; I have followed many of them with pleasure and profit; have delighted in the meticulous wit of Paul Arbelet, the inexhaustible copiousness of Henri Martineau, the poetry of Jean Prévost, the charm and devotion of a hundred different disciples who have brought little items of fact and interpretation to the altar. But the question which they have largely taken for granted is the one which I—as an outsider from a doubly insular culture (not only Anglo-Saxon but American), with an outsider's naïveté but also perhaps with his fresh eye—have thought most needed discussion. (Discussion does not necessarily imply "impartial" investigation—simply by writing on a subject one becomes partisan, at least on the score of its importance—so much as a reasoned account of one's impressions and prejudices.) It seems to me that a modern approach to this author must start, almost of necessity, with a frank facing of the

question, Is Stendhal one of those writers who have slid into a
major literary reputation through a series of fascinating but
basically non-literary considerations? Is he, in fact, a great novelist or a great . . . character?

In the context of one popular school of contemporary criticism, this is a deadly question, amounting to nothing less than
the query whether Stendhal is any good at all. But I see no need
to take the matter at such a portentous estimate; historically,
all sorts of things go into the making of a literary reputation,
and to quarrel with them is to quarrel with life itself. Naturally,
the arts of literature are judged primarily by the things which
occur on the printed page, but a special interest often attaches
to the reflections and reverberations between the polished surface of art and the ambience which we call "life-not-art"—as if
somehow the categories were exclusive. But they are exclusive
only if we make them so; and sometimes it is not worth while
to try. Only a purist would attempt to separate Marcel the narrator of A *la recherche du temps perdu* from the historical Marcel Proust—nor are the facts and myths of Proust's life the least
fascinating aspects of that fantastic, infinite production which
is the novel. The real achievement of Coleridge is out of all
proportion to the finished literary works; we properly take account of his talk, his personal magnetism, and his influence on
others, whenever we discuss his contribution. There is no doubt
a value to the satires of Swift which is independent of his fascinating, cross-grained personality; but the unity which renders
them most fully comprehensible is a personal, individual development; and to impose rigid distinctions on work whose first
principle is to defy them, has rarely seemed fruitful. In a word,
there are literary and non-literary reasons for remembering
authors and their works; there are permanent and transitory
reasons; and there are good and bad reasons. I don't feel that
any one of these categories is quite congruent with any other.
And on these terms, the question of Stendhal's precise achieve-

ment need not involve anything more than an act of intellectual clarification, an answer to the question, What is it, exactly, that we should remember him for? There may turn out to be all sorts of corollaries to this question, but the less we allow them to inhibit our consideration of the question itself, the closer we may come to an understanding of Henri Beyle and his alter ego the Baron Stendhal.

Both of these charmingly disparate figures are necessary to the story of our hero, and to the statement of our "problems" concerning him—as Cervantes found both Don Quixote and Sancho Panza necessary to the creation of a novel. To consider Stendhal the novelist apart from Beyle the man might give one an impressive hierophantic air, but would muffle as many ideas as it invited. The studies which follow aim, no doubt adventurously, to discuss abstract ideas as freely as personalities; to pursue a series of themes without regard to chronological sequence; but to connect these themes, as Beyle himself persistently and systematically connected them, with personalities and episodes in his personal history and in his fiction. This approach seems deliberately unsystematic, and may prove irritating; its wild and whirling way with lesser unities has seemed the best way of coping with one larger unity, the complex figure of Beyle-Stendhal.

Made bold by this rationale, I have not hesitated to hop around, with grasshopper casualness, from book to book within Stendhal's bibliography and from period to period within Beyle's life, going forward and backward within a single study as occasion serves and the subject requires. The reader who wants the facts in order, the life laid out from head to tail, like a fish on a platter, is referred to books already widely available. Josephson's life is copious, full of errors of detail, and critically inept, but in its own coarse way, workmanlike; dwelling more on Beyle than on Stendhal, it tends to give us a figure attuned to Rabelais and Falstaff rather than to Ariosto and Cimarosa. Professor

Green is concerned more generously with the writings, which he analyzes in considerable detail; but some of the extravagances of Stendhalian feeling are a little beyond his sober English style. Harry Levin's *Toward Stendhal* is a short but characteristically brilliant piece, critically acute and biographically informed; for all its obvious limitations, it is quite the cleverest piece of writing on Stendhal in English. In French, Henri Martineau's *Le coeur de Stendhal* in two volumes is probably the best available handy abridgement of current scholarship; and his *Calendrier* and *Petit dictionnaire stendhalien* are models of orderly erudition, if not of *petitesse*. An authority on the early life of Beyle was the late Paul Arbelet, whose classic comic studies (*La jeunesse de Stendhal, Stendhal épicier*) are unlikely ever to be superseded. *Stendhal romancier* by Maurice Bardèche is a shrewd and witty study, from a highly suspect political angle, but with much insight into the fiction and its values. Jean Prévost in *La creation chez Stendhal* has many acute and complex things to say about the mental processes out of which they were written. François Michel's collected short pieces represent, in their severity, clarity, and detailed particularity, a classic right-wing view of Stendhal (*Etudes stendhaliennes*); Victor Brombert, less dependable and more ambitious, represents a growing and potentially vigorous left-wing view (*Stendhal et la voie oblique*). Among Italian Beylistes, the work of Luigi Foscolo Benedetto, Pietro Paolo Trompeo, and Vittorio del Litto should certainly be signalized. The Divan edition of Stendhal's works, in 79 volumes, is the latest re-editing; though not so rich in apparatus as a work of its scope should be, or as older editions of particular works are apt to be, it is a monument.

In the course of writing this study I have sometimes plundered the works listed above, sometimes departed from their findings; and for the most part without leaving any specific record of my comings and goings. To write a slow, heavy book about a quick, light author has never seemed a profitable pastime; so I allowed Stendhal, whenever he would, to impose his own procedure. The first law which he decreed was no polemic and a minimum of paraphernalia. For a man of naturally contentious temper, the first of these injunctions was a hard and alien law, but it seemed worth submitting to. My aim was to present a living soul, a mind in action; and to clutter the foreground by disagreeing with Mlle. Albérès, amending Signor Carpaccio, picking at the emphases of M. Arbelet, and taking exception to detailed touches developed by M. Martineau in the course of a discussion contributed to by Herr Doktor Bergler, Professor Stryienski, and Miss Gunnell—would have been to defeat my purpose entirely.

Better an ignorant than a cluttered book—one can go terribly wrong on this principle, but if one is ever to write dangerously, what better place to start than Stendhal? So I have written from the texts themselves, which for better than two years now have been my constant and intimate companions. I have not tried to talk about all of them, or say the last word about any of them; but to question them with that humane, glancing, and speculative eye which Beyle paid us the infinite compliment of hoping for in the twentieth century, having despaired of it in the nineteenth.

Paraphernalia, though less difficult to eschew, was difficult. The literature on and about Stendhal has grown by now to the point where it is only less bulky than that on Shakespeare. From the beginning I had to exercise rigid control over this mountain of material; and did so, by the ruthless application of an intimate rule—the minute anything bored me, I put it down. This is not a good rule to follow in Milton scholarship; perhaps it is not a good rule to follow anywhere. But I dare to hope that it has been less than fatal to the writing of a book on Stendhal because the things written about our friend are extraordinarily interesting. No doubt many of them are unjust to the amazing thickness and complexity of Stendhal's psychological patterning, but still they are interesting. Read with a certain generosity of feeling, they are so nearly right as to make quarrelsome footnotes and petulant citations more than usually offensive. It is silly, for example, to talk about the *Charterhouse* as a simple fantasy of wish-fulfillment; but it is not untrue that there is a note of triumph to the book which is far less marked in *The Red and the Black*, and which is wholly missing from *Armance*. Nobody has really failed to see that Fabrizio is an essential innocent; to see that some of his corruption is also essential makes the novel a more tense and amusing structure, and gets the weight off a conflict between the individual and society which could become flat and obvious. But in criticism most of our decisions are between the more true and the less true, rather than between the true and the false.

What "outside," i.e., secondary sources I did use are most imperfectly recorded; as I did not feel obliged to refute every theory with which I disagreed, so I have not felt it necessary or possible to indicate all my agreements or even all my obligations. The field has been thoroughly picked over, and as I lay no claim to originality (what is an original critic but a fraud on his author or a metaphysician, i.e., a fraud on the public?— as well set up for an original translator!), those who are made happy by such a thought may realize that every grain of wheat has been picked over a hundred times, disputed, valued, and revalued. Thus all but the broadest outlines of the career are subject to dispute and varying interpretation—disputes and variations through which I have threaded an uneasy way which many may think mistaken in one particular after another. One prime end of scholarship is to promote uncertainty. Granted, then, the infinite complexity of that reality which I have rendered, as it were, with a whitewash brush on a postcard—yet I thought there were reasons why this vortex of complexities might be kept from bristling across every page of a work which is clearly introductory.

As for the portrait of Beyle-Stendhal which has emerged, it must be submitted to the judgment of those who know and love him. It is radical in few particulars, Beyle being so balanced a man that it is almost impossible to assert one thing about him without provoking an equal and opposite counter-assertion. His motivations were almost never pure or simple; his novels are complicated, counterpointed structures of thought and feeling. His gifts for irony and sentiment were equal. If there is one secure and fundamental principle in his life, which never changes, it is instability. The way in which he made himself a writer is the best way to make oneself his reader; not by plodding attention to exact verbal details, but by developing a habit of response to subtle, swift shifts of mood and inflections of social tone. If I have had an emphasis to add, it is that I do not think Stendhal can be read with too much energy. The lightest riffle of irony across the polished features of a count, a shade too much politeness in a phrase delivered by a bishop, and immense structures collapse. This is fine, and fun. But it is not enough to relish their fall, one must be ready at a moment's notice to rebuild them. Stendhal was not really an ironist with an overlay of sentiment, nor a sentimentalist lurking beneath a surface of irony; he was not even committed consistently to the opposition of these two principles. He was totally uncommitted; absolutely unfinal; responsive to experience in a way more fluid than logical categories can ever quite grasp. He sees a situation as sublime, he sees it as ridiculous; the sublime may override the irony, the irony undercut the sublime, or the contrast may remain, troublesome and unresolved. Stendhal loves to test his characters' reactions, and his reader's, by putting his heroes up against situations more and more difficult for their "natural" emotional bent. And there is more than a touch of perversity in the way a "natural" character sometimes reacts ironically to a situation in which even an "ironic" character might be expected to react naturally. Mosca the ironist who once served Napoleon defends the prince's statue; he would die for it. Gina the great court lady has the prince himself poisoned. Yet there is no real difference between them; the count is slightly surprised to learn that his mistress has killed his master, but the matter is not worth talking about. In the great American pastime, this sort of thing is known as "change of pace," and nothing makes a simple soul with both feet on the ground and his worldly energies at full coil, nothing makes him flounder more delightfully. The fiction of Stendhal at its best is a competition of equilibriums.* To feel "upset" by it is a tribute to the author, if not exactly to the reader.

It is probably extreme to suggest that Stendhal's novels exclude, counter, and tease the reader as a form of mimic revenge on a century which had excluded him, to the limit of its power, from the positions he sought. But the fact of alienation pervades Stendhal's life and is important in the pattern of his fiction as it is for few other nineteenth-century novelists. Looking at the questions of the day, he came up with unpopular answers; he was also unusually preoccupied with a number of almost private questions, for which he sought answers to satisfy a streaky but often meticulous conscience. He lived in his own personality to an extraordinary degree, and found it not a narrow tower but a various landscape.

Because of his peculiar commitments, he is an uneven and erratic writer, whose problem is often to write up to his best inspirations. The problem he sets himself is not to be solved by grinding up the elements of a situation, as Flaubert does, and recombining the elements imaginatively. He does not visualize particularly well, does not see society very broadly or the in-

---

* And not only the fiction—the seemingly solemn treatises and histories too are booby-trapped with poker-faced humor. How else to take the little essay on noses in the *Histoire de la Peinture?* Having established that "l'air niais" comes from little noses, Beyle goes on to argue that "à mesure qu'on avance en Italie, les nez augmentent; ils sont sans mesure dans la grande Grèce." II, 36-37.

dividual down to his abysmal depths. Pathos and piety are closed books to him; he knows no more of high moral serious- ness than of blood-and-bowels mysticism. What he communi- cates surpassingly is the fluid, vibrant feel of life lived with all the faculties, in constant change, in perpetual, shifting imbal- ance, on several levels at once. Hence the quickness and mo- bility of his style; hence the appearance of carelessness.

Because he knew himself so well, and delighted to look at himself from different speculative angles, there is an endless intimate pleasure about the autobiographical writings of Beyle. It is perhaps a special taste, but nothing in literature gives one more the sense of sharing in the life of a frank, witty, and sensitive friend. His fictional characters are extraordinarily *in- carnate*; though there is little physical description, we know the physical gestures of Gonzo, Rassi, the Abbé Pirard, Fabrizio. And so it is with the mind of Henri Beyle; its latent actions are often more vivid than those which lie on the surface of his description. The so-called "Priviléges" are a literary curiosity, a grant of magical powers made by the Baron Stendhal to him- self. (They include invisibility, altered identity, the gift of tongues, some rather modest sexual privileges, money.) But the habit of mind which they bespeak in a man approaching sixty is striking. It is a mind which wants to know what things look or feel like on the other side of various barriers which surround it—a mind restless, inquisitive, capricious. If one says it is the mind of an eternal adolescent, this is likely to sound condescend- ing to a generation which has chosen "maturity" as one of its OK-catchwords. But it is also a mind which never wears out or becomes blasé, which is perpetually open to new forms of ex- perience, as well as to the sophisticated counterpoints which can be built from its naïve exploration of differing points of view. It is, I believe, one of the rare and wonderful minds of the world, in the presence of which one feels perpetually renewed, perpetually enriched.

Thus I have written, as I read, for pleasure; carried away here and there by a bit of rebuttal, but mostly in the declarative mood. So far as libraries are concerned, I owe to them quite simply everything I know, right and wrong; they are the repositories of human nature, and the only place where it can be studied with that cool and lucid respect which is proper to scholarship. There is not an assertion in this book, the genesis of which could not be traced back to one of the following: The Cornell University Library, the Columbia University Library, the Cambridge University Library, the Bibliothèque Nationale, the Biblioteca Nazionale di Firenze, the New York Public Library, or my brother Philip's collection in the garden house at Weston, Connecticut. I am grateful to all those who kept the books for me, gave them to me when I wanted them, and put them back on the shelf when I was finished.

My education in the world of Stendhal, still lamentably incomplete, was advanced immeasurably by the accidents and incidents of a trip to France and Italy. I had the immense pleasure of encountering the Fiscal Rassi in Rome; he was, at the moment, impersonating the head of the claque at the Opera House, but there was no disguising his real nature. In the Palazzo dei Exhibizioni, I ran into Beyle himself—bold, ironic, and broad-beamed, with receding hairline, wicked black sideburns, and his hands clasped behind his back; he was looking, appropriately, at a Correggio. In Florence I knew briefly Milady G—; we discussed tragicomedy till two in the morning, and I was struck by her intuitive grasp of the subject. I have passed Fabrizio several times in the street; I think I once knew Julien Sorel rather intimately. I have not yet met Métilde, Mosca, or the Duchessa Sanseverina; but one lives in hope.

The writing of this book was suggested by Mr. Frederick Morgan, editor of the *Hudson Review*; Chapter II appeared in this periodical (Winter, 1958), and I am indebted to him for so much more, that a full accounting would be tedious. It was a *Hudson Review* Fellowship in Literary Criticism which provided the leisure for this book to grow in; it was six solitary, convulsive weeks at Yaddo, the literary-artistic foundation at Saratoga Springs, which brought the greater part of it into physical existence. I am grateful to the staff at Yaddo, and to my sponsors; among whom was the editor of the *Hudson Review*.

For various acts of encouragement and kindness during the genesis and pruning of this book I owe debts of gratitude to the Cornell Research Council; to my colleagues of the Cornell English Department, especially Professors Meyer Abrams and Joseph Mazzeo; to Professor Jean-Jacques Demorest, of the Cornell Department of Romance Literature; and to Professore Guido Corsi Agnolucci, of Rome and Montevarchi.

To Elaine and Nicholas Adams another sort of tribute is due; it is greater and sadder than words can convey.

Ithaca, New York
August 12, 1957

STENDHAL:

Notes on a Novelist

1

※

A Biographical Summary

Men do not understand how that which draws apart agrees with itself; harmony lies in the bending back, as for instance of the bow and of the lyre.

Heraclitus, 45

Justifiably, no doubt, biographies of Beyle are always bulky. The man left such an elaborate record of the things that happened to him, he analyzed his reactions to his experience in such detail, he introduced episodes from his own life under so many colors into his fiction—and, finally, he has been followed in all three directions by so many assiduous scholars and perceptive critics—that the accumulated details often seem overwhelming. Henri Martineau, cutting his narrative to the bone, managed to cram the essential facts into two solid volumes. To digest such a digest into a mere twenty pages or so smacks of a literary Spanish inquisition; it is applying to biography the boot, the thumbscrews, and the Iron Maiden, all at once. Yet some such task is inevitable. If one writes on Beyle in English, one anticipates an audience to whom the topic is in some degree exotic; readers, in fact, who are not beyond need of a quick preliminary summary of the salient biographical and critical facts. To those of my readers who find the offer of such a summary impertinent, I can only apologize humbly and offer a short cut to p. 25.

Very well; Marie Henri Beyle was born of middle-class parents at Grenoble in 1783; he died at Paris in 1842. He is best known nowadays for two novels published after he was 45—*The Red and the Black* (published in 1830, though the first edition bears the date 1831) and *The Charterhouse of Parma* (1839); but if his life be summarized in three verbs, as he tried to do it for an epitaph, "wrote" will have to take third place, after "lived" and "loved" (*visse, scrisse, amò*). Though he took turns at writing journalism, criticism, dramas, verse, political commentary, travel-books, biographies, journals, autobiographies, government reports, and short stories, in addition to the eight volumes of full-length fiction by which his reputation now stands, he was not, and never considered himself, a professional man of letters. At different times in his life he was a soldier, an administrator, a clerk in a wholesale grocery, a dilettante, a student of acting, a travelling salesman in the leather-goods line, a consul, a tutor, a lady's man, and a talker in salons. Considered as professional specialties, some of these occupations are not very distinct; but Beyle often found himself without a distinct professional specialty. At 35 he inherited some money from his father, whom he despised perfectly, but it was not as much as he had expected, or nearly as much as he needed; he was often poor, and none of his writings achieved the sort of success which might have alleviated his poverty. Balzac's puff for the *Charterhouse* came little more than a year before Beyle's death, and it was never widely echoed while he was alive.

A striking feature of his life was its perfectly unsettled and peripatetic character. During the greater part of his existence, Beyle had no settled home; he lived in furnished rooms, hotels, or lodgings; and he moved about constantly. Out of the last thirty years of his life, there are no more than four or five which are not marked by major expeditions of one sort or another. Though Paris, Milan, and (at the very end of his life) Civitavecchia were the centers from which he radiated, he often passed through them as if in a hurry to start a new trip almost before he had finished the old one. It is a rare moment when the biographer can find him, for as long as six months on end, at the same address.

Half in jest, half out of a genuine sense of persecution and desire for privacy, he shifted pseudonyms as often as residences; becoming, in his own mind, or for the edification of his intimates, such various personages as Mr. Myself, Leiméry, M. de Léry, Auguste, Alceste, Tempête, L. Roux, Chapuis, Col Favier, Dupuy, Fauris Saint-Bard, Dubois du Bée, D. Gruffo Papera, C. Simonetta, C.F. Ravet *ainé*, Harry, George Simple, Z. Joseph Charrin, Hor. de Cluny, Cher. de Cutendre, Chomont, Du Boys, Periner, Comte Change, Baron Relguir, Comte de Chablis, Dupellée, Chauvin, Lunenbourg, Louis-Alexandre César Bombet, Hector C.C. Bombet, Dominique, Junius, Banti, Choppin D'Ornouville, Condotti 48, Capeva, Cotonet, Costes, Casimir, Caumartin, Blaise Durand, Durand-Robet, Timoléon Tisset, Timoléon Gaillard, Timoléon Brenet, Timoléon Du Bois, Sphinx, Baron Raisinet, Baron Dormant, Baron Boudon, Baron Patault, Seymours, Don Flegme, Poruth, Anastase de Serpière, Léonce D., Adolphe de Seyssels, Jules Pardessus, A.-L. Feburier, Is. Ich. Charlier, Gaillard, Meynier, Roger, Tamboust, Mequillet, Chomont, General Pellet, Machiavelli B., Old Hummums, William Crocodile, Horace Smith, Edmond de Charency, Porcheron, A.L. Capello, La Borde, Chappier des Ilets, Chincilla, P.F. Piouf, Polybe Love-Puff, De La Palice-Xaintrailles *ainé*, Lavardin, Duversy, Ths. Jefferson, Rowe, Besanc.,

Ch. de Saupicquet, Tombouctou, Poverino, Smith & Co., and many others. In 1817 he tried out the pseudonym of M. de Stendhal, and because *Rome, Naples, and Florence*, the book to which he signed it, was fairly successful, he used it with reasonable consistency for the rest of his life.

In matters where secrecy seems impossible as well as uncalled-for, Beyle was still punctilious about preserving a mystery. He retained drafts of letters to a Milanese mistress, full of local allusions and particular circumstances, under a heading which indicated that they had been translated from the English. He put footnotes alongside the MSS of his unpublished novels, indicating that he thought all the subversive speeches were delivered by idiots. He wrote a foreword to his autobiography, for the exclusive benefit of the police, indicating that the MS was a novel, in imitation of *The Vicar of Wakefield*. For greater secrecy, he wrote his private papers in a peculiar gibberish, compounded of English, Italian, and French, with special code names, initials, anagrams, diagrams, and puns; the fact that his handwriting was execrable often provided better protection, but a brief sample of the dialect may serve to illustrate his procedure. "Au dernier avekon the France had given cluzion ex to the K. Kim" should be translated to read "au dernier conclave la France a donné l'exclusion contre le cardinal Macchi" (*Mélanges de littérature*, I, 78).* He was continually reading over his own prose and expressing approval or disapproval of it, with dates and circumstances carefully indicated, but often from very curious points of view. For instance, we find a note on the margin of a copy of *Rome, Naples, and Florence:* "The 4th of

---

* One can only lament the failure of François Michel to complete his contemplated *Petit manuel de cryptographie stendhalienne*—not that the paltry transpositions of our author offer a problem on which the hardened cryptanalyst needs help, but for the comedy of M. Michel's testy disappointment at the shallowness of Beyle's evasions. See "Les alibis de Stendhal," in *Nouvelles soirées du Stendhal-club*, pp. 79-104.

February, 1817, I was at Pozzuoli. Thus I saw Naples at the same time as M. de Stendal, whom I find a great liar. He's a liberal-Jacobin" (*Mélanges intimes*, II, 23-24). The handwriting is Beyle's.

Beyle had not only a passion for secrecy but also a passion for lists, dates, specific circumstances, and exact details. He liked to make notes of amorous conquests on his suspenders, and to scribble the intimate details of his life in random books, scraps of paper, old envelopes, laundry lists, or the cuffs of his shirts. There are delightful contradictions here for the psychologically minded. A man with Beyle's devotion to precise details, precut patterns of conduct, and systems of behavior is clearly standing guard against strong and unwelcome impulses from his unconscious; a man with Beyle's devotion to the unexpected is clearly impatient of the regularity he has been able to impose on his existence. A man with Beyle's passion for secrecy is not often found under the same skin with a man possessing Beyle's passion for self-disclosure and self-analysis. He was instinctively a rebel from the age of ten, because the overthrow and execution of Louis XVI foretold the overthrow and execution of his father, who also exercised a stupid tyranny with the aid of priests; but he admired passionately the *ancien regime*, was greatly impressed by aristocracy (impelling François Michel to the happy coinage, "ducomanie"), bestowed a false title on himself, and rather shrank from plebeian acquaintances. He made use of his democratic opinions, for the most part, by concealing them, pretending that they were wildly wicked and dangerous, and rejoicing in the persecutions which he either created in this way, or imagined. Always the pattern of his life was to use one of two conflicting psychological elements to conceal the other. Thus an expression of "romantic" feelings (which he tended to associate with Italian experiences, and his mother's originally-Italian family) was almost always protected by flanking demonstrations of

French irony, French rationalism, French wit and cynicism.

So far as historical incidents on the grand scale are concerned, the major episodes of Beyle's career were three. In 1800, aged just 17, he left his post as a minor clerk in the Paris war-office, rode to join Napoleon in Italy, and wangled a temporary commission as sub-lieutenant of cavalry. He did not fight at Marengo, though in later life he sometimes claimed to have done so; but he heard shots fired in what is conventionally called anger, heard Italian opera, particularly Cimarosa, especially the *Matrimonio segreto*; and saw the beautiful women of Milan fired with enthusiasm for youth, vigor, and something ambiguous called "republican virtue" as exemplified in the French army. In 1812 he went to Moscow with Napoleon; bored and frozen stiff by the countryside and by his fellow-soldiers, whom he found unbearably coarse and stupid, he nonetheless stood firm, and kept his head in the crisis. From this experience one may perhaps date a certain hardness and cynicism of temper which inured him, henceforth, to some sentimental and silly considerations which had troubled his youth. Finally, when Napoleon fell from power in 1814, Beyle fell with him—not gracefully or romantically, but with an awkward and satisfying thud. Giving up his post in the bureaucracy, his two carriages, his pretty little opera-singer, his hopes of a prefecture and perhaps even grander things to come, he retired to Milan, and lived in genteel poverty, cultivating his sensibility, writing books, and falling in and out of love. Denounced as a liberal by the Milan police in 1821, he was forced to return to Paris, where, between a pension, an inheritance, and journalism, he supported himself precariously for about a decade. Over the last twelve years of his life he had intermittent employment in government service, which he handled skilfully when he condescended to concern himself with it, and neglected as much as he dared.

His love affairs, which were perhaps the major occupation of

his life, are harder to describe. He was passionately in love with
his mother, though she died when he was only six. This was a
physical, possessive, exclusive, and devouring impulse, which he
was to anatomize brilliantly in *The Life of Henry Brulard*. It
influenced him profoundly, and in more ways than one can
readily define; but it scarcely qualifies as an *affaire du cœur* in
the ordinary limited sense. From a timid distance he cherished
an adolescent infatuation for an actress named Virginia Kubly
(she left Grenoble when he was just 15), and another for a girl
in Grenoble named Victorine Mounier (which perished for lack
of encouragement when he was about 18). But his first real
love affair was with an actress named Mélanie Guilbert or
Mélanie Louason or Mélanie Saint-Albe whom he met in 1804.
This accumulation of serried surnames suggests, correctly, a
somewhat checkered past; Mlle. Louason (her stage name, but
also the one most used by Beyle) was already accompanied by
one frail little memento of her episodic career, a daughter of
tender years. But though she herself was somewhat less than a
pristine article, and Beyle a veteran of the glamorous Italian
campaign of 1800, he approached her with all the hesitations
and misgivings of an adolescent country boy soliciting the hand
of a princess. At the age of 21, he was not, in fact, a practised or
even a competent amorist. He had read widely in the scabrous
literature, and acquired, from worldly conversations with his
libertine uncle Romain Gagnon, a most particular perception of
his duties toward the opposite sex; but he still saw them as
duties, which a strict sense of his own merit imposed on him.
Nature had not formed his spirit to be that of a roué. Indeed,
he had or developed the spirit and technique of an accomplished *frotteur* in dealing with tavern-wenches; but once en-
meshed in the higher enterprises of seduction, he was likely
to prove prolix, self-conscious, and slow. At all events, after a
lengthy courtship he was permitted to accompany Mlle. Loua-

son to Marseilles, where she was going to join a repertory company; and there, after a maddeningly sedate and chaste journey, she finally became his mistress.*

She was pretty and kind, she was an actress, and she thought he was wonderful; years later, he still thought she had been one of his greatest loves. M. Bardèche says unkindly that she was for Beyle "the mistress one has at 22, from whom one learns how to make love and how to call articles of lingerie by the right name" (p. 95). This seems a little severe; yet the fact remains that Beyle did not make a convincing move in the direction of marrying her, for reasons into which it is useless to inquire. Perhaps he simply thought her *bête*; at all events, after less than a year of irregular bliss (July 1805-March 1806), they drifted apart. He met her once again, quite by accident, amid the looted ruins of Moscow, where she had gone as the wife of a General Barkoff; Beyle helped her back to civilization, and there tried to revive tender flames; but they were dead.

The years of his public career in the service of the Empire (1807-1814) were, on the whole, years of erotic as of emotional and intellectual stagnation for Beyle. There were tentative affairs with German girls, Philippine von Bulow and Wilhelmina von Griesheim; there was a vague little creature named Babet, in Vienna. In Paris he slept for a while with a little *terza donna* from the Italian opera company which played at the Odéon, a Jewess named Angela Bereyter, with whom he set up the only ménage he seems ever to have established with any of his mistresses. And he pursued, with such stealthy precautions that she does not seem actually to have been aware of the pursuit, Mme. Alexandrine Daru, wife of Pierre Daru, Beyle's distant cousin,

---

* Paul Arbelet's *Stendhal épicier* offers the classic account of this affair; the annals of biographical devotion know nothing finer than the mingled finesse, precision, and persistence with which Arbelet managed to deduce, from certain marks on Mélanie's calendar for April and June, that she could not conveniently have been seduced during the course of her journey from Paris, in mid-May.

his immediate military superior, his protector, benefactor, and
the author of all his preferment. Mme. Daru had borne her
energetic and practical husband no fewer than six matter-of-fact
children; though just Beyle's age, she was far older in the wisdom
of the world—in fact, she was, in the dry, French way, sensible.
Even granting him some credit for frankness in avowing his own
interested motives, Beyle does not cut a very elegant figure in
this relationship. At least, he was spared the humiliations which
must, almost surely, have followed an avowal.

But, whether because they were too easy or too difficult, none
of these women touched his imagination, and none left a significant mark on his mind. Far otherwise with an old acquaintance whom he stumbled upon, almost without conscious purpose, during the summer of 1811. That was the year he returned
to Milan. Eleven years before, a sensitive and excited boy, he
had watched the turbulent Milanese make much of their French
liberators. He had admired a lieutenant, one Louis de Joinville,
and, more even than the lieutenant, his Milanese mistress.
This was a fine, handsome, black-haired girl named Angela
Pietragrua, who was about 23 years old when Beyle first saw
her; and whom he rediscovered, a fine, handsome, black-haired
woman of 34, upon his return to Milan. They met, he reminded
her of old times, said he had been in love with her, and was
charmed with the simplicity of her reply. "But why didn't you
say so?" she asked him, in a rather open invitation to make up
for lost time.

In Angela Pietragrua, Beyle found not only a fascinating mistress—bold, comic, impulsive, experienced; he found also a play-
mate who appealed irresistibly to his own sense of the dramatic.
She had a sense of danger and a sense of pleasure; she acted
with unhesitating violence on whatever impulse happened to
stir her primitive soul. And thus she became the first of his
mistresses who "carried over" recognizably into his writings; it
was around her irresistibly impetuous figure that Stendhal in

the last years of his life crystallized the magnificent image of
the Duchess Angela Pietranera who controls so much of *The
Charterhouse of Parma*. And it was evidently the fascination
which she exercised over him which brought him back to Milan
again, after Napoleon fell in 1814.

She it was who occupied his days and nights during the first
part of that glorious seven-years' idleness which was the growing time of Stendhal's soul. While he dallied in her arms, the
Hundred Days came and went; the mournful reverberations of
Waterloo drifted back to our sentimental Ulysses, beguiled in
a Fortunate Isle. Unhappily, as Angela proved more and more
difficile, the Isle gradually became less and less Fortunate. She
deceived Beyle egregiously with other lovers, she stage-managed
her affable husband into a black beast with a stiletto ravening
for the blood of innocent lovers, she grubbed for money. Finally
she made life so hard for the pliable Beyle that, after a series
of atrocious quarrels, in 1815 he gave her up.

The empery of Mélanie, the age of Angela; they were succeeded, in 1818, by the great musical movement of Mathilde
Viscontini-Dembowska. Unlike the others, she never gave herself to Beyle; unlike the others, she touched the deepest, the
most primitive, the least resolved chords of his nature. She was
a Milanese of some 28 years, possessed of two children, sepa-
rated from her Polish husband, fragile, fearless, diabolically
proud, and dimly associated with the popular middle-class sedi-
tion of carbonarism. Beyle's experience with her was almost
pure unrequited misery, for she would not have him, on any
terms at all. Several times he was on the point of suicide. Yet
there were memories—of an evening in a garden, too delicious
to be described, of a smile which gave him infinite hope, of a
phrase which might be thought ambiguous—and these lent to
his passion a depth and complexity which finally burst into
expression in a book of analysis and confession, *De l'Amour*.
His love for Mathilde, though never anything but one-sided,

continued long after the Austrian police, suspecting him of political heresy, forced him to leave Milan in the middle of 1821. It was only on the 22nd of May, 1824, that in consequence of a surprising and wholly unexpected victory over a new enemy, Beyle could pronounce himself "cured" of Mathilde. She died less than a year later, of tuberculosis, alas, and not of love for Henri Beyle.

The new enemy—Beyle's terminology in affairs of the heart was unfailingly and scrupulously military—was a plain, clever, thin, passionate woman, titled, unhappily married, mother of three, daughter of an old friend of Beyle's; the Countess Clementine Curial. "Stendhal had a grand passion to dispose of," says M. Bardèche drily; "she took advantage of it" (p. 131). With Menti Beyle carried on the richest, wildest, and most tumultuous of his love affairs. Even for a countess, she had an extraordinarily sweeping command of the invective mood. From the few samples surviving, one can see the fine flow of her 215 letters to him, unhampered alike by logic or punctuation; and her imagination was as theatrical as that of Angela herself. She hid her lover in cellars so she could wait on him hand and foot, she raved at him for liking Italian opera-singers, especially Mme. Giuditta Pasta, she relished with explicit enthusiasm his carefully-cultivated prowess in bed. Altogether, she was a rousing good cure for the dumps and depressions in which Mathilde had left him; and when Menti in turn passed on to a new cycle of lovers (June 1826), even Beyle's despair had something healthy and energetic about it. The usual term of her interest in lovers was six months; she had been with him a little more than two years.

In 1829 he had a short, passionate affair with Alberthe de Rubempré who lived in the Rue Bleue, and was therefore baptised, for Beyle's correspondence, Mme. Azur; he sometimes called her Sanscrit because she went in for esoteric learning. Her cousin was Delacroix, her next lover after Beyle was Méri-

mée, and she then settled into the happy hands of Baron
Adolphe de Mareste, who looked after her and his 22,000 francs
of yearly income for the rest of their lives. Meanwhile, the in-
defatigable Beyle—approaching fifty, corpulent, short of breath,
gouty, apoplectic, bewigged, yet still a dandy in dress and manners—was the object of new advances, made by a girl as direct
and passionate as she was perceptive. This was Signorina Giulia
Rinieri, a young lady of about thirty from Siena, who found the
old gentleman with the keen eye and acid tongue very com-
panionable and in fact deeply attractive.* One day early in
1830 she came, and, standing directly in front of him, said with
some emphasis, "I've seen for a long time that you are old and
ugly"; and, kissing him passionately, she declared her willingness
to be his mistress. It was an odd beginning; he felt its oddness
and did not dissemble his unreadiness. But after some hesitation
and with a truly touching sense of wonder at such unexpected
good fortune, he took her as she desired to be taken, and was
happy. The sex for which he had suffered so much made ample
amends in the end.

His love for Giulia was a new and special experience for this
jaded and somewhat disappointed man; and in November of
1830 he actually proposed that they should be married. But
worldly wisdom was all against the match; some specious excuses were found; and while Beyle was occupied with consular
chores at Civitavecchia, he learned that Giulia had been be-
trothed and then quickly married to a cousin of hers, Giulio
Martini. It was a bitter pill; but she managed to sweeten it, at
a subsequent meeting, by showing him in the only convincing

* After passing for many years as a child of twenty when she first became
Beyle's mistress, Giulia has recently undergone sizable modifications at the
hands of L. F. Benedetto, who demonstrated that she was born in 1801,
not (as previously supposed) 1810. See Benedetto's criticism of his own
Indiscretions sur Giulia in *Arrigo Beyle Milanese* (Firenze, 1942), 504-05.

way that her marriage had made no difference whatever in their relation.

Giulia was the last, though probably not the most deeply felt of his loves. He had subsequently a few cool-blooded skirmishes with a mysterious Roman lady whom he called Earline; he found a buxom young creature in Civitavecchia, whom, alas, he could not marry, and a mature but appreciative lady, Mme. Bouchot, *alias* La Cecchina, in whose company for a moment he managed to surprise even himself with a final flareup of residual energy. But Giulia, essentially, brings to an end the great dynasty of sultanas which Mélanie began.

This reckoning leaves out of account all sorts of minor episodes, liaisons, and passing partnerships; it takes no notice, on the one hand, of *les filles*, whom Beyle despised but sometimes patronized to the detriment of his health; nor does it regard a whole host of friends, artistes, and acquaintances of both sexes and many nationalities, with whom Beyle was on familiar terms in Paris, London, Milan, and Rome.* It is simply a listing of his major feminine preoccupations, in crude chronological order. But I do not think one need apologize either for the quantity or for the variety of emotional response which it displays. For a naturally shy man, who had to earn his living most of his life and who managed to write 79 volumes in his spare time, Beyle achieved a highly respectable amorous performance. Certain constants in the record invite our comment. Beyle rarely sought or thought of marriage. Most of his mistresses had previously

---

* For example, among the women who caught Beyle's passing fancy were such charmers as the Countess della Chiesa, Charlotte Knabelhuber, Livia Bialowieska, Mme. de Gency, Mme. Galice (7 times!), Adèle Rebuffel and her mother, Mme. Jules Gaulthier ("Bien attaquée, bien défendue, pas de traité, pas de défaite, tout est gloire dans les deux camps."), Amalia Bettini, Nina Vigano, the Countess Cassera, Miss Appleby, Rachele, Virginia, Luisina, Elisa, and enough P's, F's, J's, V's, etc. to float a bowl of alphabet soup.

been married and most had children. Beyle did not make love
to girls, he sought out mature women; they were of every class,
and he seems rarely to have been particularly attracted (or repelled) in his attachments by titles, money, or social status. As
these things go, his affairs tended to be protracted rather than
brief; and, generally speaking, his mistresses tended to leave him
before he was ready to leave them. No woman ever pined for
Henri Beyle as he pined for Angela, for Mathilde, for Menti.
His typical role was that of the unhappy lover; was not his
typical mistress one who could almost be counted on to make
him unhappy?

Psychological generalizations of this sort make their object-
victim look like an ingenious mechanism slightly out of control. To correct this impression, it might be useful to mention a
couple of dark and undeveloped aspects of Stendhal's life,
which confuse the pattern, and are hard to relate to it or to
assign an importance within it. He acquired a case of syphilis
in Milan at the age of 17, and half-cured it by doses of mercury,
sweating-baths, and exercise; but it remained latent all his life,
and was apparently responsible, in its tertiary stage, for his
death. This is an ugly underside, not only of his promiscuity,
but of his *tendresse,* and perhaps even of his much-discussed
fiascos. Equally mysterious though rather less scabrous is the
question of his relation to free-masonry. For about a year (1806-
07) he was definitely a member of a strategic, "headquarters"
lodge of free-masons, most of whom were staff-officers and administrative bigwigs for Napoleon. How long Beyle maintained
his connections and what functions he was able to make them
serve in later years are matters on which scholarship is still indefinite. He sometimes found it surprisingly easy to get pass-
ports when he needed them; his entry into the consulship at
Civitavecchia (through the granting of a papal *exequatur*) was
certainly smoothed by "connections" both high and low. Where
else did the masonic symbols enable him to penetrate? What

influence did masonry have on his concept of society as a mask concealing the warfare of disciplined but mysterious secret organizations? These are problems of considerable interest to the weaver of psychological and political patterns. But homosexuality and impotence, much mooted by the psycholettrists, seem like dead ends. Beyle suffered a fiasco now and then, he admired an occasional attractive male; only the complete innocent will see in these situations more than an ordinary experience reported with extraordinary simplicity and truth.

To weave into this tangled chronicle of his life and loves the story of Henri Beyle's writings will be a task of some complexity. His correspondence (the surviving part of which occupies ten volumes in the Divan edition) is obviously scattered over the last fifty years of his life. His autobiographical writings dovetail remarkably to present the story of his career from the beginning to 1824. *The Life of Henry Brulard* (written 1835-36, published 1890) describes the first 17 years of his life, ending with his arrival in Milan to join Napoleon's victorious army, in 1800. The *Journals* which survive (written contemporaneously, published in 1888) pick up the story at Milan early in the year 1801, and carry it through the year 1818. There are some gaps and deficiencies here; the journals of his life in Germany are largely missing, and the record is relatively scanty from 1814 to 1818, the years of the Italian sojourn, of Mathilde, of the first publications. Still, there is a gap of only three years from their final ending till June, 1821, when the *Souvenirs of Egotism* (written 1832, published 1892) are ready to pick up with the idea of carrying us from 1821 to 1830. They get us only to 1823 or so; but they are very unchronological in their arrangement, and not a great deal is actually missing. One would like to know more of Menti, of Mme. Azur, of the genesis of *The Red and the Black*; but these are a biographer's concerns. The sort of man Beyle had finally become, at the age of 40, is abundantly documented in the autobiographical writings.

It is perfectly delightful and highly fortunate that these auto-biographical works fit so neatly together. Eked out with correspondence, which in Henri Beyle's middle years swells to imposing dimensions, they provide a record of his first forty years which is quite as detailed as Boswell's, and much more interesting. But there is a caution; the first and last of these documents were written long after the events they describe. *Henry Brulard* stands at a distance of 35 years from the closing date of its events; *Souvenirs of Egotism* at a distance of ten years. Only the journals are contemporary; and the work which is first in biographical chronology is last in point of composition. This time-scheme takes some getting used to.

Aside from works of self-description and self-analysis, Beyle's literary career begins in, ends in, and often consists of a series of muddled and half-completed projects. He started to write in the conviction that he was a comic poetic genius in the tradition of Molière; he sketched many dramas and even tried to write several, but he never could manage the French alexandrine verse; do what he would, his lines always seemed to come out with 11 or 13 syllables, and in fact even his prose always retained a nervous, off-beat, and subtly irregular cadence which has a charm of its own, but a charm perfectly alien to that of the French classical hexameter. Experiments in tragedy and tragic adaptation died a-borning; immense theoretical preparations for the writing of comedy culminated in a few lines of limping verse. Finally, after seven long years of abstract theorizing and piecemeal tinkering with a comedy called *Letellier* (1804-1811), he became convinced that he had a gift neither for verse nor for drama. During his bourgeois period—1805 to 1813—he wrote little except the journals. When he started to write again, and to publish, about the age of 33, he turned first and naturally to the arts, especially music and painting, as subjects congenial to his Italian surroundings and his newfound Italian temperament. In 1815 he published some "Letters on

Haydn" supplemented by a "Life of Mozart" eked into a book with some remarks on the life and art of Metastasio. In 1817 appeared a two-volume *History of Painting in Italy*; and in the same year, a work of political observation and social commentary, *Rome, Naples, and Florence in 1817*. This last book, signed with the name of M. de Stendhal, was the first which had any success at all; the first two, aside from being tainted with plagiarism, fell almost stillborn from the press, and, far from augmenting the author's slender income, narrowed it even further.

There is no point in fussing here over Beyle's plagiarisms, which will be discussed later to the limited extent of their inherent interest; but our author's rather timid dependence on reality is a characteristic worth remarking. He likes to write about things that he has seen, and even when he has seen them, likes to rest his judgment about them on the judgment of others. His first works are not novels, not fantasies, not even inventions; they are reports, written in a carefully casual, personal, reminiscent style, of things he has seen or read about. When his ideas or even his observations fell a little short of what was needed, he shamelessly plagiarized.

Rome, Naples, and Florence is, however, his own book; it is a series of impressionistic artistic criticisms and sardonic sociopolitical observations, flavored with cynicism and wry sentiment. The author rebounds happily between the conversations of cardinals and countesses, the intrigues of mysterious policemen, and the museums. He is not too reverent about his subject or for that matter about himself; his version of Italy is a cheerful one, which brings out the happy, social side of his nature, and the book sparkles with wit. Half of Stendhal appeared in this first creation of the pseudonym; the other half emerged in the second Stendhalian book, *De l'Amour*. Unhappy in its genesis (it grew out of Beyle's miserable experience with Mathilde), unfortunate as a MS (it got lost for a year and a half in the Strasbourg postal depot), and spectacularly unsuccessful as a printed book (it sold only seventeen copies in all), *De l'Amour* is nonetheless Beyle's first book of genius. In creating it, he learned something about the sort of book which he was put on earth to write; not the rhetorical, sentimental, romantic novel, nor yet the disciplined, rational, critical treatise, but a book which combines a little of both qualities, a romantic anatomy of passion, a passionately rational philosophical romance. These books of mixed character are likely to be slow of growth; for they are the fully ripened fruit of much feeling and reflection, and there is no rushing their genesis. But the light which is at their center reflects in a hundred different directions.

When he first thought of writing a book about his experience with Mathilde, Stendhal had in mind a novel, and actually started it. But it quickly petered out for lack of basic human materials—the characters were too stiff and too rigidly set in the mold of their situation. In fact, he was not yet ready for the freedoms of fiction, and only gradually did he work up to the point of casting his thought naturally into the form of imaginative writing. He wrote a critical manifesto for the young romantic movement, *Racine et Shakespeare*, published in 1823; he turned off two versions of a quick, successful *Life of Rossini*, published the same year; he engaged to write some reviews and journalistic articles to support himself during the bad days when his patrimony ran out. It was only as a counter-measure against the despair caused by his break-up with the Countess Curial, that Stendhal undertook a full-length fiction, which was finally published in 1827 under the title of *Armance*. He had read a novel called *Olivier*, published the year before by Hyacinthe De La Touche, in which the hero was impotent. (La Touche, a practical joker, got the idea for this book from one written by and privately printed for the Duchesse de Duras; and he published *Olivier* in such a way as to make it seem the lady's. She in turn had taken the idea for her own little impotence-romance from a German lady named Caroline Pichler; its earlier history is obscure.) In any event, Stendhal modelled his story on that of La Touche. The hero of *Armance* was also called Olivier till Mérimée got his name changed to Octave; he was also impotent, and his love for the exotic Armance de Zohiloff was followed out with remorseless fatality. A modern court, considering the matter strictly in terms of what it would probably call "story-lines," might not find Beyle guilty of plagiarizing La Touche; it could not fail to note a number of peculiar coincidences, more ostentatious than necessary. But *Armance*, despite its many deficiencies, pointed a new direction for Beyle. A distinctly clinical case, its hero was elaborately analyzed, from the inside out, by means of the typically Stendhalian inner monologue; its dramatic opposition of a sensitive hero and a stupid society remained static, but was none the less powerful in its potential. The newfound novelist first polished off a fine book of travel-sketches (*Promenades dans Rome*), and then, on the night of the 25th of October, 1829, experienced quite unexpectedly "the idea of Julien." On the basis of this idea, he sat down and within the space of a few months wrote off the first draft of *The Red and the Black* (henceforth, for convenience, called the *Rouge*). Once more the kernel of his book was an item of fact; the *Gazette des tribunaux*, in its numbers of 28, 29, 30, and 31 December, 1827, had published an account of the trial, at Grenoble, of one Antoine Berthet, whose career paralleled in its rough outlines that of Julien Sorel. But Stendhal's imagination covered this rough stick of fact with a hundred gleaming crystals; filled it out with a richness of psychological insight and a dramatic energy which transformed a sad, vulgar little episode of the provinces into a work of art.

Without bothering to estimate its precise position either in Beyle's bibliography or in the world of prose fiction, one can say abruptly that the *Rouge* represented for Beyle a major liberation. In it he concentrated the pure metals of many ores which had been apparent for a long time in his life and writings, but which had remained diffuse and scattered. It was a novel written with all the fine edges of the author's nerves showing— a brilliant and heroic improvisation, at the lowest estimate, and a prophetic denunciation of a whole civilization, at a somewhat higher accounting. And it tapped resources of Stendhal's thought and feeling which none of his previous books had been able to reach.

At the age of 47, Stendhal thus created his first fully drama- tized novel and the first book in which the whole pattern of his mind and heart made itself felt. The book made no great stir in the world; "truth, bitter truth" was a strong dose to promise the novel-readers of 1830, and neither the petulant hero nor his two adoring mistresses seemed "natural" to the florid, rhetorical taste of the day. Stylistically, too, Beyle was out of step with his time; he claimed, with cheerful exaggeration, to have formed his style by a daily reading of the *Code Napoléon*; and in the *Rouge* this produced an effect which he himself recognized to be unduly brusque and clipped.

Yet he had taken a giant step; and, aside from the unpub- lished autobiographical works and a last book of travel done for money (*Memoirs of a Tourist*: 1838), the final decade of his life was given over to the writing of fiction. Novels which remained unfinished and unpublished were *Lucien Leuwen* and *Lamiel*; the shorter pieces, most of which achieved periodical publica- tion, have been collected under the titles of *Chroniques ita- liennes* and *Romans et nouvelles*. And sandwiched in between all these enormous activities, the work of a single, sustained, and splendid flare of imaginative vigor during the last two months of 1838, appeared his masterpiece, *The Charterhouse of Parma* (henceforth, for convenience and consistency, the *Chartreuse*).

It would be idle to try to describe this novel in the course of a preliminary summary; logically, one's entire case for or against Stendhal the novelist could be rested on this single book, for if it is not a fine novel, nothing that he ever wrote is. But the case is not even to be stated here, let alone argued. Let us say simply that the *Chartreuse* is a virtuoso's tone-poem on themes which had fascinated Stendhal all his life. It is a painting of Italy which boldly combines the 16th and the 19th centuries; an elegant operatic improvisation which shades together a dozen different nuances of romantic love, the shock and swirl of a magnificent battle-scene, and political commentary of the most devastating, lean, and disillusioned wittiness.

None of the books of Stendhal is very much like any of the others; yet, paradoxically, each of them is pervaded by his personality, and none of them could conceivably have been written by anyone else. A politically minded critic has cleverly suggested that among the devotees of Beyle one can distinguish a right wing of Fabrizians, a center of Julienites, a Brulardist left wing (I should prefer to call it Lucienist), and far out on the frantic left flank, a fringe of Octaviasts (Albert Thibaudet, *Stendhal*, pp. 92-93). The distinctions are real ones; yet the books written by Stendhal are all recognizably the product of a peculiar blend of feeling, philosophy, and shifting point of view, for which Stendhal himself could find no better name than "Beylism." None of the major fiction is without flaw; most of it is "impure" in a sense which one cannot apply with equal force to any other novels with which I am acquainted; and all of it arouses typically extreme reactions. I think it was Huysmans who found a novel by Stendhal so repellent to him that he could express his scorn only by throwing the book on the floor and trampling it underfoot. For the devotees of Stendhal who are proud to call themselves "Beylistes," the *Rouge* has sometimes become almost a sacred book. Paul Bourget, writing in 1883, reports hearing a pair of well-known writers carry on an entire conversation made up of "those little sentences, dry and rough like legal formulae. One would say, 'M. de la Vernaye would be at your feet. . . .' and the other would continue

'. . . speechless with gratitude' [*Rouge*, II, 34]. The game was to discover one's colleague in flagrant ignorance of a single adjective in the book" (*Essais de psychologie contemporaine*, p. 310).

The fact is that the writings of Stendhal are the product of a highly peculiar commitment to life as well as to literature; and he expected of his reader an equally special commitment. He wrote for only a few readers, and was unusually conscious of them as individuals. "A novel is a bow," he wrote in *Henry Brulard*; "the body of the violin, which gives forth the sounds, is the soul of the reader." The peculiar nature of this demand is disturbing to many readers; and there is no point in thundering critical anathemas upon them, any more than upon people who don't like Modigliani, Monteverdi, or artichokes. Still, there is an enduring vitality about the writings as well as the personality of Stendhal which makes him very much a man of one piece, and which challenges our best efforts at definition. "Il rend son lecteur fier de l'être," said Valéry in the course of his appreciation (*Variété* II, 86); in its brevity and directness, the expression is quite untranslatable. If after this one needs any other reasons for reaching after the complex and restless shade of Stendhal, one might emulate the mountain-climbers, and say simply, "Because he is there."

2

*

Métilde:

or a Lesson in Logic

Had she only. . . . But the very notion of speculation is idle. She did not love him; and that, according to the pitiless logic of these affairs, was that.

She simply did not love him; yet she dominated his life, by his own scrupulous and poignant chronology, from March 4, 1818, till May 22, 1824—from the age of 35, that is, till 41. "THE GREATEST EVENT OF HIS LIFE" was his first meeting with her, the first pressure of her hand; and time, though it darkened the tones of his feeling, never faded them. With Mélanie, Alexandrine, and Menti, his mature judgment allowed Métilde to dispute the honor of having inspired the deepest attachment of his life. In listing three great despairs (using English for secrecy), he inevitably included her name:

> Abandon of Gina...........1817
> impossible of Métilde........1820
> abandon of Menti..........1825
> all by love.

And a cryptic note overpage seems to revive the sick and despairing anguish of that "dead-blank" to which she had reduced him:

> . . . et sui eum non receperunt.
> Mét. in 1.000 ans, 1819
> La plus grande douleur.

The greatest sorrow was Métilde, in Milan, 1819. But she also did more than any of his other loves to develop his insights, shape his thinking, and form his character. Cold consolations at the time, these are inevitably the main concerns of the removed and unwrung student. And the fact is beyond question; it was under the influence of Métilde that the "Day of Genius" occurred, that day (it was December 29, 1819) when Henri Beyle discovered the first great principle of his art, that to make an experience live artistically, one must bury it psychologically. His first worthy book was De l'Amour, written about his passion for Métilde, and in a special Stendhalian sense, by her. In his own copy of it he one day inscribed a brief and eloquent note:

> 1er mai 1825. Death of the author.

Time, which has dealt so kindly by the unhappy and bumbling Beyle, has been less considerate of Métilde. After a century and a quarter, little more remains of her than a slender, proud, and pathetic ghost. Of Beyle's letters to her only nine survive, and none of hers to him or to anyone else. No portrait of her has come to light; no descriptions mark out more than a casual trait or two. Even her now-famous admirer, though he prided himself on being one of the few men to remember her more than ten years after her death, does not report more than a couple of nondescript phrases of her speaking. Indeed, from official records and passing allusions winnowed out of piles of musty Milanese scandal, the skeleton of her life can be, as it were, archaeologized. She was born Mathilde Viscontini, of a respectable and comfortable Milanese parentage, in 1790. At 17 she was married to Jean Dembowski, a Pole by birth, an Italian citizen by naturalization, a soldier of fortune by trade, and currently in the service of the French armies. He was older than his bride by twenty years.

Though he may have profited by a historical confusion with his elder brother Louis-Mathieu, who was also a general in the French armies, there seems no reason to doubt that Jean Dembowski was a competent and energetic soldier. He served in various posts—diplomatic, logistic, and administrative, as well as strictly military—during campaigns in Spain and Italy; he gained promotions and positions of trust. This, for a soldier, is success. No doubt adjectives like "rapacious," "adventurous," and "crude" were applied to him on occasion, but by themselves they would mean little. Subject peoples cannot judge fairly of a foreign ruler, and soldiers of fortune are not supposed to model their characters on Amadis of Gaul. But the discontents of General Dembowski's wife confirm the public charges of an overbearing and heavy-handed disposition. As a husband, he is said to have combined an extravagant jealousy of his own wife with an extravagant interest in the wives of other men. There were rumors of browbeating, talk of physical threats. To a woman of spirit, this can only have been irritating; and in the summer of 1814, Mathilde Viscontini-Dembowska, after seven unhappy years of marriage, took her two sons, left her husband, and fled to Switzerland. In 1816 she returned to Milan, but only after receiving assurances from her husband that henceforth she might live alone if she chose. She never resumed married life.

Casual enough in settled times, Milan society might well have forgotten entirely the behavior of General Dembowski's wife during the rush and confusion of the Hundred Days. But an awkward coincidence amplified the scandal a hundred-fold. Also in Switzerland at the time, "a compatriot in exile," was Ugo Foscolo, the umbrageous, indiscriminate romantic poet— a man with a shock of bristling auburn hair, a set of bright red opinions, and an amorous temperament which was positively scarlet. To be sure, he was at Zurich and she at Berne, but there were visits. Popular rumor had attributed to this oddly-assorted couple a previous liaison, during the winter of 1809-1810. Nothing, then, was easier than to represent Mathilde as having run off to Switzerland with her lover; nor could anything be more offensive to the good taste of those ladies who had managed to stay on easy terms with their own husbands and lovers in Milan.

In point of fact, nothing could be less likely than this scandal of an affair with Foscolo. *He* was perfectly capable of it, no doubt; nor does it much matter that he is known to have had another mistress in the period 1809-10, for in love he laid an egotist's emphasis on quantity, not quality. But she . . . ! She, who found poor Beyle lacking in delicacy, to have thrown herself, in a brief breathing-spell between pregnancies, into the arms of a blusterer like Foscolo; to have been picked up and laid aside and picked up again by this thick-skinned egotist without a murmur of audible protest! She did not have the docility to endure such an abuse of sentiment; she did not have the sensuality to be carried away without any sentiment at all; she did not have either surface or motive to feign a docility which she did not feel. Whatever lay between her and Foscolo, it was certainly not love; and most likely it was nothing more than sincere friendship tempered by political sympathy.

She was doubly wronged, then, as Beyle first saw her; by her brute of a husband, and by the shallow, conventional cynics of Milan society. Her unhappiness was a first and welcome proof of her sensibility; in addition, she was beautiful and brave. Her beauty, though unmanifested by actual portraits, Stendhal has sufficiently marked out by comparing her to the "Herodiades" or "Salome" in the Uffizi Gallery, a painting long supposed to be the work of Leonardo but now known to be by Bernardo Luini. It is a dark and melancholy beauty, languorous and feminine to a degree; with downcast eyes and withdrawn expression, Salome turns away from the head which is held toward her by a bushy ruffian. She half-grasps, half fails to grasp, the basin which is to hold the head, itself more dreamy than gruesome, of the Baptist; her expression, between revulsion and indifference and fascination, is infinitely inward and mysterious. They are beautiful features, after the heavy-lidded, voluptuous manner of Leonardo; but Beyle the aspiring amorist might have been well advised to note an element of coldness and self-absorption in their melancholy expression.

As for the bravery of Mme. Dembowska, it was exercised at first passively, in solitude, poverty, and hauteur; Beyle was not bragging when he described his mistress, through a thin veil of fiction, as "la petite tête la plus altière de Milan." But later her defiance took a more active and audacious form. For what was it but pride, an arrogance at finding society unworthy of her, which brought Mme. Dembowska into the revolutionary conspiracy of carbonarism? Some of the biographers speak of her "prudery" toward Beyle as evidence of a desire to placate society; but placatory prudes do not ordinarily wind up on the carpet in police offices, charged with high treason. Mathilde would not stoop to adultery as a revenge on society; but her conspiratorial connections suggest that it was revenge she wanted, not acceptance. And what, more than this spectrum of qualities—pride, beauty, unhappiness, and a passion for liberty

—could have made her a suitable object for the exercise of
Henri Beyle's powers of "crystallization"?

He crystallized almost immediately. To describe in detail the
campaign which ensued is neither necessary nor profitable.
Beyle pursued his fair enemy, not after the cynical fashion of a
Lovelace or a Valmont, nor even after the prudential manner
which had led him to consider, in behalf of Banti, the advantages and disadvantages of having the duchess (Mme. Daru).
He fell in love romantically, forever, to the last breath of his
being—*à la* Werther, in a word. The first of his surviving letters
to the lady ends with the following burning assurances:

> I know myself: I shall love you for the rest of my life, and
> nothing you may do will ever change the notion that has im-
> printed itself upon my soul—the notion I have conceived
> of the bliss of being loved by you—or the contempt it has
> given me for all other forms of happiness! In short, I need,
> I thirst to see you. I believe I would give all the rest of my life
> to converse with you for a quarter of an hour on the most in-
> different matters.
>
> Farewell, I leave you in order to be more with you, to dare
> to speak to you with all the abandon, all the energy of the
> passion that devours me.
>
> *Henri*

Starting on this level, a poetic lover will not find it easy to
elevate further the tone of his sentiments; and in fact the later
tenor of Stendhal's feeling for Métilde was prevailingly somber,
not to say morbid. On the 30th of September, at just 9:32 in
the evening, he was visited by intimations of ultimate success;
on the 5th of January, 1819, a friend spoke encouraging words
to him. But these fitful gleams were soon shrouded in deepest
gloom. No sooner did he dare hope a bit than he was sternly
advised to despair. Before long, the only question remaining
open for discussion was the precise amount of intimacy com-

patible with this fixed, continuing, unalterable despair. On this topic there was not much to be said.

The picture need not be drawn too black. Pursuit of Métilde had, as we shall see, its incongruous and comic moments; and while Beyle was pouring forth his griefs to his lady or his diary, he might perfectly well be, and often was, writing jovially to his Paris crony, Baron Adolphe de Mareste—condoling the Baron's latest case of the clap, reporting the latest scandals of Milan, or ruefully predicting new muddles in French politics. He took a merry tour to the Brianza with his friend the liberal Milanese lawyer Vismara. He did not play young Werther all the time; he frequently did not play it at all well; but one is surprised to find a man of his years and experience undertaking the role at all. Yet from the aspect of native temper, Beyle's part in the tragi-comedy is easier to understand than that of his inamorata. His impulse toward the melancholy, sensitive, sentimental mistress had been unexercised since the days of Mélanie Louason; but it was his natural, his deepest inclination. Alongside one of the most romantic and luxuriant of his letters to Métilde, he once wrote, "Voici le naturel *of this man*"—she had touched something ultimate and innate within him. In one limited sense only did she represent a major novelty; he had never actually loved a woman of aristocratic, "Spanish" sentiments. But since childhood he had known and admired this quality in Elizabeth Gagnon, his great-aunt. Contempt for all vulgarity, especially for money and business, combined with a whole-hearted devotion to the ideals of heroic magnanimity and moral honor as one finds them expressed in *The Cid*—these were the ingredients of "Spanish" sentiments. If not natural to Beyle, they constituted a second nature; and they too found expression in his passion for Métilde. These two deep-laid predispositions almost account for the depth and duration of Beyle's passion.

But she? Her "cruelty," such as it was, needs no explanation; she did not love Signor Beyle, and quite properly declined to be

talked into pretending that she did. Her "Spanish" disposition—
her evident lack of curiosity, and, for all we can hazard, of a
sense of humor—prevented her from taking him at a less exalted
but more amusing level. But the "kindness" which she actually
did show needs more consideration. As early as the first months
of 1819 she had seen that he loved her to the point of folly, and
decided that she could not possibly love him; why did she not
break with him, once and for all, at that time? On any of a
dozen occasions, it would have been easy enough simply to refuse further communication. But she never quite closed the door
tight against him. She might, on the score of "delicacy," an-
nounce her refusal to listen to further pleadings; yet she must
have listened a little, for she persisted in answering them, sometimes in fourteen-page letters. She might reduce his visits to one
per fortnight, but she never put an end to them. Looking ten-
derly upon him (or was this merely his imagination?), she
swore roundly that she could never love him. By way of rebuking
Beyle, she sometimes showed partiality for other men; and this
did terrible things to his self-esteem, but it also encouraged him
to think that she was not inaccessible. As he himself said sadly,
even if he were to discover her in bed with another man, he
would make excuses for her. At different times he suspected
coldness and coquetry on her part; perhaps also she was motivated by political caution. Conversations among ardent young
carbonari went on in the little house on the Piazza Belgiojoso,
and a universal mocker who had heard them might not be a
safe man to offend and then cast adrift on the shadowy waters
of Milan society. But these can only be conjectures; one might
as well question the Salome of the Uffizi on her opinion of John
Baptist as try to guess Métilde's full feelings about Beyle.

Whatever her motives then, and however much she com-
plained that he was "difficile à désespèrer," Métilde maintained
the connection; and Stendhal, whose motives were all too
patent, submitted to her decrees with a docility altogether char-

acteristic of this most docile and endearing of roués. He repelled the advances of Nina Vigano in the almost superstitious belief that this would make him more worthy "in the eyes of God" to be loved by Métilde. He counselled his fatal charmer to seek happiness in love; in supreme humility he even advised her to find happiness by loving someone else. When he vowed to adore her for the rest of his life, he had clearly meant it as sincerely as a man who deeply appreciates the sex ever means this sort of declaration; and it is almost painful to see how disinterested he could be. Yet, between his own timidity and her severity, he made only one effort, and that a half-hearted one, to bring matters to a head.

This was the famous episode of Volterra, whither Mme. Dembowska had retired momentarily during the summer of 1819, to visit her two sons who were at school there. Walking about the grounds of the college, she observed but did not recognize a stumpy figure muffled in an overcoat and further obscured by a pair of green spectacles. Evening settled over the college, and the mysterious figure, sensing that while an overcoat in June might be explained, dark glasses at night would certainly be too much, took them off, and stood revealed as Beyle. He was recognized at once by Mme. Dembowska, but out of deference to the conventions pretended not to know her. That night he wrote a first letter of explanation; and next morning, feeling calm and reflective, he went to a meadow from whose green shades he could look out, across the Tuscan plain, toward the consoling blue waters of the Ligurian sea. Did he know that this meadow was his mistress' favorite spot for a morning promenade? He protests that he did not. At any event, while languishing about here in amorous, melancholy revery, he was once more encountered by Mme. Dembowska. There followed a series of beseeching letters and angry answers, awkward scenes improvised for the benefit of the Rector, fits of jealous temper inflamed by her petulant partiality for a Signor Giorgi, and lengthy, explanatory interviews. She accused him of lacking delicacy, of trying to force himself upon her, of persecuting her; of everything, in fact, except the supreme crime in love (the only one he had actually committed), of making them both look ridiculous. Beyle at least was too civilized not to be conscious of this omission; perhaps this is one reason why De l'Amour makes such a point of contemning French wit, French satire, French regard for convention. All these qualities are stigmatized as an unworthy fear of being thought absurd, and bespeak a man well aware of just how absurd he had been. In fact, Beyle's spirit throughout the whole affair was not French, in the sense of "rational" and "moderate"; it was Spanish—sublime, that is, and ridiculous at the same moment.

Of course absurdity is inseparable from love à la Werther, and supremely irrelevant to it, as well. The man who takes love at the heroic pitch finds in passion a metaphor which he destroys himself trying to pronounce. Love is for him the key to religion, beauty, music, art, and all the wards and corridors of sympathy. As this hero occurs in fictions, a certain interest rises from the question whether he will find the proper rhetoric before he bursts; his real paradigm is Aesop's frog. But Beyle did nothing so silly with his passion for Métilde as to write it up in the rhetoric of Saint-Preux and Werther. He tried a romance, to be sure, with Métilde's cousin Mme. Traversi rigged for the role of ogress, and himself thinly disguised as a bold Polish cavalry officer who had served with Napoleon. But this was broken off abruptly and very properly, before it had endured beyond the first ten pages; for the characters had nowhere at all to go. Like Beyle in his love, they began at a *dead blank*.

A whole series of frustrations and agonizing inhibitions thus led up to the creation of Beyle's first book of genius, De l'Amour. Rome, Naples, and Florence, the Lives of Haydn, Mozart, and Metastasio, and the History of Painting in Italy are charming and enthusiastic volumes on topics which pleased him very much. They illustrate his sensitivity, at once naïve and theatrical, to certain sorts of artistic and social experiences. Yet they are as far from expressing the whole man as they are from dealing adequately with their avowed subjects. On every topic except his own soul, Beyle was the most amateur of amateurs; this is at once the crowning glory of Stendhal and a major limitation. What gives value to the first books is the sensibility which reveals itself between the cribbed passages—in the sections written from personal observation, and, above all, in the digressions. But Beyle did not have the patience to be a historian, a biographer, or a critic; and though he could assume the mask of a man-of-the-world, it muffled expression of at least half the Stendhalian sensibility.

De l'Amour, a "scientific" treatise purporting to present the anatomy of a passion, actually comes closer than any of his previous writings to catching in print the full complex of Stendhal's character. To begin with, its pretence of being "scientific" imposes a strict restraint on rhetoric. As a matter of taste, Beyle always despised rhetoric, and fought shy of themes which seemed to invite it. Over and over again, in the journals and letters as well as in more formal works, we find him dismissing an ecstatic experience in a few dry words as something which description could only tarnish, something before which all words are inadequate, and so on. His passion for Métilde was as overwhelming as a physical constraint; years after he had left her forever, he happened to see in the street a little white satin hat like that which she used to wear, and seeing it, grew faint and had to lean against the wall. While correcting proof on *De l'Amour*, in the summer of 1822, he found himself still so susceptible to the memory of Métilde that he wept over the galley-sheets; and though he was enjoying a social success in the salons of Paris, he spent many hours dreaming of that sublime and lonely creature in the Piazza Belgiojoso, halfway across Europe. Against this sort of inner compulsion it was essential to maintain strict discipline. Beyle's device of the learned treatise was useful in cropping rhetorical flowers; it served to create a fascinating and mysterious counterpoint of confession and ideology, where every axiom might be the casket of a memory, and every episode a foreshortened avenue of psychological insight. And for the first time it set in direct opposition or close conjunction Beyle's concise, cogent, and witty mind *vis à vis* the florid exfoliations of his romantic sensibility.

Even in the fully formed novels, Stendhal is always more a philosopher than a describer. He dashes at the physical details of a scene, but will hold up the most intense and blinding vision of dramatic conflict to scatter aphorisms on human conduct. *De l'Amour* employs the same pattern, but turns it inside out. Generalizations here are the apparent texture of the book, through which gleams the outlines of a narrative. These gleams are by no means elusive or obscure. A young Werther, recently dead in Volterra, by name Lisio Visconti (Métilde's maiden name, it will be recalled, was Viscontini) and another sad young man named Salviati, who has been reduced by his mistress to a single visit every fortnight, pop in and out of the book, providing by letter, journal, and anecdote, material to illustrate the fatal progress of passionate love. The words of Métilde are sometimes cited directly, though the magic syllables of her name are never pronounced; the philosopher argues with some energy that the proper age for a mature and seasoned woman to fall in love for the second time is just 28—Métilde's age in 1818, when Beyle first met her; there are even bitter though covert allusions to Mme. Traversi, who is supposed to have poisoned against love and happiness the mind of a noble and wretched young woman. If this, in Stendhal's judgment, was concealment and discretion, what must have been confession and self-revelation?

Yet we do him wrong to set these two qualities in opposition; the acts of concealing and revealing were, for Stendhal, almost identical. His puns and anagrams, pseudonyms, epithets, emblems, initials, and macaronics are all devices for saying more than most men feel it safe to say, and for concealing at the same time what has been said. His special talent for lurid dramatic chiaroscuro derives in a way from this gift for letting a ray of light fall into or rise out of the thick atmosphere of a pit. Here too *De l'Amour* works the device of the novels in reverse. As a work of ideology, the treatise on love is clear, sharp, dry, and limited; but there rise out of it and around it such clouds of sensibility, such obscurities of the soul, as make it an authentic expression of the whole man.

In effect, the art of Stendhal, like most of the things he had to say about love and even about himself, is summed up in the central image of *De l'Amour*. The concept of "crystallization," though it was not Stendhal's to begin with, and though he put it forward with diffidence, provides the key to his mind. In addition, I think it the most successful and suggestive of the many metaphors by which the 19th century tried to convey the complexity of creative art. Aeolian harps and fading coals, radiant lamps and sensitive plants, bubbling springs, deep wells, wild west winds, and open wounds—all these images yield insights into the quality of the creative mind. But the image of crystallization has so many facets and combines so many overtones, that one is hard put to bring them all out. At a venture, one might begin by saying that the metaphor implies:

1. Formality of structure arrived at by organic growth,
2. Angularity leading to luminescence,
3. Solidity giving the impression of fragility,
4. Formation, in silence and darkness, by an inner law, of structures which glitter in the light,
5. Events trivial to consciousness given splendor by immersion in the subconscious,
6. Indistinguishable conjunction of actives and passives in the creative mind of lover or artist.

Above all, it suggests without pathos or ostentation the authority of the imagination and its limits. There is a pathetic-heroic
notion deriving from Plato that beauty as it exists for the artist
or lover is transcendental and immanent; there is a counter-po-
sition, which Hobbes, Hume, and Locke must share with Meph-
istopheles, according to which beauty is primarily in the eye
of the beholder. It is an agreeable delusion, founded upon the
passions, but subject to correction by the cool voice of common
sense and the abstract ideas of general nature. Stendhal's image
of crystallization implies an inclination to the latter position.
When one crystallizes on an object, one imputes to it by association all the desirable qualities which one can bring within its
range. But this is not lawless sentiment or wilful self-delusion;
it is a way in which the mind can manifest itself to itself, a
revelation of the fact that its essential nature includes a passionate as well as a coolly cognitive strain. The truth one dis-
covers by crystallizing is a truth about the errors to which one's
mind is subject; but it is a way of seeing clearly in the end—as
Stendhal described it, of discovering the real by way of the imaginary and entering the world by way of heaven (*Filosofia
nova*, I, 16). There could be no more incisive image for a book
which proposes to treat analytically the most iridescent and
delicate of passions.

The implosive development of his love for Métilde was once
described by Stendhal as a "course in logic"; it is an odd expression, but typical of the man, for whom logic was secret,
passionate, and personal. The essence of his study was immersion in the mysterious currents of affinity. He never mentioned
Métilde to his worldly Parisian friends, never named her in the
book where her presence is implicit throughout, never in his
lifetime printed a word by which she could be identified. He
buried her far from the world of light and allowed logic to transform her—not the logic of the English tradition, but that which
Condorcet, Cabanis, and Tracy derived from the great structure

built by Descartes on the immovable fact of consciousness. *Penser c'est sentir* was the apparently inescapable corollary of *Je pense donc je suis*; and, however limited as a statement of total philosophy, or, for that matter, as a psychological conclusion, these phrases pointed an admirable direction for the man on whom literature had imposed its ulterior motives. By immersing the memory of Métilde in the strong waters of logic defined in terms of feeling, Beyle did nothing to desiccate or formalize his love; he allowed it to etch its own pattern, to grow by the laws of its own life, lit only faintly and indirectly by the glimmering light of formal categories and general experience. There is a paradox about the molecular particle whose trajectory we can never see truly because it is disturbed by the light which enables us to see it. The course in logic which Stendhal administered to himself balanced on a paradox much like this. The heart had its reasons, which reason, adroitly defined and limited, could perfectly well understand, since reason itself was so largely an activity of the heart.

Of course, this happy little construct totters dangerously, the minute one looks twice at the word "understand." Soberly considered, the position is not far from agreeable flimflam; yet it invites an audacity useful to the novelist, while avoiding the awkward boxes of copperlined categories, and for these favors we must be grateful. Leaving endorsements aside, to understand Beyle's philosophical heritage is to obviate at least one major gambit about his discussion of love. There has been a good deal of facile irony concerning the form of *De l'Amour*, as if the author had undertaken to produce a textbook or an easy outline, complete with categorical conclusions. But he was interested in the living currents of passion, not its dead contours; interested in the forms which grow out of the whole compacted and concentrated mind, not in those which by exclusion and abstraction can be carved out of or imposed upon it. The stream of Stendhal's logic is really a constant exercise in sympathy, an effort

to comprehend nothing less than little white satin hats and the
Salome in the Uffizi. To chart the currents of the underground
river, he threw himself into it.

That painting of Salome, though Stendhal sometimes used it
in general terms to symbolize an ideal type of Lombard beauty,
and sometimes declared that others of his loves or his literary
creations resembled it, belongs peculiarly to Métilde. (It is much
faded now, and if seen on any but the brightest days, produces
a glum impression of anonymous yellow-brown; but the outlines
and shading of the face are still lovely.) While looking at it
recently, there occurred to me a series of impishly logical illogi-
calities, which, if they have any substantiality at all, may illustrate the special meaning of logic for Stendhal and illuminate
one seemingly extravagant twist of his second-best novel.

Mathilde de la Mole, who is the focus of Julien Sorel's second
intrigue in the *Rouge*, is evidently intended to contrast in several different ways with Mme. de Rênal, who occupies, with almost geometrical neatness, a commanding position in the first
volume of the novel. Mme. de Rênal loves Julien naturally,
Mlle. de la Mole loves him, or must be made to love him, artificially and unnaturally. Mme de Rênal is a mother, and loves
with a mother's warm, uncritical heart; Mathilde is a mistress
who must be pursued, won, lost, recaptured, disputed—a tempting and perilous bit of quicksilver. Though Mathilde is to bear
Julien's child, he thinks only of entrusting it to Mme. de Rênal.
Mathilde is lawless, arrogant, and even in her rare moments of
self-abasement, selfish; Mme. de Rênal is humble, innocent, and
in conventional Christian terms, deeply moral. Religion is for
her a fiery barrier, which adds to her love the last element of
precious sacrifice. For Mathilde the nearest equivalent is her
demonic pride of family and person. She is passionately proud,
after the Spanish manner—contemptuous of money, birth, and
the forms of society as only a person can be who commands all
of them; indeed, she despises the whole modern world, and finds

her ideal in the heroic 16th-century warrior-courtier-gentleman who is the central figure of Corneille's tragedy. Pride is so far the ruling passion of Mathilde that Julien can control her only by affecting an even icier counter-pride and indifference. Prompted by Prince Korasoff, a Beylean man-of-the-world and a master of the difficult art of high fatuity, he throws up a smoke screen of pompous epistolary love-making about Mme. la Maréchale de Fervaques, as a way of provoking Mathilde. The cure is drastic. Mathilde is overcome by his affected cold-ness and hypocrisy, and begs forgiveness for her abominable pride. Here now the parallel with Métilde (the divine Métilde of Milan and 1819) is complete; reflecting on the experience of the campaign in later years, Beyle was apt to think a little well-placed disdain on his part might have been happily deci-sive. In the abortive "Romance of Métilde" Prince Korasoff's part is assigned to a certain Baron Zanco, who provides the un-happy Polosky with worldly advice, but the pattern is otherwise identical. Evidently the story of Julien Sorel and Mathilde de la Mole is the story of poor Dominique and his divine Métilde as it might have been played out had the youthful ardor of Beyle been guided by the worldly discretion of Prince Korasoff.*

* The woman usually cited as the model for Mathilde de la Mole is, I am aware, Alberthe de Rubempré. But, aside from proximity, what can be urged in her behalf? She did not understand or sympathize with Mathilde de la Mole; she thought Julien wicked; she did not act out of pride; did not hold herself above society; was not a secret radical; was not given, so far as we know, to Mathilde's cold and dreamy expression; and Beyle's opinion of her was contemptuous, despite his infatuation—he said she was *une catin*, not *sublime* like Angela Pietragrua, but *à la DuBarry*. This is not Mathilde de la Mole in any particular; and as for proximity (Al-berthe was almost contemporaneous with the writing of the *Rouge*, while Métilde left Beyle's life a decade earlier), when one deals with the experience of crystallization, proximity in time is not an advantage but the contrary. There is no good pulling yesterday's branch out of the salt-mines, it has gathered no crystals.

Other possible models for Mathilde who have been proposed are Giulia Rinieri and Méry, daughter of Hyde de Neuville. But Giulia was far from

Métilde is cleverly disguised under her actual name of Mathilde; she is somewhat younger, and her two boys have been transposed with a nameless addition into the family of Mme. de Rênal. Julien Sorel stands in the dark outside her window, watching the curtains being drawn and the light being extinguished, as Henri Beyle waited in the dark Piazza Belgiojoso for a glimpse of Métilde. Like her Milanese original, Mathilde de la Mole is a secret radical; her ruling passion, like that of Mathilde Dembowska, is pride. Summarizing the difference between his hero's two mistresses, Stendhal in the course of the novel itself declares that Mme. de Rênal represents "natural love," true love, love of the heart; while Mathilde de la Mole represents "love of the head" (II, 19).

But these phrases take us back, by a kind of swirling, rotary reasoning, to connect the portrait in the Uffizi, which was the very emblem, in Beyle's mind, of Métilde, with one of Mlle. de la Mole's most perverse and fascinating traits—her passionate, not to say morbid, interest in decapitation. Her ancestor had had the honor of having his head cut off, in retribution for loving a queen; she is enamored of the grandeur of this action, and of Julien when he shows himself capable of an equally distinguished destiny. The novel ends with her carrying away the head of Julien in her lap—an obscure and magnificent private ritual, which quite overshadows Mme. de Rênal's conventional

---

proud and not in the least fickle; on the contrary, she was intensely available and extraordinarily constant. Of Méry we know only that she ran away with a lover who was a commoner—an action which, in itself, scarcely accords with the behavior of Mlle. de la Mole, and implies nothing with regard to Mathilde's extravagant, morbid character. Besides, both these influences are too recent to have affected the core of Mathilde's character. Giulia became Stendhal's mistress only on March 22, 1830; and Méry eloped with her young cavalier in January of the same year. Composition of the *Rouge* has been pretty conclusively dated 25 October, 1829-April, 1830 (Bardèche, p. 176). All this is not to say that some of the Parisian flavoring of Mathilde, a certain wilful quality of *enfant gâtée*, may not have been borrowed from Méry or Alberthe.

broken heart. Love of the head, with a vengeance! Yet a grotesque and almost psychotic pun, such as this, is part of the "logic" which Stendhal learned from his course of study with Métilde. Perhaps it was an accident or a joke at first, but he used it as a sculptor working in wood uses a knot which he comes across accidentally. The train of association which carried him away intertwined pride, beauty, and contemplation with narcissism, cruelty, and a passionate desire to have the beloved's head "brought to one on a platter." Mathilde is in one sense a mechanical opposite to Mme. de Rênal; applying Beyle's own superficial categories even more superficially than he ever consistently applied them, one might be inclined to say that Mme. de Rênal represents passionate love and Mathilde vanity-love. But the course in logic did not lead to, it did not permit, any such stolid one-for-one identifications. Stendhal never says solemnly after the manner of so much modern fictioneering, "I shall make Julien Sorel a good square symbol of John Baptist and arrange round him various females representative of Herod's daughter and so on." His approach to overtones was enchantingly indirect; and one could illustrate profusely Freud's chapter on Dream-Work with examples of transposition, substitution, elision, compression, suppression, and sublimation, which set Stendhal's novels apart from the raw materials supplied by Beyle's life. Some of his finest touches are the omissions and passing glances, the open possibilities which give his novels their overpowering sense of chiaroscuro. So it was, then, with Mathilde. Her pride came from "la petite tête la plus altière de Milan"; that lofty head suggested the one by Luini, which mingled frigidity, loveliness, horror, and something completely inexplicable—an inward landscape, mysterious, evil, and enchanting, beyond anything which can be rendered in pigments; and this "love of the head" fused vanity and necrophilia in a kind of inspired and crazy metaphor, to produce one of the supreme women of modern fiction. This was logic, if you will; a logic of association as strict in its requirements and as delicate in its balances as the syllogistic tubing with which the logical positivist fastens together structures of pressure-proof, meaningless assertions. I claim for it no unequivocal allegiance, nor did Beyle. Yet it justifies itself by existing—in the novel, primarily, but thence by perfectly clear implication in those of us who find the novel dangerously full of meaning.

Danger, yes; though it is only a conventional expression. In a discussion based on discursive logic, the logic of feeling or any rival logic is "logic" only by courtesy and is dangerous by long-standing tradition. Yet, at the cheapest, we can defend Stendhal's book as an adventure in illogic. And, at a bolder stroke, we may kick the convention over any time we choose. Traditionally, discursive logic is safe; is, indeed, the only safe intellectual construct. But much of its safety has been discredited by Freud and more formal philosophers, along with its exclusiveness and above all its claim to suppress rival "logics." The logic of symbols, the logic of mythology, the logic of instinctive development, the logic of feeling, clearly have claims on us just as ancient as those of discursive logic, and perhaps more deeply rooted in our nature. "Beylism" was in effect a logic of this sort; not a complete and universal way of understanding the cosmos, naturally, but a series of linked, distinctive reactions rising from a self deliberately formed by controlled immersion in experience, self-observation, and self-analysis. Perhaps the appropriate word for the product is "syndrome" rather than "philosophy"; in any event, it served to keep the novelist in touch, remarkably in touch, with sides of our nature which it is not invariably convenient to forget. "Je est un autre" said Rimbaud, by way of expressing total alienation; but for Stendhal his ego was magnificently diffused through everything he experienced, everything he imagined, everything he thought. There is a supremely impudent footnote to the *Vie de Rossini*, Chapter 45, where Stendhal passes in four short disjointed sentences from mockery of people who "construct coherent and rational systems based upon data which they are unable to perceive," to the function of rationalism in music, to the experience of vocal music proper, to a memory of "those ragged little urchins who sang beneath our windows once in Peyrefitte on the road to Cauterets, and whom you called up into our room." Theatrical as it is, the passage shows how a personal, private experience could be incorporated for him, almost at the heart of a syllogism. His ego as it had come into existence was for him a kind of concrete logic. It was a first principle of his intellectual organization; it was a great part of what he had to organize. A single existence could not possibly suffice for all the logical realities Stendhal had to keep in touch with; he invented identities as a way of enveloping, surprising, and burrowing into the world; and his novels are often tissues of disguise and counter-disguise, of sensitive identity and protective identity-mask. There is a logic which he sets against the world, the logic of ideology, but it is a machine in the hands of that higher logic which is capable of developing the crystalline structures of Beylist feeling throughout the universe which Stendhal creates. The pure, aseptically pure, clarity of Stendhal's observation in matters of fact and feeling is famous; equally remarkable, though not so often remarked, is the perfect clarity and purity of his moral judgment—its indifference to those gross cutouts repeatedly indulged in by sentimental melodramatists like Flaubert and Henry James—cutouts like the Sincere Young Person and the Wicked Cynic. But most remarkable of all is the crystalline and mathematical purity with which Stendhal's images develop from the center out, unfolding new facets and implications of their own nature as they go. From the first, Mathilde de la Mole is surrounded by the imagery of a queen, a princess; from the first, a specially veiled and tenuous mystery surrounds the birth of Julien. He is a totally disconnected man, a dreamer who withdraws into the wilderness and takes his loftiest inspiration from the lonely flight of an eagle. All these and many other characteristics are scattered, apparently at random, through the early parts of the novel; out of them rises, gradually, and at first unclearly, the Salome-John Baptist mystery which at last establishes itself as an emotional center of the novel. Yet the central prism of feeling which joins Julien to Mathilde was formed, one presumes, before the novel was ever begun; when Beyle, thinking of himself and his treatment at the hands of the divine Métilde, scrawled in the margin of *Armance* John the Evangelist's ambiguous phrase, which may be descriptive either of the Christ or the Baptist, "*et sui eum non receperunt.*"

3

*

Tracy:

or the Advantages of Ideology

De mémoire de rose, on n'a jamais vu mourir de jardinier.

Histoire de la Peinture, II, 52

Since it was coined, over a century and a half ago, the word
"ideology" has been an outcast, a whipping-boy, a scapegoat
among the neologisms. Once a reputable philosophical term,
it was derided by Napoleon, mocked by Marx, and debauched
by Marxists; so that today the idea of "dishonest rationaliza-
tion" has attached itself to the very kernel of the word and
rotted it out. What it meant to its hopeful coiner was something
quite different, something for which we still lack an adequate
term. Destutt de Tracy was its creator; a soldier, politician,
philosopher, geometer, nobleman, correspondent of Jefferson,
commentator on Montesquieu, Scotchman, Frenchman, idol
of Stendhal and even to a limited degree his friend. The word
"ideologue" has attached itself irresistibly to De Tracy's name,

and is duly applied by historians of philosophy; but it never did him justice, and does him rather less than justice today. "De Tracy the Ideologue"; it is an ugly and misleading guise in which to encounter posterity; and he was a man too gallant and various to be afflicted with such a designation.

When he invented the term, "ideology" meant for De Tracy the study of ideas and of the ways in which they are acquired, related, and verified. As he conceived it, "metaphysics" was one word which might have been applied to this study, the examination of consciousness; "psychology" was another. But he found the first term seriously compromised by previous usage, and above all by theological and speculative connotations —it was a word too lofty by half in its overtones. As for "psychology," it was a term too general in its application, for it might refer to the study of the subconscious, of dreams, emotions, and instincts, as well as to the study of ideas properly so called. Without irrevocably dichotomizing the psyche, Cabanis and De Tracy divided its study between them, Cabanis to emphasize the emotional and unconscious aspects, De Tracy the logical and conscious. Though they dug from opposite sides of the hill, it was one tunnel at which they were working. And it was his part of the joint operation which De Tracy, by way of distinction, called "ideology."

Henri Beyle first came in contact with the mind of De Tracy in the year of his majority. On the last day of the year 1804, he went out in the snow to buy the first volume of the *Ideology* —from the bookseller Courcier, on the quai de la Volaille, as he was careful to record; and that very night, huddled in his chilly little room, he read the first sixty pages. Henceforth, he was De Tracy's man; the experience of this bold philosophic venture seems to have been for Beyle what the discovery of Marx was for Bernard Shaw, it made a man of him. Not till thirteen years later did he make the personal acquaintance of M. de Tracy, when the philosopher had turned (for reasons we shall appreciate) somewhat sour and bitter. But he never lost his admiration for the philosophy or for the man, even when his affection was ill-reciprocated, and the philosophy was in discredit.

The reasons for his admiration are not obscure or difficult. Beyle had a natural gift for mathematics and exact reasoning; he admired also a plain, unpretentious style and direct expressions; and he was passionately concerned with the quality and character of consciousness. Partly this emphasis on the plain, clear, mechanical elements of human nature existed in Beyle, as it were, for its own sake; as the child of an enlightened century he believed in clarity, simplicity, order, and rationality. Partly also he found in this temper a weapon against the irrational authoritarianism of his father and his father's church. On both counts De Tracy appealed to him, though less satisfactorily on the second basis than on the first. In the role of substitute father, indeed, he did little more than repeat Cherubin Beyle. *De l'Amour* he thought a lot of nonsense, and, in the peevishness of old age, he gave credence to malicious stories against Beyle, whose admiration for the philosopher had rendered him, as usual, inarticulate. Yet he also saw something valuable in the young man, and expressed it, gruffly enough, when he described his disciple as a "fractious horse." The tribute at least implies the possession of spirit. In the end, Beyle needed a philosopher, if only as a trace to direct and a snaffle to curb his sensibility. The sort of philosopher he discovered in De Tracy (solitary anachronism though he was) did much to determine the sort of novelist he was to become.

In effect, De Tracy was a philosopher in a sense much broader and more genial than German transcendentalism has since allowed the word to assume. Not simply a technician of the thought-processes, a plumber of leak-proof self-evident propositions, he undertook to be a legislator for the thoughts and affections of men. We shall see him most truly under the aspect of a military commander. Like Kant's, his family was Scotch by national origin; and the philosopher descended from one of four brothers named Stutt or De Stutt, who in the middle of the 15th century came to France with the Douglas to help defend Charles VII (Joan of Arc's Dauphin) from the English. They stayed, joined the Scotch Guard, acquired estates, and, through the property of Tracy in the Nivernais, the title by which they were to be known. Antoine Louis Claude Destutt de Tracy was born in the year 1754, and destined from childhood for the career of a soldier. His father died in battle when the boy was 9; his mother exacted from her son a vow that he would go for a soldier, and she (being a true French mother of the prudent, managing breed) so smoothed the world's rough road for her boy that he was a colonel in command of his own regiment by the time he was 22 years old. This circumstance impressed Stendhal hugely, and left its mark, perhaps, on the reactions of Julien Sorel to the young bishop of Agde and to Count Norbert de la Mole; it is certainly responsible for a significant phrase in *Armance*, Chapter 2, where an envious provincial deputy, snubbed by Octave, dreams of humiliating the damned aristocrats—"we no longer wish to see you colonels at 23, as we used to, while we remain captains at 40."

Influence—one might almost say, compulsion—made De Tracy a colonel; chance and inclination combined to make him a philosopher. Stationed at Strasbourg, he began to attend lectures, to read metaphysical essays, to discuss the grounds of intellectual certainty. Who his first preceptor was has been debated; but the point does not really matter much, for none of the available candidates could have influenced De Tracy in the direction which he shortly took. His most striking qualities as a philosopher are those which remind us most tellingly of the general staff officer. He is bold, clear, decisive, and limited. Both virtues and faults are on the surface, for all to see; and it would be cruelly gratuitous, in this day and age, to make

game of a man who in 1800 fondly imagined that his intellectual system had embraced all human experience. At the same
time, it is difficult to take him seriously when he writes, for
example:

> In following the path which I have taken, it is hard to mistake
> one's way. I studied even as I wrote; I did not know my field
> of study when I began, for it did not even exist; I had no
> prejudice; I did not know where my conclusions would lead; I
> observed the human mind without any previous presumptions,
> and noted what I saw without any idea of reaching a foregone
> conclusion. Every time I saw that I was being led into ab-
> surdity, I retraced my steps; parts of my *Logic* I reworked as
> many as five times, and I never failed to discover the spot
> where I had gone astray, that is, where I had made a bad ob-
> servation. In short, without any suppositions, gaps, or logical
> flaws, I have been led to an intellectual result which I neither
> foresaw nor desired. It is plausible, it accounts for all phe-
> nomena, one cannot fail to yield it a full and complete confi-
> dence.

Alas for the confidences of philosophers! And yet this armed
and resolute confidence of De Tracy's was by no means the
offspring of an easy or unquestioning acceptance of things. Slow
of growth, obstinately disputed at every stage, it crystallized, so
to speak, in De Tracy's mind under the most exigent and doubt-
provoking circumstances, amid the desperate threatenings of
a revolution run amok.

From the beginning of the great uprising of 1789, De Tracy's
part had been that of a sympathetic moderate, a critic of emi-
gration, and a supporter of the abolition of feudal rights and
tithes. In a word, he was a loyal and enlightened lieutenant of
Lafayette. When Lafayette resigned his command for the third
and final time in the summer of 1792, De Tracy also retired
to what he hoped would be a life of philosophic speculation.

But revolutionary governments, as we now know, do not like lean men who think too much, whether they call themselves active or retired; and such a dangerous thinker De Tracy was soon judged to be. Arrested by a corporal's guard of sans-culottes on the stock charges of disaffection, conspiracy, and sympathy for the aristocracy, he was remanded to jail for execution. His appointment with the guillotine was announced for 11 thermidor of the year II (1794). On 5 thermidor he noted down, in his cell, the grand outlines of that philosophical system on which his fame depends; and between the second date and the first, on 9 thermidor, Robespierre was messily done to death, the Terror came to an end, and De Tracy was freed.

However anxious the moments of its genesis, De Tracy's system was by no means the expression of a "conversion" psychology; nor did he rush into print with it. Years of study, analysis, and testing followed, of conversations and disputes with his friend and colleague Cabanis, his friend and student Biran. Practical applications of the philosophy were not forgotten. Called upon by Napoleon to help reorganize the French educational system, De Tracy had a chance to develop to the full his flair for casting abstract ideas into lucid, impeccable, yet slightly informal prose. Thus, when the first volume of the *Ideology* appeared in 1804, De Tracy was a man of 50, possessing considerable experience of the world and as much experience of the conditions of abstract thought as he was ever likely to acquire.

The program of this magnificent, and now melancholy, intellectual undertaking deserves preservation, if only as a curiosity, though biography has now given it an inadvertent pathetic interest, as well. M. de Tracy planned to proceed in a steadily ascending order of abstraction, from the rudiments of perception to the most refined constructs of which the mind is capable; and so divided his great work into three sections of three volumes each. Elementary ideology, grammar, and logic would be treated in the first section; will, morality, and legislation in the second; and physics, geometry, and calculus in the third. At various times the author toyed with the idea of a final chapter in which all the erroneous structures of knowledge would be contrasted with the pure and shining temple just created; but, long before this stage was reached, construction had ceased, and the mighty tower of learning had been abandoned.

The manner of this giving over can only be described as odd. With easy confidence and elegance of exposition, M. de Tracy wrote his way through the first three volumes, publishing them in 1801, 1803, and 1805 respectively. "Logic" turned out to require two volumes, and parts of it had to be rewritten (as many as five times!), but it appeared on schedule. However, a lengthy pause now followed. Ten years passed before another volume appeared, and when the first volume of the section did finally come forth, its form was strange indeed. "Will" and "Legislation," the first and last parts of the section, were complete, though physically they occupied only a single volume; a single chapter had been written on the last part of the section, "Morality." This one complete chapter dealt with "Preliminary Ideas"; and then, abruptly, after two pages on the topic of "Love," and in the middle of a sentence, M. de Tracy broke off his treatise with a plain declaration that he would never pick it up again. In fact, he never did.

At best, it is an embarrassing place for a philosophy to break down, especially a mechanical one, as De Tracy's fundamentally was. The example of Lucretius, who had been through it all some time before, was mournfully relevant, or may well have appeared so. To be sure, there were public circumstances to account, at least partly, for M. de Tracy's discontinuance of his great project. The course of public affairs after the fall of Bonaparte disgusted him profoundly; his intimate friend and cherished colleague Cabanis had died in 1808; he underwent an operation for cataracts, which was only partially successful; he was growing old. And yet these circumstances, though they explain much, do not fully account for De Tracy's abrupt decision. For in fact he did not stop writing his treatise just where he stopped publishing it. The chapter on love went on, in MS form, and completed itself in terms of its rather unpromising beginning; it has since been published by M. Gilbert Chinard (1926). When one starts by defining love as "friendship embellished by pleasure," there are not many directions left to go. Still, De Tracy wrote more of his treatise than he allowed to appear; and he broke it off, with a gesture worthy of Stendhal himself, in such a manner as to convey a distinct sense of mystery.

A sentimental mystery, such as this appears to be, may be thought incongruous with that figure of De Tracy which has come down to us from his last years. Scotch severity combined, during those years, with philosophic resignation, to produce a truly formidable old personage. Dressed all in black, wearing a huge green eyeshade, lean, dry, meticulous, and terrifyingly forthright, he presided and sometimes tyrannized over his wife's salon like an armored, invulnerable presence. Yet the fact was, M. de Tracy had suffered a disappointment in love, one which the respectable of his time and above all of his family did not like to talk about, but which Stendhal knew of, and has communicated to us, in the *Souvenirs of Egotism*. Madame la Duchesse de Praslin had been De Tracy's neighbor at Auteuil; their gardens communicated through a little gate in a large wall. She had also been his dear friend, and in fact his mistress, after the quiet French family way, for many years. "Friendship embellished by pleasure" indeed; yet, one may surmise, it was not till her sudden death, just a single day before that of Cabanis, that De Tracy realized how much more than either of these two edifying sentiments was involved. It was a triple catastrophe, of friendship, of love and of philosophy; and this collapse, no less than his political disappointments and logical difficulties, finally reduced the gallant colonel to silence and was hinted at in the abrupt and mysterious termination of his project.

He was silent, as far as publication went, for the rest of his life, a silence rather dour than genial with regard to Beyle. Like Pierre Daru—like most practical men, one is tempted to say—he did not appreciate Stendhal's writings. One could scarcely expect a man who defined love as "friendship embellished by pleasure" to take much pleasure in a lyrical rapture like *De l'Amour*. Yet Stendhal's book may be compared to a sort of revenge inflicted by De Tracy's philosophy on the passion which had silenced it. To capture Don Quixote, one must be a little mad oneself; and Stendhal, in *De l'Amour*, ventured far down the path of imaginative sensibility toward a world of private values. But his aim was to understand, to release, to control; his success, though imperfect, was greater by far than his preceptor's; and his spirit was quite as enlightened and humane.

For what Beyle derived from De Tracy was essentially an ideal, an attitude, and only the mask of a manner or method. He accepted, as De Tracy, along with almost all the French *philosophes*, had done, both Newtonian physics and the intellectual method which they exemplified. De Tracy, further, brought his special gifts of clarity, confidence, and energy to the immense task of applying this physical method to psychic phenomena. He was neither the first nor the last laborer in this vast, ungrateful vineyard. The discovery of uniformity behind multiplicity, the reduction of chaos to simplicity, which Sir Isaac Newton had recently accomplished for physics, beckoned to all students of the mental processes; and since the splendid act of uniformity long since imposed by Descartes, all Frenchmen were, perforce, students of the mental proc-

esses. If thought were a guarantee of existence, nothing could
be supposed to lead more directly to a definition of existence
than an analysis of thought. By reducing the thought-processes
to their simplest elements, one might see both the truth and
the means by which one had perceived it—a double surety.
By way of economizing on one's assumptions, it might be well
to see how far one could understand the working of the mind
as a matter of simple sensation. Descartes himself had written
off animals as merely ingenious machines—a view less removed
than one might suppose from contemporary Pavlovian be-
haviorism. But the chief use of positing such a mechanism,
for Descartes as for most of the respectable non-behaviorist
thinkers who followed him, was that by accounting for the
primitive elements of sensation on a mechanical basis, one distinguished the human soul as an organ devoted to higher and
more spiritual functions. No mere quantitative distinction
would do here; it must be a qualitative one, setting the soul
apart, not merely as a specially capacious vessel, but as an
active, responsible, divine agent. The only basic flaw in a logical barricade of this sort, erected with great pains and energy
by the 17th century, was that its very existence posed a challenge to the destructive, economical spirit of the 18th century.

The necessity for the hypothesis of a soul is a question only
one step removed from the necessity for the hypothesis of a
God; and, with many different motivations and emphases, the
philosophes of the 18th century were concerned to push back
the frontiers of both concepts, limit their functions, and at-
tentuate their existence. As physics tried to account for the
world without God, so ideology tried to account for man's
brain without a soul. An aspect of this impulse to reduce intellectual life to its first elements with which the intransigent
De Tracy was particularly associated formed about the catch-
word, *"Penser c'est sentir."* To think is simply to perceive; the
acts denominated perception, memory, judgment, and will are

in fact but four different applications of the same mental activity. One possible effect of the argument may be to vulgarize and oversimplify the quality of mental activity in order to make "perception" cover it entirely. Another effect, not quite so suspect, may be to lend a measure of dignity to the emotional life, and so to render directly meaningful the observation of psychological quirks and oddities. When all thought is sensation, all sensation may include elements of thought; feeling, whatever else it may be, is not irrelevant embroidery on an impersonal process of mechanical molecular agitation. No doubt the bumping together of physical particles served to explain the original materials of some of our sensations; the study of these objects, or presumed objects, and their motions might properly be assigned to the science of physics and the disciples of Sir Isaac. But metaphysics (or psychology, or preferably, ideology) was the study of the same objects in the light of their effect upon us; its aim was to work from the familiar to the indefinite, adding as little as possible in the way of new hypotheses, and accounting for the maximum of facts with the minimum of theories.

For those to whom all reality is essentially spiritual or intellectual, these presumptions no doubt seem to beg a major question; but, such as they are, they are the presumptions of De Tracy, Stendhal, and the modern world in general. And, in the end, it is doubtful that they need much defense or apology. To organize one's thoughts and feelings as thoroughly as possible; to cultivate a rigid economy of assumption; to beware of explaining one obscurity by another; these are the first principles of any intellectual program worthy the name, and if they are too sensible to be very exciting, at least they provide a sort of guarantee against the verbal flatulence of a naturally ornate sensibility. One may think the ideals of ideology respectable, its methods enlightened for the day, and its illusions far from essentially corruptive; and yet consider the creed most valuable to Beyle as he held to it with a certain levity, not to say perversity.

For though they are often ideologists, his heroes are never simply ideologists. The world of sympathy, mystery, magic, and instinct is never far away, especially in the novels; it is always running up against a cool, mechanical rationalism which both deters and assists it. Fabrizio del Dongo, thinking of his addiction to astrology, asks himself if there is anything real in this science. "Why should it be any different from the others? A certain number of imbeciles and clever fellows agree among themselves that they know Mexican, for example; they impose in this matter on society, which respects them, and on governments, which pay them." And he goes on to reflect with bitterness that astrology may be, "like three quarters of the non-mathematical sciences, a mixture of enthusiastic fools and supple hypocrites, who are paid by those whom they serve" (Chapter 8).* This doubly-ironic logic, which seems to throw doubt on all sciences, ends by affirming that astrology is no worse than the rest, and perhaps a little better, because at least there lies at the root of it an emotional fact, an otherwise incomprehensible intuition.

So far as it works defensively for him or his heroes, Beyle takes ideology perfectly seriously—that is, so far as it concerns the social behavior of men expressed in norms, averages, and manipulative probabilities. The practical ideologist is seen at his most remarkable in the figure of Conte Mosca, a social engineer of the most sublime and casual practicality, who is at a loss only when he runs up against the absurdities of his own bewildered heart. The contrast sets his ideology in high relief —it is pure defense, simple social reflex. But figures like Julien

* Other examples of Fabrizio's superstitions are his private tree (ridiculously Freudianized by some commentators), the omens which he reads in the flight of birds, and his devotion to the number seven (see especially the *Chartreuse*, 12).

and Fabrizio, who find in their destinies something more lofty and complex than ideology can discover, treat it more casually —with a bland and careless duplicity, indeed, which neither requires nor receives theoretical justification. Because the world is so easily fooled and manipulated, the happy few can concentrate happily on developing their own sensibilities; because most men cannot look truth in the face for very long, but feel obliged to dress it in verbiage and pseudo-profundity, even the assertion of obvious facts may become a cryptic, a conspiratorial form of communication. Both faces of the ideology (its simplicity, its subtlety) can thus be used to foster the coterie-consciousness so dear to the heart of Beyle; both lend themselves naturally to that odd sort of insiders'-disillusion which seems, these days, so typically French. The humblest workman in the grimiest Parisian suburb knows that politics is a racket; the simplest citizen cultivates his sensibility, with cheerful disregard of public weal, under the aspect of petty graft. Such cynicism makes an appeal of its own; simple, straightforward, and utterly unashamed, it verges on the naïve—it has, sometimes, the luminous, fragile perfection of a rare poisonous flower. And the fact is that Stendhal, about all of whose intellectual operations there lingers a faint aroma of the shallow and the factitious, often has for this very reason a precociously naughty child's charm. His reflexive irony, his inward and devastating clarity, alone, would have stripped the illusion of profundity from a man much more interested in creating and sustaining that illusion than he was.

His heroes use the ideology, it might be said, as they use the walls of prisons; both are sounding-boards, off which they bounce the reverberations of their own personalities, and so define the character of their own beings. Perhaps the most enchanting and yet terrifying thing about the heroes of Stendhal is the sense that they define their own beings only provisionally and temporarily, in conflicts of thought and action,

in negations; without enemies, they are almost without natures, and wither away, like Fabrizio, when deprived of danger.
I think it is this vision of human nature which allies the novels
of Stendhal most closely with the great, hollow, reverberant
structures of Joyce, and the legerdemain cardhouses of Gide;
the fact that all systems of thought and feeling are tangential
to the natures of their heroes is linked to the circumstance
that their central natures are themselves a dark and hollow
mystery. From this aspect, there is no core or center to the
Stendhal fiction, as there is none to the fiction of Joyce; the
more little anagrams and puzzles of correspondence one solves,
the less one finds actually being asserted. What the novel
means is its shape, its surface, its structure; the arcana of society, like those of thought, are simply emptinesses which return
us to the surfaces of life and the solitude of the cynical individual.

In Stendhal's artistic wardrobe, the ideology is a tawdry bit
of makeshift lace—agreed; yet he wears it with a difference. But
I am very far from including Stendhal's atheism in this round-
about, left-handed, weak-kneed commendation. That seems to
me a higher form of spiritual conviction altogether; an exaggerated form of anti-clericalism, in its essence, such as derives
from too lofty (rather than too shallow) a conception of the
Christian church and the Christian god. Beyle refused to believe in God because he did not want to impute to the Al-
mighty the wickedness or weakness of having made the world
such as it is. He had a cruel Gallic wit, which he did not at
all mind using on the professionally good; he despised the pious
cant and sanctified greed which passed in his day, as in ours,
for religion. But the real seed of his atheism was planted the
day his mother lay dead, and Henri overheard the priest saying to his father that her death was God's will. From that
moment, Beyle hated his God with the anger of a jealous,
supplanted lover; the priest himself had said God was respon-

sible; wherever he turned, God was made responsible for in-
justice—by the same direct logic which made witches in the
middle ages, Beyle became an atheist. There have been ages
of the church when such a position was the most religious one
available. At least, if one accepts Pascal's terminology of faith
as a bet, disbelief is the more responsible position. But Beyle
could never quite attain to a good religious conscience, never
quite reconcile the simple sincerity of an effusive nature with
the jealous and sarcastic irony through which he was forced to
express it. Precisely this knot of tangled sentiment, with the
bitter bad conscience to which it gave rise, constitutes an element which Beyle could never have learned from De Tracy.
Ideology aimed at, and ordinarily did promote sentiments not
much more distinguished than those natural to Benjamin-
Franklin deists. Cool, calm, rational, and in its own austere
way constructive (whatever desert it made of human life was
undeniably peaceful), it aimed to lay bare the passions, and so
to gain mastery over them. It was an Apollonian philosophy,
implying throughout a belief in the therapeutic value of sun-
shine, open air, and rationality. Stendhal's art, like his thought,
is a *tour de force* of light and dark—a shimmering web of
bright, geometrical consciousness weaving transparent patterns
over the caverns of unconscious association. The picture he
paints may be described as a clash of black on white, in which
the clear but limited truths of ideology oppose the black, un-
limited Machiavellianism of jesuitry—and out of which there
strides without warning a streak and ripple of royal purple, a
king's color and a kingly gesture, set unexpectedly against a
sparse and angular background.

Ideology provides a dry and limited framework for Stendhal's
ideas; his observations and emotions are constantly escaping
from it, returning to it, correcting it, mocking its insufficiency,
teasing the reader's eye with things which are beyond its ken.

Ideology, then, is a foil. But it serves more positive and more complex purposes as well, which one might approach by way of the observation that Stendhal is an extraordinarily repetitious writer. Not exactly in his situations and episodic inventions, though there is often a general similarity from novel to novel. As a striking example, the likeness between Julien and Fabrizio, already considerable on the surface, is enforced by subordinate parallels between Mme. de Rênal and Gina, Mathilde and Clélia Conti, Abbé Chelan and Priore Blanès. Falling off a horse indicates the same thing about Lucien Leuwen in his relation to Mme. de Chasteller as it does about Julien Sorel in his relation to Mathilde; the same world-weariness combined with the same exaggerated suspicion of other people's motives torments Octave and Lucien; Julien at Besançon and in Paris picks or is on the point of picking the same sort of cafe-quarrel as Fabrizio at Geneva and Henry Brulard at Lausanne. A false letter deceives Octave de Malivert as a pretended pregnancy deceives Lucien Leuwen; a falsified letter causes the downfall of Julien, and a forged letter leads to the capture of Fabrizio. The dying daughter of Clementine Curial, who gave rise to such remorse in her mother, is repeated as Mme. de Rênal's sick son Stanislaus and Clélia Conti's sick child Sandrino. These are distinct varieties of repetition in Stendhal, little units of narrative invention, if you will, with which he filled out the structure of his fictions, and sometimes used twice over, or thrice.

There are also similarities in the language which frames his episodes. For example, the famous "*N'est-ce que ça?*" turns up in the *Rouge*, I, 15, and II, 6, in *Lamiel* (Chapter IX), in the Waterloo episode of the *Chartreuse* (where it is not quite word for word), and of course in its original (yet final) expression, in *The Life of Henry Brulard* (Chapters 45 and 46). And there are other examples of catch-phrases, as it were, which summarize a particular dramatic action for Stendhal, and so are repeated. "Speech was given to man to enable him to conceal his thoughts"; the epigram appears in *Armance*, Chapter 25, and as an epigraph to the *Rouge*, I, 22, where it is attributed to one Malagrida, S.J. That books are a lottery on which the winning numbers will be declared by posterity, that one cannot describe supreme pleasure without spoiling it, that despair in love causes one to want to "burn one's brains," these are Stendhalian commonplaces.

But the repetitions I have in mind are more gratuitous than this. They are almost philosophic in character, they are little verbal tags which turn up over and over again in the course of the novels. For instance, there is just one opinion concerning America which finds expression in all Stendhal's writing. It is a routine counter, it occurs over and over again in the travel-sketches, in the novels, in the criticism. America is a land where public opinion reigns supreme, where the grocer must be courted as the arbiter of destinies, and where pleasure is dead. Sometimes these bits occur together, as in the *Chartreuse*, 6 and 24; more often separately as in the *Rouge*, I, 1 and 23, or in the second and third prefaces to *Lucien Leuwen*, and Chapters 6 and 65 of the same work; or in *Racine et Shakespeare*, Chapter 8; or in *Promenades dans Rome*, 22 August, 1827; or in a dozen other passages which could be culled from the canon. Comments like these on America are neither inappropriate, as a rule, nor contemptible in themselves; simply, having heard them before, we are struck in a peculiar way by their repetition. Primarily we are made aware of the author, who by this rather indirect and backhanded means makes an appearance as a commentator and generalizer existing outside the novels and from novel to novel. This authorial mouthpiece is not a fully dramatic figure; now and then he slips into something as simple and straightforward as an avuncular narrator. M. de Rênal had widened the main avenue of Verrières by more than six feet, admits the narrator of the *Rouge* (I, 2);

"although he is an ultra and I myself a liberal, I give him credit for it." This is clearly ironic. But mostly the narrator is more elusive. Sometimes he is omniscient as authors in their books can always be. Sometimes he is Beyle, historical M. H. Beyle, come down from Paris to Verrières overnight, and still dreaming of the brilliant social life of the capital, as he watches the turbulent flow of the Doubs (*Rouge*, I, 2). The author of *Armance* is said to be a lady whose MS the fictional figure Stendhal has merely edited; the novel itself has no character requiring, or even consistent with, this sort of author. Most frequently the author, without necessarily appearing as an explicit "I," is responsible for a series of semi-philosophic or critical commentaries on the action, half-serious, half-ironic, like those which Byron makes on the action of *Don Juan*.

These repeated commentaries on the action are a major means of establishing the character of the narrator, which is dry, decisive, rationalist, and limited; and of separating him from the narration, which is complex, intuitive, and passionate. Many of the most telling commentaries on the action are brief and grammatically subordinate; but they lift the subject, for the moment, quite out of context, flash it in a new profile against another light or sometimes two contrasting lights, and without another gesture allow it to slip back into its original position in the narrative flow. Julien Sorel, in a famous passage, is bargaining with M. Valenod in the patois of vulgar fatuity; on the one hand this, on the other hand that, but we most never forget, on the third hand. . . . "Julien," says Stendhal, "attained such a degree of perfection in this style of eloquence, which has replaced the swiftness of action under the Empire, that he ended by boring himself with the sound of his own voice" (I, 22). The flare of light from that little passing phrase is like a match struck in the darkness and quickly extinguished; yet it is the outside world that it lights up, not Julien.

Elsewhere the author is viewed, or even views himself, more

ironically, even when he seems to be moralizing straightfor-
wardly; his qualities, then, sharply bound his vision, so that
what rises to sight outside that vision, or in opposition to it,
seems to have a special authenticity. Whenever Julien shows
any sensitivity, perceptiveness, or sincerity, he is stigmatized
as foolish, ridiculous, weak, or naïve; when Mathilde, yielding
to a genuine impulse from the heart, has written to Julien
for the first time, she is overcome with pride, shame, desire,
scorn; the commentator has nothing to say but, "Fortunately
such characters as this are very rare."

Ironic comment by the narrator serves to deprecate the passionate narrative, to set it in a perspective, to contrast its glowing colors with the neutral common-sense of the speaker in the
foreground. But a defensive arrangement like this gives way
frequently to direct attack upon the narrator, his audience, and
the century of which they are representative. A *propos* of the
Conte Mosca's arrangement for Gina to marry the Duca Sanseverina-Taxis, the narrator breaks into the following paragraph
of apology:

> Why should the historian who faithfully follows the details
> of a story as it was told to him be held responsible for it? Is it
> his fault if the characters, seduced by passions which he, un-
> fortunately for himself, by no means shares, descend to actions
> which are profoundly immoral? It is true that things of this
> sort are no longer done in countries where the only passion
> which has survived all others is that for money, as an excuse
> for vanity (Chapter 6).

The logical progression here is extraordinary; it is dialectic
carried to the point of perversity. *I am an impartial recorder of
evil passions, which I wish I shared, and which are called evil
only by those who are wholly given up to worse ones.* The
passionate truth of the story is affirmed by inventing someone
to sneer at it, and then sneering at that person. Like a nest of

Chinese boxes or an onion, the core of truth is surrounded by a whole mass of alternate, conflicting falsehoods and counter-truths. Compression of these perspectives sometimes leads to sentences so wild and whirling that they dizzy the reader with flashes of ironic light from two or three directions at once. When Fabrizio has escaped from the tower, public opinion is much occupied with his story, each faction having its own interest to serve. "Several liberals known for their imprudence, among them a certain Doctor C***, an agent paid directly by the prince, added, but compromised themselves in so doing, that the atrocious police force had had the barbarity to execute eight of these unhappy soldiers who had assisted the flight of that ingrate of a Fabrizio" (Chapter 22). The sentence is deliberately shaped as awkwardly as possible; it gloriously imitates the stuffed mouth of a bold, cautious liberal, who wants to make known both his earnest indignation and his perfect political reliability. It also includes extra "outside" ironies—Doctor C***, the "imprudent" liberal, whose imprudence, so familiar in modern life, compromises only his colleagues; and the fact, held in suspension till almost the end of the sentence, that the liberal indignation is roused to its keenest pitch by the death of purely imaginary beings. Passages like this are responsible for Valéry's characterization of the Stendhal manner as a "vaudeville"; and perhaps there is no better word for them. But they are not the whole style, and the more usual, more patent use of the defensive gesture is to safeguard the passion of the narrative both from deliberate enemies (the frozen souls) and from the insidious assistance of *"enflure."* Something like this may be responsible for the famous likening of politics to a pistol-shot in the middle of a concert, which Stendhal used so much. The phrase occurs in three of the novels (*Armance*, 14; *Rouge*, I, 21; and *Chartreuse*, 23), as well as in *Racine et Shakespeare*, Letter 5, "De la censure." But of course in its most famous contexts it is quite wrong, perhaps deliberately misleading; politics is no interruption of either of the great novels. They are saturated in politics, political feeling is the breath of their being; but it is insurrectionary, heroic politics, which was a kind of music to Stendhal's ears. By disclaiming what he once called the politics of taxation, he aims to avoid responsibility for a kind of politics he could no more avow than he could avoid using it.

We shall find nothing elsewhere in Stendhal to equal the reverberations of that pistol-shot; but the in-and-out of quotation and authorial comment suggest a peculiar sort of interplay among planes of reality which produces some other odd effects. Stendhal's use of epigraphs is particularly notable. Most of them are perfectly straightforward citations from reputable authors. Some of the quotations are invented, translated, distorted, or incorrectly attributed; but this is less to our purpose than their occasional habit of turning up in the text itself. For example, Chapter 8 of *Rouge* I carries as epigraph a dictum attributed by Stendhal to the historian Saint-Real: "A novel is a mirror which travels along a busy road." Aside from the fact that Saint-Real never said anything of the sort, this is a fine epigraph; but in I, 19, the statement is repeated as an element of the author's argument. And the same comparison is found in the Prefaces to *Armance*, and *Lucien Leuwen*, as well as elsewhere in the writings—it is a particular bit of proverbial wisdom, which is not in fact true of the novels of Stendhal, any more than the remark about the pistol-shot. If these are mirrors, they distort strangely. Elsewhere, characters in the novel itself are cited in the epigraphs, even though the events in the course of which they are supposed to have made the statements have not yet (in the novel's time-scheme) taken place (*Rouge*, I, 18, 25). So in the *Chartreuse*, the epigraph to Part II is taken from Chapter 23 of the same Part II, where it appears in the course of a speech by Conte Mosca. And the epigraphs make connections which the text itself does not dare undertake—for example, the epigraph to Chapter 25 of *Rouge* I, shows that the same meanness controls the seminary at Besançon as the poor-house kept by Valenod at Verrières.

The appearance of the novel's characters as from a realm outside the novel implies a view of them as "real" people which recent criticism has taught us to despise. "How many children had Lady Macbeth?" She is a character created out of words printed on paper, she is incapable of parturition—it is perfectly obvious common sense. But Stendhal would not have felt the question to be absurd; he himself as an actual person evidently inhabited, was inhabited by, and was able to extend at will the world of his fiction; so that, almost as in Cervantes, the novel itself could come to play a part in its own actions. There is a notable alteration in the *Rouge*, I, 30; instead of the leaf of a tree, supposed to have fallen from the Abbé Pirard's letter as a sign to Julien, Stendhal substituted a blot on the thirteenth word. His reason, assigned in a marginal note, was that the spy (whom every reader would assume as existing and having access to the letter) might have forgotten to replace the leaf when he opened the letter. Clearly there is no limit to the action which he imagines as taking place; around the action described in the book, Stendhal's imagination, and that of the reader, are invited to weave a whole web of intrigue and coun- ter-intrigue. Thus the whole experience described in the novel is recessed in depth, within Stendhal's mind, and behind the printed page, infinitely.* Partly this quality may be attributed

---

* Striking examples of these techniques are cryptic footnotes from Beyle's private life affixed to certain chapters of Stendhal's novels. For example, the *Rouge*, II, 13, ends with a note, "Esprit per. pré. gui. II.A.30," which is easily decipherable as "Esprit perd préfecture. Guizot. 11 août 1830." Rather more puzzling are notes to the *Chartreuse*, XXV, which read, "4.9.38.26.x.38fir.s.6.f. last 26 m.39." and on a separte line, "3 Ri d. f. g. D. ha. s. so. p." The first, describing dates of composition and proof-correction for the *Chartreuse*, evidently reads, "4 novembre 1838 to 26 décembre; first sheets 6 février, last 26 mars 1839." The second

to Stendhal's early habit of making a complete list of every character's actions, a dossier, only a few items of which might ever be used; but I think it capable also of an esthetic rationale, which Beyle would not have hesitated to invoke in behalf of his stories, any more than Byron or E.T.A. Hoffmann for theirs; that is, the rationale of recessed realities, *trompe-l'oeil*, and open form used for comic ends.

The elusive but haunting presence of Beyle-Stendhal in the world of the novel is then to be assumed; and his constant intrusion, by means of the repetitive generalization, confirms that strangely double situation by which the events of the novel take place inside his mind while he himself appears within the framework of the fiction. There is a kind of double mirror at work here; if it is to work properly, the reader must be kept aware of the limitations, if not the limits, of each mirror. The consciousness of the narrator is clear, definite, precise; he is the man who repeats his pat, ideological little opinions. Sometimes he is an avuncular man of the world, who comments good-humoredly and urbanely on the follies of his young hero. But the fiction contains and pervades the narrator, even as he claims to summarize it; and the reader slides from angle to angle, from reflection to reflection of reflection, without ever being sure of his author or his author's work or his author's intention.

Such a mistake could never be made in the case of Flaubert or Fielding; Flaubert who keeps out of his novel, and Fielding who gambols all over his, have the same kind of respect for the tissue of the novel as such, which leads the one to refrain from violating it and the other to violate it distinctly and emphati-

---

is more resistant. "3" may refer to the date of Beyle's first admiration for Giulia Rinieri, which was 3 February 1827; "d.f.g." has been conjecturally read as "di fortunata Giulia" and the last five abbreviations "Dominique has secured son pucelage." Since the situation of Fabrizio and Clélia in the novel parallels markedly certain relations between Beyle and his Giulia, the latter reading seems persuasive; I am not sure that "3 Ri d. f. g." has yet yielded its ultimate message.

cally, for comic effect. Neither does Stendhal use the limited consciousness quite in the way that James does, ironically, dramatically, sometimes with four or five limited and polished mirrors maneuvering and reflecting one another within a single drawing room. Stendhal is almost always concerned with a single consciousness at a time; but he gets some special effects, and some variety of effect, by a deliberate fluidity of outline, arising from indefinitely recessed reality-planes, and a fluid, pervasive, half-dramatic use of his own personality in the fiction.

He is not unfailingly successful at this game; or at least his successes are not always of the unequivocal sort one can tot up on a critical adding-machine. Take for example the scene where Fabrizio, after his scuffle with Giletti, has killed him, escaped, and gone to a church to give thanks for his good luck. There is no real way for Stendhal to handle the accumulated contrasts of this scene—the naïveté of his hero, the ironies to which a vulgar or a self-conscious mind would subject it, the religious fervor which overrides those ironies without effort—except to write in his own person a little essay on the subject, complete with dummies to represent the limited points of view.

"What is remarkable," the essay begins, "is that he never thought to count among his faults the project of becoming archbishop simply because the Conte Mosca was prime minister. . . ." His religion, Stendhal continues, had absolutely nothing to do with thinking for oneself; the idea that he had committed a sort of simony never crossed his mind. "If you had suggested that he give a hundred louis to become first grand vicar of the Archbishop of Parma, he would have rejected the idea with horror"; but he never reflected that accepting the prime minister's influence amounted to much the same thing. "A Frenchman," Stendhal concludes, "who was raised amid the personal interest and irony of Paris, might in perfect sincerity have accused Fabrizio of hypocrisy at the very moment when our hero was opening his heart to God with the fullest sincerity and the deepest feeling" (Chapter 12).

Here the explanatory author intervenes to reconcile a "low" advocate of bribery and a cynical Parisian to his religious Italian. Stendhal does this, not ironically, but with a cool, comprehensive vision which holds in one equal hand both the truth of Fabrizio's feeling and the social truth of his critics. The tone is scrupulously fair, and the point is brilliant. Still, an insight so deep and calm may well destroy all sorts of potential consistencies in lesser author-dummies who have been used to make comments, more or less understanding, on the action up to now. We have to see, evidently, that there is no formal program or limit to Stendhal's intervention in the affairs of his novel. He roves in and out, assuming precisely the character he chooses, and trusting the reader of discretion to follow his maneuvers. Repetition of ideas is, in one sense, a substitute for sameness of character, feeling, tonality; because he modulates so fluidly in the quite unaccustomed band of feelings, attitudes, reality-levels, and authorial identities, Stendhal need make no bones about a sameness of ideas. They are *only* ideas.

Indeed, Stendhal has imposed on his readers in this matter of ideas. His repeated comments on the oratorical style of his contemporaries are correct enough in themselves, and when he says that rhetoric serves George Sand or Chateaubriand chiefly to cover up a paucity of ideas, he is perfectly right. But there is an implication that he, who does not use the rotund style, has plenty of ideas; and this is quite wrong. Stendhal did not have many ideas; his abstract ideas were few and almost spectacularly limited.* Henry Brulard is close to the truth when he remarks

---

* Harry Levin, following Paul Bourget, says Stendhal is a writer of ideas, not images (*Toward Stendhal*, Pharos #3, Murray, Utah, 1945, pp. 30 ff.); and, as it applies to the texture of his prose, this is certainly true. Yet it opens up a series of paradoxes. Stendhal was a philosophical novelist who

that "By instinct my moral life has been spent in careful consideration of five or six principal ideas, and in trying to see the truth about them" (Chapter 2). Beyle was a philosophical anachronism almost before he started to think, his learning was pure façade, and his real talents lay in another direction entirely. One is reminded of Byron, who was great by virtue of his feelings. Stendhal too is better in the realm of feeling than in the realm of thought; but he is best of all in the realm of inexact observation. He had at his disposal immense resources of social situation; he was responsive to subtle nuances of impulse and behavior. And one of the qualities which contributes to his special gift is an ability to make thought reflect feeling and vice-versa—to frame a tale of deep and complex feelings which contrast with dry, clear, abstract ideas of the utmost obviousness—to show and to conceal himself with such adroitness that one is never sure how far one is to read beyond the printed page, only that there is somehow something more.

This indefinite recessing of the book beyond its ideas and beyond even the construct of its words constitutes a principal source of Stendhal's "impurity". He is in love with the open possibility, with the chance for whole new areas of life behind the areas described in the book; and he does nothing to close them off. Only consider as a single example the teasing which goes on throughout the *Rouge* regarding Julien Sorel's paternity. He is the son of old Sorel, a peasant carpenter; but he is something additional or something else. The Abbé Pirard thinks he is "the natural son of some rich man" (I, 30); and when Julien takes naturally to Paris life asks "Can it be his blood coming out?" But then Norbert invents the same story for Julien, to account for his participation in a duel—that he is the illegiti-

---

had few ideas; a social observer whose literal details were invariably inaccurate; an egotist whose genius lay in the delineation of the passions. Each of these paradoxes relates to, and is explained by, the difference between public and private "lo-gi-que."

mate son of a wealthy nobleman in the Franche-Comté (II,6). M. de la Mole makes ironic and sceptical commentary on this story when he hears of it; when he gives Julien a cross, he gives him, for use with it, another pseudo-genealogy, he is to be the son of Duc de Retz (II, 7); but later M. de la Mole tells the Abbé Pirard, apparently in all seriousness, "I know the truth about Julien's birth, and I authorize you not to keep this confidence secret."

It is a nice question, who is deceived in all this; whether the Abbé Pirard alone is mistaken and M. de la Mole is ruthlessly exploiting this mistake for the benefit of his protégé; or whether M. de la Mole too is mistaken; or whether both of them are not right, and Norbert's story, idly invented as a joke, is not the truth. Even more charming is the question of who is aware of the import, the clear implication of all this fencing and feigning in the novel? Julien only becomes aware of his artificial parentage and seems ready to believe in it, when its complete falsity and artificiality are most apparent (II,35); and the narrator, though he recites the story, either forgets it at once or ignores it, for he says nothing which would confirm such an idea and a good many things which militate against it. In terms of the story, it does not much matter whether Julien is legitimate or illegitimate; what does matter is that Stendhal went to such pains to raise the issue in the reader's mind and to keep from closing it—that he left even his narrator in the dark (if he can be supposed to have had a distinct narrator; a sizable fragment of himself, if he cannot). A good ideologist, whose opinions on life in America, politics in novels, the novel as mirror, and other similar subjects are always ready to hand, might be expected to take a certain interest in obtaining clear and distinct ideas on a topic like his hero's paternity; but no, it is part of Stendhal's art to be full, clear, and explicit on topics which are immaterial, but to say nothing, or as little as possible, on matters where the busybody reader wants genuine, practical information. It is the triumph of a jesuitical education, says Stendhal, "to form the habit of not paying attention to things that are clearer than daylight" (*Chartreuse*, Chapter XII); if this is, indeed, jesuit education, Stendhal himself exemplifies it passing well. He has made Fabrizio's paternity even more dubious than Julien's;* Gina's highly ambiguous and questionable feelings for Fabrizio are never resolved. For the greater part of the novel, we never know why the Charterhouse of Parma, appearing only on the last page of the book, gives its name to the whole. What alternatives are indicated by the Red and the Black? Without information from outside the novel, one would never be able to guess what is the matter with Octave de Malivert. In one detail after another, Stendhal deludes the reader in matters of essential information. He clearly intends to do so; it is part of his method. Fabrizio sends to Clélia a handkerchief on which was printed a sonnet of Petrarch—"it is true that a word was altered in this sonnet"—we are told no more. Again Fabrizio, receiving a forged passport from the duchess, notes "the little spot of red ink dropped, as though by accident, at the foot of the sheet, near the right-hand corner." Only the definite article and the subordinate phrase "as though by accident" make this a countersign. And it seems to me that this whole hide-and-seek procedure grows naturally out of the evident deficiencies of ideology as a body of conclusions, its remarkable advantages as a preparative for psychological study. Like most rationalist philosophies, it tells us brilliantly what we already knew before we started to philosophize and do not particularly need to hear again; unlike most other rationalisms, it encourages us to feel as much as possible in order to understand as much as possible.

---

* François Michel flatly denies (*Etudes stendhaliennes*, pp. 241-242) Fabrizio's illegitimacy; the same astringent scepticism which is his glory as a biographical investigator serving here to shut him off from Stendhal's system of hints and allusions. If he is not begetting Fabrizio, what the devil is Lieutenant A. doing in the novel at all?

The ironies of the first situation counterpoint brilliantly the lights and darks of the second. A plethora of useless, self-satisfied clarities is just the springboard necessary for a diver whose chief delight is "the unexpected."

Editors, of the critical works especially, have sometimes made heavy going of Stendhal's cavalier attitude toward intellectual systems. He likes to have handy a couple of broad theoretical definitions, which, as in *Racine et Shakespeare,* can be used to put the opposition permanently in the wrong. But they are not really devices of dialectic or even of communication, so much as shields behind which his own wayward personality and hedonistic responsiveness are left free to develop. German music, he says in the *Life of Haydn,* "is correct, it is learned, it is elaborate; it has only one fault,—it makes us yawn" (Letter XIII). Such distrust of the systematic and correct is, in one form, a critical doctrine running back to Longinus; but for Beyle it is simply an expression of his overpowering need to stay close to immediate psychological facts. As he reads, or listens, or looks, the important question at the front of his mind is always: "Am I really enjoying this?" Our own age, typically involved in building metaphysico-critical cloud-castles, must necessarily find his directness and simplicity altogether unnerving. The last question in the world to occur to the modern critic is whether he is really enjoying his book, or himself. After all—*subjectivity!*

From the aspect of exalted critical theory, if one wants to assume this aspect, there are hundreds of reasons for disapproving of Beyle. Not only is he incapable of systems, he scarcely pretends to be interested in them. Yet his criticism represents interesting literary work, held together as it is by his detachment, his irony, his attitudes. An inquisitive mind with sudden subtle perspectives and a sense of total relevance joins with considerable delicacy of response to make a truly free critical agent. It took some courage in that age of pompous system-builders to be frankly impressionistic; it still does in our own day. And yet who before Beyle ever put together such a collection of insights and ideas about the novel as can be collected from his marginalia? In theory as in practice, Beyle's 18th-century sense of human limitation stood him in good stead. He never tried to say more than a human mouth can utter, and thus managed to maintain the bloom of experience, actual as well as imagined, in its pristine and indefinite iridescence.

As novelist, then, and even as critic, Beyle drew advantage from ideology precisely because as philosophy it was so inadequate; which is to say, that some major functions in life he never expected ideas to perform. His mockery of the great intellectual systems of his day, Liberalism, Catholicism, German Transcendentalism, rationality itself, contains an element of the perverse; but it contains too an element of that feeling for free possibility and open choice which ultimately made a novelist of him. The decision received sanction from a quite unexpected source. "The only way to achieve truth nowadays is in the novel"; it was old M. de Tracy who told him this; and so bequeathed, as it were, to the irresponsible and wayward form of the younger man's imagination what had slipped through his own too-rigid fingers.

"*Faute de mieux*"; it is a motive for creation perhaps more widespread than is generally recognized. If Beyle had not lived in an age of philosophical decay and decadence, and shared its intellectual deficiencies, he might never have had to become a novelist. Caught between a limited and all-but-useless certainty on the one side and a great ocean of doubt, confusion, mystery, and open possibility on the other, he never really made up his mind to accept wholly, or reject finally, either. Passion cut across his concept of character like a lightning-flash; a boy's cynicism balanced a child's credulity. Outmoded 18th-century philosophy lit the edges of his stage brilliantly, and plunged the center in the most dazzling and enchanting blackness. Both thought and feeling then became toys in the game which he spent all his life playing—the game of looking into darkness and trying to see it without disturbing it. The essential comedy of this routine hardly detracts from its value for a novelist—or, to be sure, for any man whose imagination is to remain flexible and alive. Most of us, I think, are given incongruous materials from which to patch up lives; but to join a fallacy and a curiosity to create great novels is really a *tour de force* of that improvisation which for Stendhal was the breath of life itself.

Yet better materials might have proved just intractable enough—perhaps one ought even to say "reliable" enough—to yield a worse product.

4

*

Angelina:

or the Duplicity of the *Chartreuse*

Force is only a desire of flight.

Leonardo

Angelina or Angiola Borroni Pietragrua, known to her associates and intimates as Gina; and Angelina Cornelia-Isota Val-
serra del Dongo, Contessa Pietranera, Duchessa Sanseverina and
Contessa Mosca della Rovere—also known to her associates
and intimates as Gina—; between the promiscuous wife of a
minor clerk in the Milanese bureaucracy, who happened to exist
in historical flesh and blood, and the eternal duchess of Stendhal's imagination, there lies an evident abyss. Perhaps the
best way to cross it is with some vague, promissory reference to
the creative imagination, some casual comment on "crystallization." This is the indicated approach; for the glitter that Stendhal contributed to poor Beyle's fascinating bitch is all too
evident. On the one hand we have amours which veer between

the squalid and the pathological—intrigues without tenderness or even style, carried on by an infinite series of tricks, traps, and deceptions which ended by disgusting even Beyle, who was not squeamish about such matters. On the other hand, that figure of gleaming defiance, impenetrably mannered, irresistibly witty, mercurial, passionate, tender, and brave—the very model of Castiglione's court lady. It is a magnificent metamorphosis— no less interesting for its economies than for its extravagances.

The fulness of the transformation requires little development. It was by raising her rank, imputing to her a truly Spanish, and perfectly original, disdain for money and convenience, by exaggerating the quickness and ferocity of her responses, and augmenting her age to an Indian-summer brilliance, that Stendhal did most to convert his mistress into a heroine. Of these alterations, the responses which cut right across conventional morality are undoubtedly most exciting. Stendhal's proceedings here exemplify one ancient paradox about fulfilling art by disdaining it; they suggest a new one about the strongest beat in a rhythm-sequence being the one that is missed. He neither made Gina exemplary, in the sense of living up to a code, nor traded on her violation of codes to make her a romantic outlaw. He granted her, in fact, no sense of guilt at all; in this respect she is wholly unlike most heroines of the romantic age, and a figure scarcely to be paralleled in fiction. It is her special quality to be unconscious of or indifferent to the codes which her conduct violates; those violations are neither defiant nor principled, but simple and direct outgrowths of her perception. To see is to feel, to feel is to act; the Duchessa Sanseverina never hesitates to be perfectly and completely herself, and there is an almost archaic severity and simplicity about her attack on life. She acts, at her best, in the very highest style, taking perfectly for granted her inalienable right to do exactly what she wants; and justifies all her conduct precisely by her sublime refusal to condescend even to begin to justify it.

This is a traditional and probably a correct view of the duchess; but one is bound to notice in this context a tendency of recent criticism to enlarge Stendhal's irony and "double consciousness" at the expense of his sublime and "natural" impulses (H. W. Wardman, "*La Chartreuse de Parme*: Ironical Ambiguity," *Kenyon Review*, Summer, 1955). The argument takes its start from an assertion of Stendhal's that Mathilde de la Mole needs a public, an audience. But she does not realize that France after Waterloo, instead of applauding the sublime, ridicules it. Therefore Stendhal's drawing of Mathilde includes an element of the comic, so far as she has made a mistake in the pursuit of happiness. So far, so good. But the argument now goes on to assert that the Duchessa Sanseverina has made the same mistake; and also that she has crystallized on social success, aristocracy, in a way which keeps her from being ironical about it—and that this is Stendhal's judgment of her.

Note, though, that there is an audience for much of the duchess's histrionics; it is the villagers of Sacca, it is Ludovico, it is Ferrante Palla, it is her ladies in waiting, who applaud at the end of her long operatic duel with the Prince—it is, to look no further, the happy few. Thus the Duchessa has not mistaken the path to happiness as has Mathilde—she does not need an audience, though she has one which responds perfectly to her performances. Her most acute struggles, those over Fabrizio, are played out without benefit of audience, and she betrays no need of one. Yet there is, in fact, a half-comic judgment against her; it is that she plays her hand more strongly than she needs to. Not that the values for which she is playing are negligible—positively they perhaps are, but negatively the penalties of losing are real. Whatever one feels about the Parma court and citadel, there is no irony about poisoned food or twenty years in the Spielberg with irons on both legs. So the Duchessa is playing for real stakes; but she overplays her hand both with Fabrizio and the Prince; falls helplessly in love with a nephew 20 years younger than herself and has to honor, to her dishonor, a sordid contract with a stupid man. Pursuing happiness the hard way is to her credit, but pursuing it too hard is not. Mr. Wardman concludes his case against the Duchessa for being too sincere and naïve by saying her "grotesque association with [Ferrante Palla] leads to his attempt to overthrow the system on which her ambitions depend" (p. 456). But this is an easy literalism. She poisons the prince, acting as an outlaw and with an outlaw; she is in vendetta, but everyone knows a republic is, in practical terms, hopeless, and she is not trying to help Ferrante set it up. Her passion, like a good deal of sublime feeling, is self-defeating in practical terms; she cannot help deepening the conflict at every exchange. She teaches Fabrizio the need to conform, but the game she is playing has more in common with Russian roulette than with whist. There is a judgment here, but it includes the observation that constant danger is necessary to development of the superior person. Thus I think irony tempers a basic sympathy for the sublime, in our feelings about the Duchessa, rather than *vice versa.**

In part, it seems likely that Stendhal was led to this image of the Duchess' character (as he was to that of her prototype) by a preoccupation, common in the early 19th century but rather outworn now—the myth of the Noble, Natural, Simple, Sensitive Soul. Beyle was no more than typical of his age in his concern for a people, untainted by civilization, who could find access to their emotions without hesitation or self-consciousness. Being himself the most self-conscious of men, he found the attractions of simplicity and directness particularly strong; but indeed they were felt by many romantic writers. Words-

---

* On this general theme see Henri Martineau's inaugural address, on the occasion of the Journées Stendhaliennes, held at Grenoble in 1955—the address titled, "Sincérité et dissimulation de Stendhal." (It was on this occasion that the lycée de jeunes filles at Grenoble was admirably retitled, "Lycée Stendhal.")

worth made much of the North-Country yeoman, and Chateau-briand of the red-skinned Cherokee, Mérimée idealized the Spanish gypsy as Shelley idealized the proletariat, ancient and modern Greeks were variously popular, and savage peoples in Africa, Asia, and the South Seas were frequently rigged for the role of spontaneous children of nature. For Beyle as for Byron the promised land was Italy; and, having determined to see the Italians in this light, the romancer did not fail to find the qualities for which he was looking. It is one of his great demographic commonplaces that the Northern countries are full of cold, reserved, formal, and rational people; the Southern ones are simple, sensuous, and passionate. "In the North, in America, for example, two young people experience love for one another only after discovering, by means of twenty evenings spent together in cold reasoning, that they have the same ideas of religion, metaphysics, history, politics, the arts, novels, dramas, of geology, the formation of the continents, revenues by indirect taxation, and many other matters. At first sight and without any metaphysical reasoning, a statue by Canova will move a young Italian woman to tears" (*Promenades dans Rome*, II, 24).

A passage like this implies some very odd ideas about America, young Italian girls, and the art of Canova; and indeed the whole notion of the cold north and the impetuous south has something distinctly factitious about it. Still, such as it is, Stendhal shared in the illusion, and drew upon it to give his duchess her peculiarly vibrant and passionate disposition. His own severe taste enabled him to avoid the temptations of rhetoric and deliberate display, obvious to anyone in a novel like Madame de Stael's *Corinne*. *Le naturel* is an ambience for Gina, a circumstance, not a *geschaft*.

Of course the Duchessa Sanseverina has other elements in her character than the Natural Italian. She is of the Spanish temperament, which Beyle had admired in his great-aunt Elizabeth; Corneille's *Cid* had a part in her making. She is also an aristocrat of a great Roman family, and of an age when aristocracy carried all before it. Her original, in the chronicle around which the *Chartreuse* grew, was Vanozza Farnese; and the grandeur of the house of Farnese, in all its severity and arrogance and taurine energy, has left its mark upon her conception. Still another parallel may be worth mentioning. In her brilliant moral obliquity, it is possible that La Sanseverina owes something to that blunt, artless, 17th-century teller of courtiers' smutty stories, the Sieur de Brantôme, whom Stendhal had long admired. How blandly does Brantôme introduce us to a story of blackguardism, cuckoldry, and intrigue, by assuring us that he once knew a very honest, handsome woman, who. . . . Brantôme's "honnête femme" is proverbial; and the quality which distinguishes her is not very remote from that which marks the individuality of the Duchessa Sanseverina.

Thus there were two main forces working on Stendhal's imagination when he set about transforming the petty official's wanton wife into a dazzling duchess. He must make her more aristocratic and splendid; her disregard of the conventions must be instantly charming and sympathetic, never savage or ugly, so that she need never hesitate or fumble, apologize or explain. At the same time, he must make her more natural than nature itself, giving her, beneath the aristocratic polish, a perfectly untamed and unspoiled sensibility. In some measure the two projects are complementary; because she conspires so happily and naturally with a servant like Ludovico, or suffers so miserably and naturally the pangs of love for Fabrizio, Gina's court behavior shines at once more brilliantly and artificially. Mosca enjoys the same duplicity, talking one language to insiders outside the court circle, and quite a different, "official" tongue to the outsiders of the novel, who are the inside circle of the court. But his character does not reach beyond the limits of an easy and comfortable—occasionally a cruel—cynicism. Gina draws out both points of the dichotomy; at the height of her bent, she is both a mischievous, susceptible girl and an invincible princess, a magnificent lady and a child. This, I venture to say, is the sex fulfilling its most enchanting potentials. In the novel, at any rate (to narrow the assertion remarkably), it works supremely well. By drawing out the figure of Gina in two opposing directions and by boldly ignoring anything which sounded like meat-and-potatoes reality or middle-class morality, Stendhal went a long way toward creating from a feckless trull one of the most glamorous and vital women of modern fiction.

The same pattern applies to other aspects in the drawing of Gina's character. Eros impels her in two contrary ways, both apart from the socially approved channels. Her tender, motherly affection for Fabrizio almost but not quite conceals a profound physical attraction for that delightful but socially tabooed young man. The equivocations of this maternal-mistress relation had been delicious to Beyle since his early youth; any resolution of it is quite out of the question, but the very fact that it cannot be avowed is a prime reason for making this passion the mainspring of the book's chief action, Gina's plot to release Fabrizio. The intensity of this darkness at the heart of the novel is heightened when her love of Fabrizio is made to cast a shadow over her relation to the Conte Mosca. By comparison, the arrangement with Mosca is a fairly straightforward attachment. Technically, it is a bit irregular, owing only to a purely arbitrary sentence of Stendhal's, which grants to the Count a living wife with no other function than to keep the lovers from getting married. This wife disappears even more conveniently and silently than the Duca Sanseverina-Taxis, as soon as there is no further need for her. Stendhal's choice here is, of course, far from arbitrary in terms of the effects at which the novel aims. The deepest relations he knows are built on passion and are intolerant of formalities; they are the creation of free agents, not of partners to a contract. The heroic, the decisive, and the personal are exemplified in Gina's relation to Mosca, as in Mathilde de la Mole's relations to Julien.

In the details of her dealings with Mosca, as with her other admirers, the Duchessa is only to be likened to Cleopatra, as Shakespeare showed her dealing with Antony. She is fractious and subtle, various and devoted—a mistress of superlative policy and instinctive attraction. Only General Pietranera, that first husband in the background, serves like Fabrizio's real father General A—to represent the straightforward way of things, a contented growing in life taken on its own terms. But Gina, either as an elegant lady at the Court of Parma or as a poor widow in retirement at Grianta, is a person with a gift for making more of life than its elements seem to allow. She is, in effect, an actress, instinct with the creative imagination which forms every incident into a dramatic scene. When she dismisses her cowardly lover, Limercati, it is with a little flick of scarifying contempt, which cuts and curls to the heart. When she acts out her great scene with Mosca and Ranuccio-Ernesto IV (Chapter 14), it is under the aspect of an operatic scene, complete with costumes, stage-entries, arias, recitatives, applause, and curtain-calls. And in this quality at least, she does not transcend but follows obediently after her humble prototype. Though she never appeared behind footlights, Gina Pietragrua, from all we can learn, was a woman of the theater *par excellence*; a natural actress, whose instinct for dramatic behavior would have put to shame little Mélanie Louason, Beyle's tragedienne. Mélanie was a professional actress, poor girl, but she had not a fraction of the natural *brio* which Gina infused into her most casual relationships.

The observation that Beyle always liked histrionic women comes perilously close to saying merely that he liked women. Still, there are gradations, and it is clear that Beyle showed a marked preference for theatrical women and sometimes women of the theater. From the days of Kubly, Louason, and Bereyter to the sere and yellow season of La Cecchina, he cultivated the society of actresses. Even his attachments with women of rank may be seen as a version of this impulse to the histrionic, which is itself part of his deep concern for artificial identities. At one time he exercised himself in the art of the comedian; as often as he ventured into society, he was apt to prepare a part, an appearance for himself; and he was never unappreciative of a fine performer, on or off the boards. Gina played up to that side of his genius from the first time he saw her.

For one thing, her perfect frankness about pleasure had, upon a shy and inhibited young man, the effect of the most dazzling *disinvoltura*; this characteristic she shared, in Beyle's mind at least, with all the other ladies of Milan. They appeared with their lovers—*cicisbei, cavalieri serventi,* or whatnot—at La Scala, at private parties, in the cafés, wherever good society foregathered; and by behaving with a bold simplicity, freedom, and naturalness, they succeeded in making the perfectly obvious completely invisible. This sort of social legerdemain delighted Beyle; and Gina, who liked to send messages to her lover by the hand of her son, take trips to meet him in the company of her husband, and introduce him to Lord knows how many of his predecessors and successors, seems to have cultivated it with the care of a virtuoso.

She played, too, a fascinating role in her own person. Alternately tender and savage, timid and fearless, coy and experienced, she could look as majestic as a sibyl and fight like a cornered vixen; yet when she melted into amorous pliability, no one could be more seductive. She was in fact a thoroughly practiced coquette, past mistress of the art of encouraging a lover and putting him off, a versatile, volatile libertine of a woman. Kissing Beyle passionately, she pleaded with him to leave Milan forever, leave, leave, leave, lest she find herself too weak to deny him the supreme happiness. When he seemed too importunate or longwinded, she denied her presence, or played him against Widmann the Venetian lover, or Turcotti the local product; in the tangled game of social love-making, she was as quick to see a wrong step or a false counter as he was. Moreover, her retributions were as indirect as his, and her storm-clouds were as easily dispersed. She liked to see him knowing, gay, confident, twirling his cane like a man of the world; she liked to hear him talk of painting, and it was under her aegis that he conceived that History of Painting which he dedicated "To Milady Angela G———." But she could bring out a tender, reminiscent strain in him too. One need not sub-scribe to the rather hydraulic psychological theory involved (it was borrowed from Cabanis) to find something quite remark-able in his attributing to Gina and Milan the whole artistic bias of his spirit.

> Certainly, had I been loved in Milan, my character would be very different. I'd be much more of a ladies' man, and I wouldn't have that residue of sensibility *che puo servimi pell'arte* (which may be useful for art). In Marseille, my head was too occupied for love to be the master of everything; I was beginning to observe. I was reading Tracy and Say.
>
> The two years of sighs, of tears, of sentimental and melan-choly effusions which I passed in Italy, without women, in that climate, at that period of my life and without prejudices, are probably what gave me this inexhaustible source of sensi-bility which today, at the age of twenty-eight, makes me feel all, down to the slightest details, and makes me capable of dictating fifty pages of an artist's observations of the passage through the mountains this side of Isella, for instance.
>
> I compare this present sensibility with a liquor which pene-trates to the tiniest veins of the body into which it is injected. It suffices for everything, abounds everywhere.

Whether all this is so or not, the recognition which flooded over him at six o'clock on the 11th September, 1811, that he had fallen in love with Gina, produced an extraordinary gloom and rage in Beyle's soul, which he explained interestingly. The charm of Milan suddenly disappeared as the thousand little springs of happiness which reside in memory abruptly dried up, and he felt the sharp necessities of that warfare which he always assumed must be the preliminaries to what he could only define as a "conquest." The memories which had been planted in 1800 were infinitely richer than the crude new experiences of 1811; and he resented the need to divest himself of the former in order to pursue the latter. At one point he found himself thinking with something like horror of his mistress' physical person. But the remarkable thing is that she, for her part, understood something of this quality in her "little Chinese"; she saw that he must have a chance to remember her if this conquest was to be permanent. And so she teased and tantalized him as the time approached for his departure; she promised and then bridled, she gave him "semi-favors" and squeezed his hand, she appointed rendezvous and missed them, she wept, implored, admired, regretted, talking endlessly—and so postponed the decisive encounter until half-past eleven of the morning of the day he was to leave. Then, at last, the second time he walked by her house, a paper showed at her window; it was the signal. "After a very serious moral conflict, in which I shammed unhappiness and almost despair, she was mine at half-past eleven." Next day at half-past one Beyle left Milan.

In these dramatic circumstances their affair began; it was continued amid cloak-and-stiletto theatricals which both parties adapted freely and joyfully from the 16th century and their own black imaginations. Signora Pietragrua had a fine taste for dangerous people and perilous situations. In the Brera one day she described for her lover the character of Giuseppe Bossi, undistinguished painter and historian of painting; her supreme accolade was, "He was a genuinely dangerous man." Stendhal remembered the name as well as the tribute, and used it as a

pseudonym for Fabrizio, under which he receives a false passport and signs a scornful challenge to the Conte M——
(*Chartreuse*, 13). Not only Bossi was dangerous; the long-suffer-
ing Signor Pietragrua, a mild and melancholy husband if ever
there was one, developed, when and as it suited his wife's purpose, a most ferocious streak of jealous savagery. Duels, hired
assassins, and treacherous spy-networks darkened the atmosphere; and the most elaborate precautions must then be invoked
to protect the pure blood of innocent lovers. Their signals became codes complex beyond man's ability to remember, codes
of windows open or half-open, with one, two, or no towels hang-
ing from them, representing different hours for the assignation.
She arrived for these assignations veiled and afoot, having thrice
transferred from carriage to carriage in order to elude pursuit.
She sent Beyle midnight notes from the very center of intrigue
—guarded, cryptic, intimate communications, hot with the
breath of passion. She shuddered at the perils her lover ran, and
behaved with what would have been the wildest imprudence if
there had, in fact, been the slightest danger. She invented
imaginary obstacles or transformed real ones, for the pleasure of
dramatizing her love by overcoming them; she sent her lover
abruptly to Genoa or Venice, ostensibly to keep him out of
harm's way, but more immediately to have a free hand with her
other lovers. Then when he did not write often enough to suit
her, she grew angry and jealous, declared the illusion shattered,
the rupture complete. Gloom struck at his heart, but he took to
work at his writing in order to distract himself, and new reconciliations always turned up in time to save him from complete
despair. She had her quirks, her fancies, her jealous streaks; a
watch which his little opera-singer in Paris, Angelina Bereyter,
had given him, bore on its face a sentimental inscription; to
satisfy her, he smashed it. Storms and sulks, melting smiles and
passionate reconciliations thus made up the texture of her days;
and in these pleasant, squally doldrums, tempered by absences,

journeys, and estrangements, she kept the fancy of Henri Beyle elaborately occupied between the years of 1811 and 1815.

If the matter-of-fact calendar be consulted, and "togetherness" (odious word!) be interpreted simply as residence in the same city, they were together for about a month in 1811; for something less than two months in 1813; for two weeks in August and intermittently over the last two months of 1814; and with increasingly violent scenes and prolonged estrangements, till the final rupture at the end of 1815. But this is the least of it; from 1811 to 1816, she was rarely far from his thoughts, and on the snowy steppes of Russia, she was often closer to him than on the Piazza Belgiojoso itself. Their affair ended with a series of wholesome bangs and very few whimpers. Through the good offices of a chambermaid, Beyle was able actually to observe the lady's "unfaithfulness" with a later arrival; he and Gina had a series of furious and depressing quarrels over the money involved in a junket to Padua, Verona, and Venice; and finally, at the Brera itself, she put on a last dramatic show, kneeling before him, begging forgiveness, weeping gustily, and finally accepting her dismissal with a sad yet noble resignation. With that scene ended the affair which, liberally speaking, had dominated his life for at least five years.

But a woman like Angela does not easily relax her grasp on the imagination of a man like Beyle. She held him by her beauty, which he described in one of the finest passages of the Diaries, as having an element of terror in it:

Milan, Albergo della Citta, November 2, 1811.—Undoubtedly the most beautiful woman I've ever possessed, and possibly ever seen, is Angela as she appeared to me tonight while I was walking with her through the streets by the light of the shops. I don't know how she came to tell me, with that naturalness that distinguishes her and without vanity, that some of her friends told her she frightened people. That's true. She was animated tonight. It appears that she loves me. YES-

TERDAY AND TODAY, SHE HAS HAD PLEASURE.
She's just had coffee with me in a solitary back shop; her eyes
were brilliant; her half-lit face had a suave harmony and yet
was terrible with supernatural beauty. It was as though she
were a superior being who had chosen to be so beautiful because that disguise became her more than another, and whose
penetrating eyes read your soul. That face would have made
a sublime sibyl.

She held him also by a quality which the Beylistes have not
been anxious to attribute to her: a quality of mind. No doubt
it is odd to think that an uneducated Italian woman of lascivi-
ous habits could have a good mind; certain of the critics would
doubtless be much happier if Beyle could have managed an
affair with a lady professor—of jurisprudence, say, or one of the
more solemn of the social sciences. But whether Gina had a
good wit herself, or was chiefly the occasion of wit in others,
one fact is beyond dispute; those pages of Beyle's *Diaries* which
deal with her or were written in her vicinity are the most
thoughtful, subtle, and inventive of all his intimate writings.
Rich in psychological reflections and aphorisms of conduct, they
coincide with the development of an interest in the noble land
of Mocenigo, a land of pure and exalted imagination to which
one attains by the assiduous practice of Beylism. And if one
doubts the part played in these developments by poor, shabby
Gina Pietragrua, the last word must be given to Beyle himself,
who wrote, "I find nothing better to say about my liaison with
the Comtesse Simonetta [his pseudonym for Gina, borrowed,
evidently from the Président de Brosses] than this reflection of
Duclos: 'In the long run, only a mind serves to nourish a mind;
left to itself, it does not produce for long' (Duclos, Vol. II, page
37)" (*Diaries*, September 25, 1813).
   She did much, in fact, to transform his rather literal and
flatminded approach to love, an approach which sometimes
verged on the mechanical, into those enchanting indirections,

those unpredictable, erratic, yet irresistible bounds of passion
which are found in the fiction. All his life long he saw romantic
love under the aspect of warfare. But he came to Gina as one
undertaking a siege from fixed positions; entrenchment, forti-
fication, and the slow, deadly attrition appropriate to a Valmont
or a boa constrictor, were the highest reaches of his tactical
imagination. She introduced him to the war of maneuver, showing him how to deploy his cavalry, his skirmishers and recon-
naissance troops, delighting and baffling him with the multiplicity of her maneuvers, the roaring violence of her unpredictable assaults. The role which she created in Beyle's mind was
one to which later women in his life merely adapted themselves
more or less successfully. Menti, Alberthe, and Giulia all had to
accept and exploit, with their varying skills and differing ac-
cents, the part created by Gina. Métilde alone stood outside it,
as she stood apart, in so many ways, from the rest of Beyle's
experience. With Métilde he made the heartbreaking discovery
that the deepest sincerity in affairs of the heart is often less
effective than that playful and cynical duplicity which is not
above keeping an eye on the momentary effect.

For he shammed with Gina, as she with him. Her first
"surrender" was made to a hypocrite who was pretending unhappiness and despair; at the height of the affair, the highest
compliment she could pay her lover was that he caused things
to happen "like a novel"; and the only way he could end the
relation was by feigning a coldness which he did not feel. From
start to finish, dissembling and artifice were the natural ambience of these two; they played a fantastic, sophisticated game,
to which each egged the other on. Follower and leader are
hard to distinguish here. She was not a bold bad woman who
taught him, an innocent novice, to apply to love the strategies
of Machiavelli; he knew something of the game already, and
showed a natural talent for the rest which came close to
rendering tuition superfluous. But she did give him the idea of

a woman whose style was light and disconcerting, whose feelings were primitive, and who, in the great games of love, war, and politics, *took the lead.* The women of Stendhal have a tendency to be placed permanently on the defensive when they are not (like Armance or Mme. de Chasteller) completely on the anonymous periphery of things. Partly this is because the great principle of feminine modesty makes many of their motives obscure or undramatic. Stendhal, as a thoroughly masculine and self-conscious novelist, is often absorbed in and limited by the psychology of his heroes; very much as Donne, the most masculine and self-conscious of poets, usually represents feminine psychology as a fascinating and perhaps empty enigma.* But the Duchessa Sanseverina, without bating an ounce of her

* Mme. de Beauvoir, who sees things from a distinctly militant angle, celebrates the free energy of Stendhal's women, their ability to exist as independent, authentic beings; yet she also points out that Stendhal's sympathies for his heroines are greater, the more closely they are confined, especially by their own scruples, modesty, and limitations of outlook. So that in effect there are bold, active women in Stendhal's books, who are admired for their boldness and activity; and there are timid, modest women, who are admired for their timidity and modesty. They are either creatures of impulse or of revery; but what Mme. de Beauvoir does not mention is that this is equally true of Stendhal's men.

On the other hand, women are not simply people for Stendhal, but special organisms, far more complex and subtle than men, against whom the most complicated campaigns are often launched in vain; and who refuse their own highest happiness for motives which are simply impossible to fathom. "Feminine mystery," says Mme. de Beauvoir, is alien to Stendhal; woman is merely the product of her training. But if this is so, her training in modern society is so deep and thorough as to amount to a second nature. *De l'Amour* never hesitates to attribute to the sexes wholly different psychological patternings, simply on the basis of the sexual difference. See also the complete and deliberate exception to Privilege 21; the privileged one may know the thoughts and see the actions of whomever he chooses—except for the woman he loves best.

But these criticisms are ungenerous; for, setting apart the feminist argument and bias, which is easy to do, the few pages of *The Second Sex* which are consecrated to Stendhal are among the most elegant and sensitive of modern tributes.

essential femininity, is magnificently on the attack; and some part of this heroic energy is undoubtedly owing to her proto-type, Gina the lesser, and the idea which she fostered in Beyle of histrionics as a form of competition, a mimic war.

Our notion of Beyle as a person of duplicity, an artistic arranger of even the baldest realities, owes a good deal to the late Paul Arbelet, whose studies in the early life can scarcely be sufficiently praised. Arbelet is one of the chief reasons why the life of Stendhal seems at first glance to have brought out all that is finest in the French tradition of literary discussion. His studies are richly embroidered with the sallies of a charming and cynical wit. Benign, sardonic, immensely detailed, and always supremely lucid, his textured prose is beautifully illumi-nated by the wise humanity of his comment. But the historian's dry scepticism, which was perfectly appropriate and productive of many insights where he applied it, may easily be carried over into areas where it is less relevant. *La jeunesse de Stendhal* ends, with *The Life of Henry Brulard*, at the opening of the new century; ends, that is, just where the primary document ceases to be that written 35 years later, by the mature and artistically formed Stendhal. When we move into the world of the *Diaries*, which, with the exception of some correspondence, are Beyle's first intimate writings, we find a mind much more primitive than that of Henry Brulard. Our young man is simple and literal-minded; when he omits some fact of consequence, it is usually his vanity which has suggested the omission; when he alters the outline of a story, there is no particular reason to think he is exaggerating the highlights or darkening the shadows for dramatic effect. As a matter of fact, his story has few high-lights or shadows, and no dramatic effects; it is the story of a young man with distinct amorous ideals and ill-defined social ambitions, which he tries, unsuccessfully, to satisfy at the same time. Art, for this young man, is the career of the "bard"; gloriously conceived, but represented in actual practice by *Le-*

tellier or *Les deux hommes,* two "tapisseries de Pénélope" [the phrase is Henri Martineau's], from which he keeps hoping that ultimate comedy will someday flower. Observing traits shrewdly and combining them cleverly represent the apex of his artistic strategy. But Moscow, Gina, and Métilde were three revolutions, which, between 1812 and 1818, shook this smug young sprout to the roots. It is important that two of these three earth-shocks were defeats; a material defeat before Moscow and in the bureaucracy of the Empire, a spiritual defeat with Métilde which cast him deep into the caverns of his own spirit. But for the art of Stendhal, which is essentially comic and resilient, it was even more important that the "victory" over Gina took the form and came at the time that it did. She helped him, in effect, to become the triumphant, aggressive, and rhapsodic liar whom Arbelet discovered in the writer of *Henry Brulard,* and whom Beylistes have long known and cherished as the author of the great fictions.

The idea that Beyle became a literary creator in consequence of a series of worldly defeats and erotic experiences is peculiarly and delightfully easy to document out of the biography. Wherever one turns, there is a worldly defeat or an erotic experience at hand to be thrown into the explanation-hopper. In fact, so many "causes" of this character are available that one's chief trouble is likely to be explaining why the *Rouge* had to wait till the author was 47, and the *Chartreuse* till he was 55, before getting themselves created. Clearly literary causation is a complicated matter; and, being so, clearly it cannot be established by a simple assertion of biographical fact. The fictions themselves must help us out; and so they do, for both the *Rouge* and the *Chartreuse* contain passages in which the crucial scenes of Beyle's spiritual life are strikingly re-enacted. When they are placed under strict physical constraint, delivered from the compulsions of social ambition and social warfare, the souls of Julien Sorel and Fabrizio del Dongo turn instinctively backward and inward with a great burst of serene joy; and then flower for the first time into literary creation.

That burst of joy which the Stendhal heroes feel as the prison closes around them must sometimes seem perverse to the unprepared reader. But it is simply an inversion of the despair and rage with which Beyle himself discovered, in 1811, that he was in love with Gina. The wells of memory suddenly flow; the thousand sources of pleasure which are hidden in revery begin to enrich the mind. In prisons and caves, especially when they are perched on towers or mountainsides, high in the air, the Stendhal heroes come into possession of their souls. Here they find an escape from the business of the world, which is transacted at its worst with stupidity and malice, at its best with dry, urbane, and cynical intelligence; but which is incompatible, under either aspect, with genuine sensibility. Only in prison does Julien Sorel achieve his apotheosis. Perhaps it is simply a coincidence that the terms "crystallization" and "arrest" can be used almost interchangeably to describe the way in which the mind's structure imposes formality and significant emphasis on experience. Still, it is true that prisons are good places for Stendhal heroes to crystallize, and that their crystallization in jails usually has an artistic aspect to it. In prison, all the poetry Julien ever knew comes to him in a flood, and his rhapsody against the 19th century in the name of honor, simplicity, and tenderness merely confirms the author's observation: "Never had that head been so poetic as at the moment when it was about to fall."

Fabrizio del Dongo also comes in prison to know the self, the love, and full expression which society has done its utmost to deny him. There is an old Fabrizio to be buried here; the lover of Marietta and Fausta, the handsome young man with an English horse, a carriage, a charming apartment, a half-dozen mistresses and an acute case of persistent boredom. But Fabrizio's dungeon is not only a place of burial, it is a two-hundred-

and-thirty-foot erection, a cavern poised atop a tower. It serves Fabrizio as a pinnacle for emotional flight, a seedbed for the generation of his sensibility, a summit of power and happiness, a refuge from and a fulfillment of passion. Within the prison, which is his new and deepened self-consciousness, is accomplished mysteriously the crystallization of his soul and his love; within the prison he becomes an artist, a poet not merely in words but in feelings. The triple knot of Stendhalian sentiment, erotic, Narcissistic, and creative, is tightly tied in the depths of the dungeon and in the isolation of the lofty tower. As a result, Fabrizio becomes more whole and secure of feeling than ever before. As he crawls over the parapet to escape, "How different I am," he says to himself, "from the fickle, libertine Fabrizio of nine months ago!" He has been in jail just long enough to pass through a complete cycle of rebirth. In the new Fabrizio elements once discordant are firmly welded together; the "Journal" of Salviati assures us that only after being in love for a year did he understand the "heroic simplicity" of Livy's Romans (*De l'Amour*, xxxi). So it is with Fabrizio. His piety, his ambition, and his love are combined, under the impulse of a new artistic unscrupulousness, to give him the vocation of a popular preacher; and the vehemence with which he publicly implores mercy of his mistress gains him credit with the unthinking for the utmost sanctity, just as his ambition is best served by the wearing of a shabby black coat. By the inversion of art he has been made, in Donne's phrase, "one of all."

Undoubtedly there lurks in this solution or resolution, a germ of the exquisite Stendhalian irony. The arrangement with Clélia, which hides just around the corner, has sardonic overtones which can scarcely be tied down to one circumstance. Having sworn before the Virgin that she will never see Fabrizio again, Clélia delicately conducts her affair with him in the dark. Touches like these fall just short of burlesque; and Fabrizio's whole church-career is not hard to see as a triumph of that legerdemain which amounts to rendering black white, white black, and black-and-white invisible. His crimes, if one wanted to spell them out sobersides, would be almost as many as those of Gina herself. But crimes are not all and equally crimes, for Stendhal; in the circumstances of a corrupt society, when performed with energy and without "lowness," when they are "interesting" and "passionate." . . . In the specific circumstance of Fabrizio, there is an element of seriousness in the observation that, where the business of society is to misuse language in its interests, the revenge of the artist is to make his own special perversions of speech in his own interests. The phrasing should not, ultimately, be cast in such vindictive terms, though vindictiveness is one element of the total reaction. The artist creates a refuge from society, he also does pleasure to society; and at the same time he sets it at secret defiance. This triple quality of the artistic response is, I think, a distinguishing and triumphant quality of the artistic subversion which Stendhal brilliantly exemplifies, and which he learned or at least developed during the years of his delinquency with that most disreputable of bad little girls, Angelina Pietragrua.

To say this is not to imply that there is ever, for Stendhal or his characters, a stasis, a point of permanent and unchallenged rest. A voluntary system of balanced but radical instabilities is the best one can hope for—passion leading to revery and wisdom, logic placing itself in the hands of passion, not only to light but in some sort to help form its subterranean crystal-caverns. A glance conveys so much, a mood shifts so quickly, the very material circumstances of Stendhal's world are so liquid, that there is no assurance of outward continuity; and the inner life, while enriched by the intimate conjunction of thought and feeling, is for that reason infinitely reverberant and unstable. M. Richard puts the matter with Gallic wit and precision when he says, "Health for Stendhal is formed out of the conflict of diseases, and truth, far from being found in some wise middle-way or other, must always be sought in the impassioned association of extremes and contradictories" [*Littérature et sensation* (Paris, 1954), p. 115].

One peculiar flavor of Stendhal, by which we distinguish him from any other novelist, derives from his concern with the calculated stupidities of Europe under the peace of Vienna. Organized stupidity is a theme vastly relevant to our own day and capable of infinite applications. But absolute power, in the most tyrannical of states, can be exercised only as a last resort. It is too lawless to be economical; the routine work of government must always be done with symbols, not swords; by persuasion, not compulsion. It is in this area of manipulated terminologies, of formulas and phrases and verbal conformities, that Stendhal's ironies find their most elegant and limber play. Our own day has seen the enormous growth, in numbers and influence, of those social and psychological engineers, those manipulators of words and values, whom Stendhal described as the governing classes of Parma and France. With practice, immunity, and division of labor they have become not only more proficient but more daring; and modern motivational research is supposed to provide keys to the human mechanism for the use of chewing-gum salesmen as well as social planners, politicians, and religion-venders. The more limited exercise of Stendhal's characters is yet a strict and complex one. The players take for enemies not only one another, but the stubborn knotty texture of physical facts, which they delight in twisting, altering, or obliterating entirely.

If you read our *Gazette* [says the Conte Mosca, with perfect aplomb], you will see that a clerk at the citadel, named Barbone, has died as the result of falling from a carriage. As for the sixty odd rascals whom I dispatched with powder and shot, when they were attacking the Prince's statue in the gardens, they are in the best of health, only they are travelling abroad. Conte Zurla, the Minister of the Interior, has gone in person to the house of each of these unfortunate heroes, and has handed fifteen sequins to his family or friends, with the order to say that the deceased is abroad, and the very definite threat of imprisonment should they let it be understood that he is dead. . . .

This the way the world runs; ragged rascals attacking with stones and catch-words a dead man's statue; cool, unscrupulous rascals having them shot down; and simple rascals or (worse yet!) simple simpletons reading innocuous, improbable stories in the *Gazette*. Given such a world, who could find it in his heart to condemn Fabrizio's little ventures in hypocrisy, simony, adultery, blasphemy, treason, and murder—especially when they are carried out in such excellent taste?

One way or another, the truth counts for nothing in Parma. When Fabrizio has escaped from, and so "disgraced" the prince's citadel, the police invent a story about twenty soldiers bribed by the Duchessa to provide him with ladders. By making his escape seem commonplace and easy, they minister to their own pride. The Liberals, only nominally the opponents of the regime, would do nothing so radical as tell the truth; led by Doctor C*** the police agent, they add the liberal embroidery that eight of these soldiers were shot by the barbarous police. Thereupon everyone happily joins in condemning Fabrizio for having caused by his imprudence the death of eight poor (imaginary) soldiers. On another occasion, the prince, having made a significant utterance to the Duchessa, agrees at once with her civilized response that she would never dare look the Conte in the face afterwards.

"I should be as much out of countenance as you," says Ernesto-Ranuccio IV. "The dear Conte! My friend! But there is a very easy way out of that difficulty, and I have thought of it: the Conte would be put in the citadel for the rest of his days" (Chapter 7). The more impudent and obsequious one's lies, the better they suit the taste of Parma; a special phrase for jail-breaking gains currency after Fabrizio's escape, and is highly thought of—it is "removing oneself from the clemency of a magnanimous prince."

If only as revenge on unscrupulous society, then, the unscrupulous behavior of the Stendhal heroes makes a place for itself in the reader's mind. And there is more to it than revenge, as we have seen. If anything, the reaction of the Stendhal heroes to the world laid bare by the Stendhal cynicism is too choked with overtones, too rich, almost, to be altogether viable. It may seem ungenerous, then, or too demanding, to point out one major bare spot in the fiction, one key in which it does not reverberate at all. The *Chartreuse* comes as close as anything ever written to being an amoral or immoral novel; it seems better to call it immoral.

The function of morality in a fiction presents issues of rather more delicacy than 19th-century critics usually perceived. Sainte-Beuve thought the Duchessa Sanseverina's behavior in having the prince of Parma poisoned was an altogether shocking act of misconduct; he blamed the lady for doing such a thing, and Stendhal for abusing Italian morality by imagining it (Alain, *Stendhal,* pp. 25-26; see also Martineau, *L'Oeuvre de Stendhal,* p. 473, note). Alain picks up this judgment and rather cruelly contrasts it with Saint-Beuve's easy and completely unjustified assumption that Balzac must have been bribed to render such a favorable judgment of the *Chartreuse.* The juxtaposition, he finds, reflects far more discredit on Sainte-Beuve, his policeman's morality and his coarse conscience, than on Beyle: "The exterior rules of morality I despise; and in this, no doubt about it, I follow close in the footsteps of Stendhal. The force of a soul, its truth to itself, that is virtue." Certainly it is closer to a fictional definition of virtue than obedience to any external code.

The fact is that morality in fiction is at best an auxiliary device for attracting sympathy. But as it is true that in art the lion, morally speaking, lies down with the lamb, so it is true that sympathy-judgments correspond only to a limited degree, and under the impulsion of a distinct and deliberate purpose on the part of the author, with morality-judgments.

It is perfectly evident that the *Chartreuse*, like any other fiction describing modern society, takes cognizance of a goodly number of complex moral states. One could no more describe the 19th or 20th centuries without morals than 19th or 20th century man without trousers; they are an essential part of the décor. Perhaps a moral novelist, then, is simply one who is able to see six feet beyond the end of his nose, and recognize that moral ideas do play a part in modern life. But in any sense much more exalted than this, it will be hard to claim a position for Stendahl as a moral novelist. He does not reprobate the conduct of his characters when they are unsocial or self-willed; or if he does so, he lets us see immediately that it is the voice of society speaking, and that he considers it stupid. He does not think his characters' behavior is particularly virtuous, either; he lets it speak for itself most of the time, without defence or explanation or comment of any but the most casual sort. His own standards for behavior are evidently primitive; he approves of energy, sincerity, sensitivity, and a sense of personal style. These are strikingly interior qualities, to begin with; none of them represents a very distinct guide to social behavior. In addition, Stendhal endorses them with a kind of haphazard ambiguity which he makes no apparent effort to rationalize. He approves of hypocrisy as well as sincerity; he shows that energy can be extreme and self-defeating, as well as admirable; he feels that personal style is compatible with, and in fact dependent on, a complete deficiency in vital ideas. Of the four qualities noted, he probably endorses sensitivity with fewest qualifications, though not without any; it is furthest from being a properly moral quality. Many of the distinct qualities which his characters display are without moral overtones of any sort; they might just as well be displayed by a solitary castaway on a desert island, who does not exist in the moral sphere, except by memory or anticipation. The isolation of the Stendhal hero, however, is but one circumstance making for his moral indeterminacy. Stendhal does not point up or direct the incidents of his story in a moral way; he does not declare, even indirectly, that he is avoiding moral issues or ideas. In a considerable part of the fiction he appears to be simply deaf to the moral overtones of his action. Very often he writes in the character of a student of behavior, examining the choices available to his characters and recording with perfect indifference the results, such as they happen to be. And if this were the uniform character of his work, as it occasionally is of Joyce's and often is of Stephen Crane's, one might satisfactorily write Stendhal down as an amoral author.

But there is one more aspect to the matter. It is no accident that, when one adds up those actions which in a western, Christian society are customarily called "crimes," Fabrizio, Gina, and Mosca appear, to the startled reader, as moral monsters. One had not realized, one does not realize, while reading the novel, just how many of the commandments are being fractured. They are not fractured out of good intentions, as Tom Jones expands and bursts a few of the major commandments while adjusting to his own exuberant temper. They are not broken out of premeditated villainy, or to illustrate any moral quality, either good or bad. They are overridden in passing, and scarcely noticed. Stendhal deliberately (one can hardly think so consistent a performance other than deliberate) rakes our sympathy-judgments across the teeth of our moral judgments. There is a perversity about this brilliant performance which probably entitles the *Chartreuse* to rate as a thoroughly immoral novel.

Of course any zealot among the literary critics who put his mind to it could drag back Stendhal, or the devil himself, if the devil wrote novels, into the fold of grace. At a time when Baudelaire is practically a candidate for canonization and the Mar-

quis de Sade is being rehabilitated as a great moralist, anything
can happen. All an author has to do is be outstandingly disso-
lute and display a few marks of bad conscience, and one has
qualified him as a great religious writer. His dissipations are
promptly explained as an exalted "adventure in evil," far more
profound than the facile actions of the merely good; one may
freely impute to him a desire to expand the moral consciousness of his audience, and even a latent satirical purpose, for
which no particular evidence need ever appear. These are but a
few of the available and currently popular gambits. If anyone
wanted to haul Stendhal into the fold, it would be by the lin-
gering shreds and remnants of his religious conscience. These
are apparent in the *Chartreuse* as in other fictions; and Stendhal
delighted to use them for the contrasts of emotional lights and
darks which they made possible. By his standards, no mistress
really loves one so much as she who thinks hell-fire is the pen-
alty of her actions; it was he who reported the charming and
typical reaction of an Italian princess who had just been presented with a sherbet: "But it's delicious; what a pity it isn't a
sin!" This is one use, and perhaps the typical use, to which he
puts religion in the fiction. But when he was not standing
Christianity on its head to gain a black and morbid perspective
for his characters, or representing its agents as double-dyed villains and hypocrites, he disregarded it entirely. That is, he paid
little attention to the Christian moral conscience. No doubt he
fell a little short of being antiseptically pure of all moral feeling whatever; but he was always uneasy in the moral ambience,
either contracting morality to the narrow limits of the utilitarian
platitude ("Morality," he had learned from Helvetius, "is simply the knowledge of the means men have found for living together as happily as possible.") or spreading it over the entire
range of esthetic dispositions. Hence his curious aphorism,
"Painting is simply structured morality." This is a way to dispose of morality, not to glorify it. In this context, one might

usefully distinguish morals, which are codified rules applying to social behavior and with which Stendhal is strikingly unconcerned, from an ethic which is individual, intuitive, and which interests him intensely. In any event, there are clearly few works of literature which take such pains as the *Chartreuse* to flat the moral note.

Does this spoil the fiction for us? There is no reason for such a booming conclusion. The English middleclass novel has a long tradition of joining morality with sympathy judgments; and this happy combination (perhaps the finest flower of insular existence) undoubtedly makes the *Chartreuse* seem particularly acid and prickly to the Anglo-Saxon reader. But from a larger perspective it is clear that while fiction of its own nature has a good deal to contribute to morality, morality is by no means a necessary friend of fiction. That good people are often dull is not the point at all; nor is the insidious impulse to preach precisely the root fault of moralized fiction. Rather, obsolescence is the deepest peril, to which all moral systems are subject; the artificial security of an apparent moral ultimate is a temptation to sentimentality more dangerous than mere selfish striving for effect. Besides, the great commonplace, the liberal, tolerant, do-unto-others creed, is capable of having a thoroughly soggy influence on a novelist's notions of human nature. The English middle-class novel has, typically, something easy and unstimulating about it; the agreeable people turn out, after just enough difficulties to make a volume, to be the morally acceptable people, and very often the socially successful people as well. For austere tastes this may be rather too much of a good thing. Yet to increase the moral complexities of fiction is to place upon the novelist a burden of persuasion and explanation which may bear down the emotional action of his fiction altogether. Indeed, it is hard to see how moral scruples of great delicacy can possibly be weighed with any accuracy in a work which has as many other things to do as a novel. Give a character a fresh turn of speech, allow him to open up a fresh line of thought, and the fact that he murdered his mother will shortly be forgotten. From a very different point of view than Stendhal, Ibsen had a somewhat similar conviction that an audience only deceives itself with flabby likings and dislikings when it tries to stand in both an esthetic and an ethical relation to the characters of a fiction. Kierkegaard is only part of the intellectual background here; there is also a cold, lucid, and infinitely remote perspective supplied by the eddas and sagas of those pagan republics which flourished in medieval Iceland.

But on the other hand, Stendhal's notion of morality has clearest affinities with the special Renaissance conception of *virtù*. A distinctive quality of this concept was the momentary fusion of two abstractions familiar to the ancient Greeks as *areté* and *dynamis*. *Areté* often had itself connotations of "manliness" and particular excellence, it was no woozy combination of all the conceivable nicenesses; add to it an emphasis on energy, power, and behavior typifying a specific social character, and one has something like *virtù*. A warrior, a lover, a courtier, a politician, a mother, each would display *virtù* in a different way, and in fact each would have a different *virtù*, a different principle of action. Thus the Renaissance Italian tended to think of love, war, revenge, the state, courtliness, and the self itself, under the aspect of a work of art. A beautiful revenge, a *bella vendetta*, was one carried out with the finest possible combination of physical ferocity and crushing, humiliating ingenuity; and to carry out such a vendetta was to display *virtù*. This concept of virtue may be described from two aspects, as either ruthlessly realistic or supremely imaginative. It identifies one's entire personality with a social role, and in this sense represents a kind of imaginative heightening and purification of one's existence; on the other hand, it seems to make a supreme value out of almost mechanical consistency. Thus the Italian, whom outside observers are likely to stigmatize as "operatic" in his reaction to a particular situation, thinks of himself as being perfectly natural, and sometimes as demonstrating a "*virtù*" too obvious even to need explanation, when he accepts a conventional role in a social situation. A spirit of terrible lucidity and distinctness, of bitterly realistic particularity, inhabits these "child-like," "operatic" Italians. It was the aspect of their existence which most thoroughly entranced Beyle; it is the aspect which recalls us most movingly to the archaic lucidity of the early antique world, to its peculiar, wiry energy and utter lack of sentimentality. The greatest French and Italian authors have always had a major strain of the sparse, specific, and distinct in their work; only the German and English traditions are naturally florid.

However this may be, the *Chartreuse* stands out against the prudent novel of moral speculation and moral theory with a glistening and pristine freshness; for it is immediate. A reader knows intuitively whether he has observed a low action, or one performed with what Stendhal boldly called a Roman worthiness. But the dreary windings of principle and logic—on the one hand this, on the other hand that! The shifting categories, the triple but not mutually exclusive alternatives! Men have been more deceived by moral deductions and general concepts in novels than they will ever be enlightened. Looking at things as they are is, in itself, a dispiriting pastime; but recreating them in the refracting prisms and mirrors of a personality which is itself largely deliberate gives depth of perception and the bloom of emotional richness to one's world. In such a world one does not need morals, for one has the guidance of one's self and the ethic it creates, in the light of which the self itself may sometimes be regenerated. And it is good to see, once and for all, that by throwing away moral standards, we throw away the terrors they inspire, too. There is nothing so awful about the amoral-immoral world of the *Chartreuse*; on the contrary, its Etruscan clarities are far more invigorating than the gloomy, obedient miasmas of the English middle-class novel.

If the *Chartreuse* is not a thoroughly immoral novel, we shall have to invent one; simply for the pleasures which such a *donnée* can yield, in the first place; and in the second place, to give all the moral novelists a sense, of which they must be sorely in need, that they have exercised an option. It is the dreariest of trades to be doing out of serious obligation what all other people are doing naturally, or for fun, or simply because they can't help it.

5

*

Montlosier,
Raillane, Machiavelli

All the Cilicians are bad men.
But amongst the Cilicians, there is
one good man, Cinyrés.
But even Cinyrés is a Cilician.

Greek Anthology, DCXLIII

Startling as it is, the opening of the *Chartreuse* simply recapitu-
lates the biography of Beyle. He burst into Italy as heroically as
Lieutenant Robert encountering the ladies of Milan, as naïvely
as Fabrizio del Dongo encountering Waterloo. If we view only
the strategy of living, these qualities cancel out in bashfulness
and blundering; confirming thereby the ancient wheeze that
youth is wasted on the young. The arrangement of the novel,
too, which looks permanently odd from the aspect of slowly-built
climaxes and prepared effects, is thrown off-balance; but this is
all to the good. At least the reader is given to understand that

the unexpected is everything in this fiction; he need not huff and puff in preparation for a climax a hundred pages off. And perhaps in this first slashing episode the reader as well as the hero gets rid of something—a virginity, Stendhal called it indelicately—which is worth disposing of abruptly. Once fleshed in this sort of action, we are ready for something rarer.

By contrast, the *Rouge* opens slowly, amid diplomatic negotiations. One major incident which is functionally analogous to Fabrizio's Waterloo does not turn up till the middle of Volume II; and it is muted, tentative, confusing. Julien's mission to the Duke of ———— is a curious incident in itself; it occurs without previous preparation or motivation, and has no direct effect on the "plot," such as it is, of the novel. Julien is deep in the toils of his affair with Mathilde when, at the beginning of II, 21, he is called upon by M. de la Mole to attend a conference of political intriguers, take down a record of their rather disjointed sayings, digest the sense of the meeting, and carry four pages of political proposals to a Duke, unnamed in the novel, probably the Duke of Wellington or possibly, as M. Liprandi argues, a Russian duke or an agent of Metternich's. Despite efforts to intercept him, he makes the journey to Mainz, delivers his message, and returns to Paris, where II, 24, finds him once more pursuing and being pursued by Mathilde. The only event of his journey which leads to further results is a chance meeting at Strasbourg with the Prince de Korasoff, who gives him love-letters to copy out for Mme. de Fervaques as a way of gaining the upper hand with Mathilde.

The political episode is curiously inconclusive, then; but this may well be intentional on Stendhal's part, a consequence of his natural view of things. He revelled in the divine unexpected, and would not have minded the sardonic implication that political projects undertaken in the spirit of high fatuity sometimes serve no other end than to forward the love-affairs of the underlings involved. But the incident is odd in other ways besides its inconclusiveness. Elaborate precautions are taken to preserve the anonymity of the participants; yet Julien, who is a complete outsider, recognizes all the important ones. Julien himself is introduced to the circle as "a young Levite devoted to our sacred cause"—a character which he could only have acquired through M. de la Mole, who had several reasons to know its incorrectness and none to assume its accuracy. He knew Julien was not in orders, and he knew him as a protégé of the Abbé Pirard, described as a "jansenist" and bitterly hated by the jesuits and ultramontanists who are represented as taking part in the plot.

Indeed, there is something peculiar about the plot itself, about the aims which it assumes and the opposition it encounters. It is represented as the work of arch-reactionaries; its participants are members of M. de la Mole's social circle, bishops, dukes, generals, a cardinal. The cause seems to involve a military occupation of France by the allied powers, to be supported by a political party, a priestly clique, and a military organization within France itself. The great enemy is assumed to be Jacobinism and its offspring—the middle classes, popular journalism, bicameral legislation, individual judgment, and the city of Paris. Against these enemies the Throne, the Altar, and the Nobility are to be leagued together in eternal struggle. To be sure, nobody ever says distinctly what the Duke of ——— is supposed to do about the situation; it is frankly admitted by all that England is too badly crippled by taxation to support another war. Still, the general aims are clear enough. All the speakers indicate essential sympathy with monarchical and clerical ideas, though their emphases vary and their mutual jealousies are apparent. Yet the enemy whom Julien encounters on the road is no republican, no Jacobin, but the Abbé Castanède, a jesuit father represented as mysteriously impeding a jesuit plot.

To be sure, the plot itself does not seem to be viewed with deadly seriousness; its hatching is described as a rather nebulous and uncertain affair, in which none of the participants is quite happy about what the other ones are conspiring for, or clear about how the Duke of —— can help them get it. Their deliberations are disorganized, illogical, and disturbed by personal bickerings. Despite their theatrical precautions regarding secrecy, the loyalty of several to the common cause is highly precarious, and it is accepted that there will be traitors and spies among them. Yet all speak with the most amazing frankness, as if they were trying to make their ideas as objectionable as possible.

Indeed, M. de la Mole specifically warns Julien that he may be intercepted on his journey to the Duke by some agent of these disaffected conspirators. But if this is the case, and the Abbé Castanède (who was last seen in II, 27, teaching Sacred History in the Seminary at Besancon) is really an agent of a recalcitrant conspirator, why is he looking for papers? Julien was introduced to all the conspirators as a man of unfailing memory who would transmit a *verbal* message to the Duke of ——. And why, given the fact that Julien was introduced by name to the conspirators as "M. l'Abbé Sorel," why is this omniscient Abbé Castanède so poorly furnished with the idea of Julien's identity that he suspects even the Neapolitan tenor Geronimo? "An exseminarist named Sorel, now working for the Marquis de la Mole"—surely that would have been description enough for a secret agent of even moderate intelligence who had had such a student in his class less than a year before. But Professors of Sacred History are evidently ill-adapted to employment as secret government agents.

Whichever way we turn, the confusion is impenetrable. No doubt the conspiracy was something of a joke in Stendhal's eyes; we can scarcely question his hatred of the political outlooks represented, and it may be that the mode of satiric dislike has slipped just a trifle under his hand and become burlesque. He introduces the conspiracy with his stock deprecatory phrase about a pistol-shot at a concert; he assures us that this episode is boring and stupid but necessary to his chronicle. The speeches of the conspirators are said to have been "of an incredible simplicity," and the Duke of ————'s answer so disconcerting as to squelch the whole conspiracy outright; for we never hear of it after the first sentence of II, 25.

On the other hand, if we take it as an unmitigated joke, the episode casts M. de la Mole in a ridiculous role, undercuts much of the novel's own satire, and even reflects on Mademoiselle de la Mole—for her father's ideas in the conspiracy are precisely hers when she thinks of her fashionable suitors: "They will let themselves be slaughtered like heroic sheep, but of real active energy, they betray not a trace." Quite aside from his position as agent, Julien Sorel is involved in the conspiracy to this extent, that his words are quoted by M. de la Mole (without acknowledgment) in evidence that the young men of France are anxious for war and eager to follow a new Napoleon. And these words themselves have an echo in the writings of Beyle, who talks in his own person of 200,000 Julien Sorels who are thirsty for a revolution.*

Thus, to view the conspiracy as an entire absurdity (even an absurd conclusion drawn from a sound analysis) is to compromise all the novel's main actors and some of its leading ideas in the absurdity. If energy is really a sublime thing, it cannot be wholly absurd to display energy even if one does so in an impractical manner. If the only alternative to the heroism of sheep is the heroism of idiots, there is nothing so degraded about the well-intentioned, empty-headed mediocrities, like M. de Croisenois. Even if the plot were purged of its adventitious absurdities, it cannot be allowed to show up too darkly in the tonality of the novel, lest Julien be entangled in an enterprise completely wicked or completely foolish. For if the work once breaks down

---

* See letters to Sutton Sharpe of 10 January and 15 August, 1830. All these passages echo phrases in the original "Note Secrète" of 1818, though there are few other direct parallels. The points are summarized by Louis Aragon, *La lumière de Stendhal*, (Paris, 1954), pp. 35-37.

into intrigue for its own sake and melodrama without motivation, everything for which the strict style and distinct habit of
observation have fought will be irretrievably lost.

There is, undeniably, a sense in which even Mathilde de la
Mole is foolish and comic, as there is a sense in which she is
judged unworthy of Julien. Her soul, *"sèche"* but *"hautaine,"*
has a comic need of display, a theatricality which is reproved in
Julien's alternate preference for Mme. de Rênal. But the point
must not be overstated, or she will become merely a Parisian
doll. Mathilde understands very well that the audience available to her is not that which she needs; she is sublime as well
as ridiculous in her scorn of the 19th century, and if a nation
of dead-center sheep will not applaud her, the happy few will
have to. The barbaric ritual cortege at the end of the book is
there to make their lot happier. More explicitly even than the
Duchessa Sanseverina, she is playing an historical role; yet precisely when she is following out that role most fully, and surrendering to its artifice most naïvely, she appeals to us most
deeply. I cannot feel that there is any major irony about her
commitment to the ideal of Boniface de la Mole. To finish
the novel on such a bold, raking, confident chord may have been
an artistic necessity; but no novelist of stature would or could
have done it without something close to complete credence in
the emotional value of the gesture. If one doesn't feel this, there
is no way I know of to demonstrate it.

On a much simpler level, the Machiavellian (cloak-and-
dagger) view of Beyle implies an acceptance of intellectual and
ethical insignificance in every context; yet, apart from the fact
that the Machiavellians unstring many of the essential tensions
of adult fiction, their position does draw a sort of authority from
the life and work of Beyle. Julien Sorel, like Fabrizio and Mosca,
like Lucien and Coffe, has a striking willingness to serve the
machinery of social power which he despises; and this suggests
a total unscrupulousness which is, melodramatically, at least,

powerful stuff. Beyle enjoyed the pose of ruthless cynic, and the heroes of Stendhal also lay frequent hold of it, both as a practical strategy and as a dramatic role. Moreover, this cynicism about such matters as the politics of bicameral legislatures accords gracefully with a passion for aristocratic manners, convictions about the value of living dangerously, and a love of heroic individualism. But in this entire complex of thoughts and feelings, rather familiar nowadays than curious, opportunism is pretty surely a subordinate element, a defensive weapon in the service of other sentiments rather than a complete outlook in its own right. Though he often poses the questions of a ruthless egotist, Julien Sorel is never happier than when his meditative spirit leads him to a lonely, lofty cave from which he can contemplate the possibilities of his destiny. He is a Napoleon *manqué*, not a natural Talleyrand. Neither Fabrizio nor Julien ever comes to attack openly and without hypocrisy the social problem as they understand it; but their hypocrisy is virile and defensive, serving, in alliance with an impenetrable scorn, to defend the sanctity of their own spirits. These ideal heroes of Stendhal's are not opportunists in the service of any cause so much as free spirits in the service of none. (The depth and complexity of their commitment to action, combined with their general scepticism about the causes they serve, suggests some modern parallels in the literature, if it can be so described, of "engagement.") In one sense their dramas involve a renunciation of national destiny, social responsibility, the active life; this is accomplished with *mépris*. Then, afterwards, they become complete individuals when they have learned the generous emotions of love and sympathy. So far as the conspirators are represented as striving in a spirit of *mépris* for the whole 19th century, Stendhal must have taken them with at least partial seriousness. And at least one conspirator, M. de la Mole, makes an attack on the vices and weakness of the servile 19th century which is altogether in the spirit of Stendhal's own sentiment.

It is that of an anti-jesuit ultra, a heroic anachronism, a liberal reactionary.

Closeness to actual life, satiric indirection, and a careful tempering of rough edges to accord with the larger outlines of the novel are all much in evidence here; we may appreciate the mixture better by comparing the final structure with one of the "pilings" on whom Stendhal evidently built it. This underground support, many of whose political variations and contradictions over a period of years are telescoped in the character of M. de la Mole, was an actual political figure, François Antoine Dominique de Reynaud de Montlosier, better known after the Restoration simply as the Comte de Montlosier.

The title of Chapter 21, *Rouge* II, "The Secret Note," points a long finger at the Comte de Montlosier. For he was popularly credited with having drafted, in 1818, a "Note Secrète" which represented to foreign powers the political sentiments of an ultra-royalist group. This group, known from its meeting-place in the Tuileries, as the "Bord de l'Eau," seems briefly to have contemplated a *coup d'état* in the name of "Monsieur," the Comte d'Artois, Louis XVIII's younger and more reactionary brother who was later to become Charles X; the victims of the *coup d'état* were to have been the moderate royalists. In the event, the conspiracy was abortive; the "Note" was uncovered and published through the collusive machinations of Baron Decazes, the minister of police for whom Beyle's intimate friend Lingay was a secret agent. (The epigraph to II, 21 is quoted, significantly, from a friend's letter.) And both note and conspiracy were irresistibly associated, in the public mind if not in historical actuality, with the Comte de Montlosier.

The Comte de Montlosier would go far toward explaining brilliantly Stendhal's figure of M. de la Mole, if there were only some good explanation of the Comte de Montlosier. His enemies and his friends agreed, with different intonations, in finding him "singular" and "bizarre"; and so in fact he was. He was born, the twelfth child of a singularly loveless marriage between a mother who came from the common people and a father who occupied the last and lowest rank of French gentility—a *chevalier* by the skin of his ancestors' teeth and force of his own determined and arrogant character. (Some say that the count's father was a mere "notary," but the word is malicious. One of his fifteenth-century ancestors had in fact been admitted to the minimum order of chivalry by a British knight whom he had been lucky enough to capture, and who was irked at the idea of surrendering to a plebian. In the course of three centuries, the descendants of this lucky fellow had done nothing to elevate their status; on the other hand, they had been tenacious enough not to lose their humble foothold entirely.) Yet the Comte de Montlosier typified with passion and brilliance the aristocratic principle in French life. His own title was genuine enough, though it dated only from the days of his exile, that is, from the last decade of the eighteenth century. But, like his convictions, his style, and his whole character, the aristocracy he professed was a product of his inner nature. He never acted but from impulse; he never lacked for violent impulses on which to act; he was from birth the incarnation of a petty nobleman from the Auvergne, heroic and absurd, erratic and immovable, but always and completely his own man.

The Count was an aristocrat, then, though never a courtier; a man of absolute independence though never of great wealth or calculated influence. He was an opponent of the revolution while it was taking place, a refugee from it, and a counter-revolutionary against it, implacable, aggressive, and imbued with the stern concept of a preventive war; yet under the Restoration he urged with great eloquence that a revolution of French dimensions is a fact, which must be accepted. Hereditary privilege was a sacred principle to the Count; who therefore advocated a truly representative government and a written constitution granting complete security to all the different estates of society.

"Hierarchy with liberty" was his ideal. He was a liberal among the ultras, a reactionary among the revolutionaries, and a man of immense hauteur and intense pugnacity wherever he went. After a thundering defence of the church and its rights before the Constituent Assembly in the eighteenth century, he revealed himself to be anti-clerical, anti-jesuit, anti-*congregation* in the nineteenth. Every evening he read a chapter of the *Imitatio Christi* to his assembled tenants; but he hated with deadly hatred a priest in politics (inventing the elegant, invidious expression, "parti-prêtre"), and had moments when he doubted the existence of God. At his political high-point he was an outspoken, angry defender of the rights of the individual (to whom in the aggregate he referred ingratiatingly as "the *canaille*"), a kind of feudal liberal, if this combination is not too indigestible.

Add to these traits a passionate intellectual curiosity which led him to dabble in chemistry, the geology of volcanoes, anatomy, theology and patristics, philosophy, law, and constitutional history; also a truculent and savage independence in the exercise of criticism, which spared nobody; and one has a notion of the Comte de Montlosier. It was altogether characteristic that as he lay dying, in his eighty-fourth year, he was squabbling with the *curé* over the terms of his repentance; and in effect he died without receiving the sacraments rather than give up an inch of his argument. This was the man who, as a child, could not bring himself to learn Latin by the usual methods; and so invented his own system of instruction and his own version of the language, rather than submit to the regulations of "pedantry."

Wherever he went, whatever he did, the Comte de Montlosier seemed bound to place himself in the party of opposition. The family crest was pleasant, but unworthy of him; to express the Comte de Montlosier, it should have borne the blazon, "Au Contraire." He stood against the revolution, against Napoleon; and when the Restoration seemed to have ended those quarrels, he stood against the Bourbon princes, their priests, and their ultra supporters. His rural estate at Randanne near Clermont-Ferrand had clearly been intended by an all-seeing Deity to raise a crop of dry heather and volcanic dust, eked out by a few bumble-bees. But the Comte de Montlosier set himself in opposition to this manifest destiny, too; and by pouring in plants, trees, animals, water, fertilizer, buildings, people, and in places the very soil itself, he managed to augment the annual output of his acres by some momentary crops and permanent lawsuits. On public issues, as on private ones, he was perfectly intransigent. He fought duels with republicans whom he had criticized too rancorously, and duels with *émigrés* who thought he had stayed too long in France, criticizing republicans. When he himself emigrated, he did not sneak off meekly in the night; but demanded of the revolutionary government that it provide him, as deputy, with transportation to Coblentz instead of Clermont-Ferrand. (It is a tribute to the French sense of humor, even in a revolution, that this demand was granted.) He appealed his individual quarrels to magistrates and from magistrates to ministers; he carried appeals over the heads of ministers to the people at large, to the crowned heads of Europe, to the ancient nobility of France. Though he fought for the rights of the clergy in 1789 and against the abuse of those rights in 1827, he was not essentially an inconsistent, an unpredictable, or even an extreme man; but he stood definitely outside of all parties, responsible to no organization or institution except his own conscience. "*Au milieu du nouveau régime*," wrote a contemporary, "*c'est un chevalier des anciens temps, un véritable paladin.*"

A fine story—told by a satiric witness, to be sure, but an intimate of Stendhal's, Victor Jacquemont—suggests one particular paladin as the image of the Comte de Montlosier. Coming to inspect the great agricultural-reform project at Randanne, the visitor was cordially received by the Count, and offered the rough hospitality of the farmhouse. While they were passing through the baked fields, admiring the dusty soil and weedy crops, the visitor noted that the clock in the farm-tower indicated six o'clock, while his own watch said only four. Much agitated, the Count immediately called his bailiff.—What did this mean? Had the course in clock-repairing, to which he had been sent at great expense, meant so little? Did he not realize the danger of misleading travellers? (M. Jacquemont assures us that from horizon to horizon he was the only traveller in that barren countryside.) No, said the Count, no excuses, my man; you have been remiss; see that the matter is put right at once.—Next morning Jacquemont rose early and, while wandering about the farmyard, happened to climb the tower. Behind the face of the clock there were not, there never had been, any works.

In a word, there is a kind of Quixotry about the character of the Comte de Montlosier, which must have been very appealing to Stendhal; of which we find more than a trace in the Marquis de la Mole; and which invites us to some rather delicate disentangling of the mingled threads of mockery, affection, and respect which went into this portrait.

The preliminary and separate incident of Julien's spelling *cela* with two l's, though it had nothing to do with the Comte de Montlosier, has a touch of relevance. The episode derives, as we learn in *Henry Brulard*, from a memory of Beyle's own experience with Pierre Daru. The word "benefactor," used repeatedly by Julien of M. de la Mole, is Beyle's word for M. Daru; and the whole complex of feelings is analogous. For Beyle respected Daru as a man of industry and ability, served him in the affairs of an office faithfully, accepted from him promotions and preferment gratefully; and yet felt ashamed and unworthy before him, and aspired to cuckold him. Already there is a touch of revenge in the Stendhal love-affair; sex is a backhand blow by which a resentful underling touched with divine passion revenges his weakness on the world's practical wisdom. One may note, in passing, a variant on the same theme in the Fabrizio-Mosca conflict of the *Chartreuse*.

The Daru connection suggests that a young man's revenge is not incompatible with respect and affection. But in the *Rouge*, the practical enterprises at least of M. de la Mole are not treated with respect or affection; they are the object of satire and critical exaggeration. The most "ultra" ultras never talked as frankly and cold-bloodedly as Stendhal's conspirators of the necessity of foreign invasion. The most jesuitical of priests never announced his party's and his country's political dependence on the pope in quite such flat and uncompromising terms as Stendhal's cardinal uses. Deliberate civil war was no part of any ultra's political program in 1830; and while a sacred struggle against Paris had sometimes been proclaimed, it was only by isolated individuals, at the height of revolutionary turmoil, and not by any means with the cold, principled, deadly hatred which Stendhal attributed to the young bishop of Agde. Among the scoundrels and madmen taking part in Stendhal's plot, the Marquis de la Mole is probably intended to seem least contemptible; for while he counts on foreign help and does not wholly scorn the priestly party, the burden of his advice is to form a "royalist militia" and take to the field as men did in the sixteenth century. An army of chivalrous gentlemen, loyal retainers, and devoted peasantry, on the march against the whole nineteenth century; hearts of oak, as someone once said, and heads to match. It is the Quixotic mode in essence. The Marquis does not even despair of catching the imaginations of those "two hundred thousand young men of the petite bourgeoisie," mentioned earlier by Julien on his visit to England and here reintroduced at the climax of M. de la Mole's speech to the conspirators. How he expects to convert young men who are ready to fight *for* liberalism into a militia organized *against* it, he does not say. Thus the essence of his proposals is simple, dangerous, attractive madness; and Stendhal expects the reader to see this. His scene consti-

tutes an *exposé*; the characters, supposing themselves unob-
served, are made to give away the secrets of their inmost hearts
with a frankness which is almost parodic. By comparison with
the blackness of the ecclesiastics, M. de la Mole seems almost
admirable. As for the opposition of the Abbé Castanède, so
dimly motivated in the novel, it derives tacitly from the Comte
de Montlosier's overt anti-jesuit program, and constitutes, for
Stendhal, a kind of partial, inverted benediction on the Marquis
de la Mole.

Thus the reader, imitating Julien and Stendhal himself, is
expected to dislike M. de la Mole for his ideas, his emptiness,
his arrogance; but to admire him for his style. His plottings are
absurd, discussion in his salons is conformist and reactionary to
the point of perfect tedium, his only ambition for his daughter
is the perfectly empty one that she should marry a duke. He is
himself a political and social anachronism; but his style is strict
and noble, almost jansenist in fact. He nothing common does,
or mean; and in this strictness and austerity of manner, Julien
Sorel the parvenu is more fully his heir than Comte Norbert,
the idle, empty squadron commander. Respect and mockery
are intimately blended. One is reminded of the author's attitude toward Ranuccio-Ernesto IV, in the *Chartreuse*; without
even the virtue of M. de la Mole's courage and independence,
the ruler of Parma has style. It is not his own style; he has copied
it from Louis XIV (out of Saint-Simon, no doubt), but when
he puts it on and looks like a monarch, it is nevertheless impressive. So with M. de la Mole. His style is an exterior and limited
quality; it makes respect comprehensible, but gives no reason
for self-sacrifice or loyalty. Thus Stendhal eats out the core of
Julien's devotion to M. de la Mole beforehand, without making
the master quite ridiculous or the servant altogether contemptible. And thus the seduction of Mathilde, in a world dominated
by inhuman, reactionary follies, becomes at least understand-
able and almost sympathetic. Finally, Julien's service to a cause

in which he does not believe is skillful enough to lessen his look of ineffectuality and heighten his potential danger.

In all this matter, the critics have naturally been eager to assert that Stendhal throughout the details of his conspiracy was recording fact, writing social history. If the *Rouge* is a *roman à clef*, the three conspiratorial chapters undoubtedly constitute the *clef*. But there are many locks in these three chapters, and even more keys to fit them. Alongside the Montlosier-de la Mole parallel, for example, one may set a whole threadwork of parallels which link Julien Sorel to his success-shadow the young bishop of Agde; and both to a seventeenth-century ecclesiastic, the Abbé, later Cardinal and Archbishop, de Retz. As a young churchman but not yet a priest, coadjutor to the Archbishop of Paris, de Retz was sent abroad on several secret political missions, once to Sedan; and before becoming a cardinal (at the age of 37) he was, precisely, bishop of Agde. The "duc de Retz" carries his name and the thought of his *Memoirs*, the memoirs of a young man made priest in spite of himself, into the *Rouge*. In connection with the "Bord de l'Eau" conspiracy, one might also compare Julien's journey with a mission carried out by M. de Vitrolles to England in 1818. The proposals which he carried differed, to be sure, in many details from those of Stendhal's conspirators; but the novelist's inflamed Jacobin eye might well have "transposed" them, under the circumstances of 1830, into some such terms as the *Rouge* represents. Simply to save the pun, one would like to limit M. Hyde de Neuville's appearance in the novel to the figure of M. de Nerval whom others relate to the political figure named Polignac; but he may well, in the multiplicity of his characteristics, have supplied a trait or two for M. de la Mole as well. The urbanity of the Marquis, his Parisian wit and sophistication, small dry figure, and intellectual barrenness all set him apart from the volcanic Comte de Montlosier. Either M. de Neuville or M. de Tracy himself may well have been placed under contribution for one or several of these characteristics.

Thus we have social history, to be sure; but so unliteral as to amount to a kind of inspired, associationist poetry. The truth is more complex than any combination of facts. At least as remarkable as the way Stendhal reproduced and recombined the social materials of the Restoration and of his reading is his free adaptation of them to the needs of his novel.* Though the Comte de Montlosier was a historical fact, he defied all the probabilities and decorums of character in a way which would have made him quite useless for some novelists and for others (one thinks, shudderingly, of Dickens) useful only as an amiable eccentric. Stendhal adapted and civilized him; made him rich and a Parisian instead of poor and provincial, and reduced his eccentricities, leaving them without emphasis or diffusing them through a whole class of men where they were necessary to keep Julien from showing too blackly. And in order to provide that fillip of purple peril, of mysterious, deadly opposition which he required of every conspiracy, he invoked the everpresent aid of the jesuits.

Here too he was imitating history, if the Comte de Montlosier be history; but it is a case of a master-imagination following an essentially pedestrian one, with the still more prosaic facts of history buried completely in the background. The Comte de Montlosier delivered a number of philippics against the jesuits, and they make entertaining reading; but for the reader who approaches them with the sinister figures of the

---

* A striking example of political inversion is provided by M. Liprandi's demonstration that materials for the king's visit to Verrières came from a liberal celebration held in honor of Lafayette during the summer of 1829 ("Un roi à Verrières," Le Divan, juillet-septembre, 1950). A phrase used in pseudo-jacobin context by Beyle the political reporter is smuggled into the Rouge under ultra auspices (Louis Aragon, La lumière de Stendhal, 38-39). Why not look for the original of the scene where the boy-bishop of Agde tries on his mitre in the coronation of Napoleon?

Abbés Castanède and Frilair in mind, there is something disappointing in the charges which the Comte de Montlosier, drawing on material collected from all of France, has to bring against the Society of Jesus. They have not only established schools—as, indeed, our accuser concedes they had a perfect right to do; they have taken pupils by the day—as, he says, they should not have done. The point might be proved a dozen times over without constituting high or even low treason. But there is worse to come. A priest—it is not alleged that he was a jesuit or under jesuit influence—spoke roughly of a girl who had attended a dance; said he would drive her out of the church if she dared appear there. This is offensive language and silly morality; but it is far from the sly subversion of universal liberty which Stendhal attributed to the priestly party. In fact, whatever it shows about the individual priest, evidence of this sort may even be thought to negate, in some degree, the very hypothesis of a priestly party; for parties which have secret ends to gain are usually less flagrant about offending public opinion. These are typical counts in the long indictment; they are closer to popguns than howitzers. And yet the Comte de Montlosier in his accusations against the jesuits was accused of exaggerating his facts. If the facts themselves were in the order of 1, and Montlosier's exaggeration of them something like 5, then Stendhal's version, in the *Rouge*, must be close to 500.

The Abbé de Pradt is more satisfying to our sense of jesuitical theatricals; for like Stendhal, he identifies the jesuit principle with spiritual tyranny and predatory priesthood pursued for their own sakes. But even he, though he ransacks the history of the Society from its first founding by Ignatius Loyola, does not come up with anything particularly horrendous in the way of actual behavior. Thus to some students it has seemed idle to seek a specific public or, so to speak, macrocosmic source for Stendhal's jesuit phobia. His image of the jesuits crystallized, we are told, around a childhood tutor, the Abbé Raillane, probably with some assistance from the early life of the Abbé of Perigord, later known as Talleyrand. Perhaps so; but if this was the way of it, his phobia was a long time in finding its way to expression, after first being formed when he was just ten years old.

For the early life and writings of Beyle show no special antipathy to the Society of Jesus. Young Beyle is much taken with the comic possibilities of Tartufe; he hates priests, especially strict and hypocritical ones, with a fervor that relates rather oddly to his own deliberate cultivation of hypocrisy. But it is only after 1825 or so that he passes beyond a mild and often jocose anticlericalism. When the word "jesuit" finally enters his vocabulary, he applies it freely to figures whom he had known earlier in life, figures such as the Abbé Raillane. *Henry Brulard* puts the matter so forcefully, indeed, as to have convinced some of the biographers that the Abbé actually belonged to the jesuit order. But this is impossible; after the abolition of their organization in 1773, the jesuits were not reconstituted in France till 1814. When Beyle applies the word to his tutor, he is thinking of a type of character. But the word, and this use of it, are of 1835 vintage. The early writings have words enough for a deceitful or bigoted ecclesiastic; but "jesuit" is not one of them. Jesuitry has no generalized meaning for young Beyle, and does not start to have one till the popular anti-jesuit agitation of the mid-twenties has got under way. Between the two editions of *Rome, Naples, and Florence* (1817, 1826) a major change has taken place; and much, which in the earlier edition was ascribed to priests generally or not mentioned at all, is laid in the second edition on the doorstep of the fathers of Jesus. And with the Chevalier de Bonnivet, in *Armance* (1826-27), we are fairly embarked on a line of malignant, supple, and corrupt clerics which represents for Stendhal the blackest tone of which his palette is capable.

Useless to seek an early antipathy to the jesuit name in Beyle's

writing; useless even to seek in his early biography a propor-
tionate experience of the anti-ecclesiastical complex, such as it
was or came to be when "jesuit" became identified in Stendhal's
mind with "priest." The Raillane tyranny, though it has been
estimated at as little as nine months, may perhaps have lasted
intermittently as long as twenty; but evidence from outside
Henry Brulard suggests a far from malignant disposition in the
man who exercised it. Simple in his domestic arrangements, old-
fashioned and courtly in his manners, sincerely and fearlessly devoted to his pastoral duties, the Abbé Raillane appears, outside
Henry Brulard, about as jesuitical as Saint Paul. In his character
as pedagogue he was doubtless strict, perhaps narrow, even doc-
trinaire; but it is a rare teacher, and perhaps not a very good
one, whom his fractious pupils do not consider a tyrant. That
Beyle was fractious everyone remarked; and the Abbé Raillane's
success with other pupils, the Perier children for example, and
their cousin Philippine Duchesne, suggests that, even if an ogre,
he was not an ineffectual one. At all events, a teacher who is a
fugitive from justice, placarded in the public streets for his convictions, may be conceded a little strictness in dealing with a
sulky and resentful ten-year-old.

Beyle suffered, then, at the hands of the Abbé Raillane; but
not very much or very long or in any way which the impartial
reader (any more than Beyle himself at the time) would think
of calling "jesuit". Least of all was he pushed, like his best-
known heroes, toward an ecclesiastical career for which he felt
no inclination; indeed, now and then in *Henry Brulard* he
verges on blaming Raillane for not having courted and wooed
him sufficiently for the service of the church! Geometry may
have been necessary to get him out of Grenoble; but it was allowed to do its work with little interference or opposition. This
was a deficiency in experience which Beyle had opportunities to
remedy vicariously. The early career of Cardinal de Retz furnished him with one example of a resentful, high-spirited,

worldly boy made priest in spite of himself, and his youthful
interest in memoirs had made the episode perfectly familiar.
The story of Talleyrand's first years, though the formal *Memoirs*
were unwritten as yet and would not be published for years to
come, was common knowledge, and may well have given another nudge to the novelist's imagination. Yet both these
princes of the church went through something much closer to
Fabrizio's experience at the seminary than Julien Sorel's and
actually milder than the experience of either. Unperturbed by
doubts or intrigues, they pursued a course of self-education according to the classic dichotomy of books and mistresses. They
suffered no jealousies, no repressions, no discouragements, no
humiliations; they were never enjoined that blind obedience
and absolute empty-headedness which is such a striking feature
of theological education as Stendhal represents it.

No, the genesis of Stendhal's jesuit-phobia must be sought at
once closer to home and in something more generalized than a
specific text. I think it was Joseph Lingay who first presented to
Beyle a spy's-eye view of French politics, such as gives much of
its flavor to the *Rouge*. Ugly, clever, venal, and as undomesti-
cated as Stendhal himself, little Lingay was reputed to know all
the deals and detailed arrangements by which power and profit
were actually divided in France. What Vidocq was to Balzac,
Lingay was to Stendhal. He was a spy and a counter-spy; one
who managed publicity both favorable and unfavorable, in the
interests of those who paid him. He had the peculiar quality,
notable in the Conte Mosca as well, of being perfectly devoted
to whatever minister happened to be in power. Stendhal said
Lingay would have sacrificed his life for any of the men he
served, as long as they were in power when the sacrifice was
called for. A total absence of logic, a perfectly supple conscience,
no more idea of "civic duty" than Beyle himself had of angelic
communications—these were supplemented in little Lingay by
a perfectly chivalric devotion to his friends. Stendhal, whose

private name for the minister Decazes was "Maison" (from *casa*), called Lingay, Decazes' creature, by the charming nickname of "Maisonette"; and he seems in fact to have been a little minister, who managed to stay in office as long as he wanted by his perfectly unofficial flair for being the best-informed man in France. Thus he was in a position to do for Beyle's view of politics what Angela Pietragrua had done for his view of love. When someone spoke of the lofty liberal principles of M. de Jouy, Lingay could simply go to his files and take out the autograph letter in which M. de Jouy humbly begged from the Bourbon administration the cross of St. Louis. Intrigue and counter-intrigue on this scale are heady subjects for a man of Beyle's imagination; the combination of Lingay's inside dope with the vast public furore which arose in the mid-twenties over the activities of the jesuits and the *congregation* did much to ripen that distrust of the clergy, which dated from an early, peculiar, and yet an oddly distinct reaction to the clerical mind.

For, like figures as oddly assorted as Talleyrand, Joyce, and Chillingworth the English theologian, Stendhal's reaction against the Roman church took the form of deliberate imitation. Perhaps apostasy seems for men like these the logical culmination of an intellectual method which they cannot doubt; perhaps also they learn to admire, by fighting it, the style of the church which they must hate in order to leave. Their cool, dispassionate, elaborate unravelling of the sleeve of evidence, their pursuit of real rather than merely sentimental interests, and their careful observation of their own psychology, leads them to follow the jesuit intellectual method scrupulously away from the conclusions which it was designed to support. Beyle, at least, never laid eyes on a jesuit father who was, in the realities of the word, as big a jesuit as he, who affected to despise the order.

English readers who encounter anti-Catholic prejudice in fic-

tion are likely to see it first in novelists like George Borrow and
Charles Reade—honest, red-blooded, Anglo-Saxon penmen,
flushed with bluff indignation at the insidious Latin equivocations of the jesuit order. But this is to use clubs against rapiers;
even if one wins, the victory does not make a pretty spectacle.
In all the essentials of jesuitry, Stendhal paid his jesuit opponents the sincere, the supreme tribute of direct imitation.

There are, it would seem, three distinct sides to being a jesuit;
one is ruthless power politics, one hypocrisy as a deliberate policy, and one the art and practice of equivocation. In theory, all
these elements go back to a single first principle, an intellectual
commitment which requires that every act be interpreted as
either for or against one's own party. Hence the justification of
power politics; one's actions are inflexibly determined by a
loyalty which admits of no rivals, no alternatives, and no more
mitigation on the score of "reasonableness" than will serve
one's best political advantage. Temporizing and casuistry are
ways of seeming to mitigate this rigidity without actually doing
so, of seeming to consider alternative attitudes and points of
view without risking positive contamination; while hypocrisy
is the inevitable result of seeming to deal with men in the
day-to-day terms of the world, while maintaining in reserve an
intellectual commitment which renders perfectly vain all day-
to-day considerations.

Nothing makes Stendhal's jesuitical proceedings more apparent than a straightforward account, such as Mr. Josephson's,
of the novelist as liberal. In order to draw this picture at all, one
must omit so much both of Henri Beyle and of the romances of
Stendhal, as to make caricature inevitable. Actually, liberals
play an uneasy, ambiguous role in both the great novels. At first,
the *Rouge* seems about to offer them a straightforward role of
opposition to the ultras and arrivistes typified by Rênal and
Valenod. We hear of Valenod seeking their support for reasons
of his own, but no shadow falls upon their motives; and in fact

the general odium in which they are held by accomplished
rascals casts an indirect but honorable light on the liberals. The
author or his spokesman says that he is a liberal himself. But his
basic dislike for the breed is not long in making itself felt. Time
and again he represents the liberals as a faction more sanctimo-
nious and less successful than the ultras, but in no way superior
to them. When the king visits Verrières, the liberals find excuses
to illuminate their houses even more brightly than the ultras;
when Julien is admitted to the Guard of Honor, these preachers
of equality are profoundly horrified; when he recites the Bible
in Latin, they are stupefied with admiration. Liberals crawl
lower and intrigue more basely than anybody else; Stendhal invented a M. Sainclair, a famous liberal, and brought him into
M. de la Mole's salon for the exclusive purpose of making this
point. Surely Stendhal glances at the liberals when he speaks of
"those conspirators in yellow gloves, who profess to reform all
the conditions of life in a great country, and would be horrified
at having to undergo the slightest inconvenience themselves."
In fact, being a liberal is for Stendhal merely another way of
feathering one's own nest; it is simply one more snug and servile niche in that society with which his heroes are perpetually
at odds. At Parma, when Ranuccio-Ernesto IV is succeeded by
his son, the liberal party automatically becomes ultra and the
ultra party liberal, without a word being said by anyone.

Two extremes of liberalism which seem to be viewed somewhat more leniently than the orthodox creed are anarchy and
dictatorship, as represented in the novels by the poetical brigand
Ferrante Palla (modelled on Ferrante Pallavicino with, perhaps,
touches from Silvio Pellico) and Napoleon. These alternatives
to liberalism are not explicitly criticized, it is true; but neither
are they compatible. Both exemplify heroic energy, both are
outside the realm of responsible politics; and if that be taken
as a conclusion in itself, it is nonetheless a conclusion not
frankly avowed but dissembled. Palla and Bonaparte are sticks

to beat the liberals and ultras; but in themselves they lead only to the well-known dead ends of America and the Directory.

No less dubious and a little more disturbing than his "liberalism" is Beyle's equivocal attitude toward France itself after 1814. He stood firmly enough by the regime of Napoleon, active and inventive to the end, even while earnestly soliciting those "crosses," the appetite for which he was capable of mocking so acutely. But after the cause was lost, what happened? His version of the story, as it accumulated and solidified in later life, was that he left for Italy in disdain, full of a noble *mépris* for Louis XVIII and all his works. The facts invite a sizable modification of this view. He signed an oath of allegiance to the new regime, which has survived; it is dated April 19, 1814. His friend and cousin Colomb tells us that in 1814 Beyle was expressing the greatest pleasure at the overthrow of "the despot who had stolen the liberties of France." He made deliberately vague the dedication to the first edition of the *Histoire de la Peinture*, so that posterity has generally assumed it was directed to Napoleon; actually, it was a veiled effort to flatter Alexander, Czar of Russia, and Napoleon's recent conqueror (Martineau, *Le Coeur de Stendhal*, I, 368-69). From his old friend, Edouard Mounier, from a relatively new acquaintance, the Comte Beugnot, and from a perfect stranger, one M. Blacas, he solicited employment in the new administration, whether at Paris or at an Italian consulate. For reasons which are completely obscure but undoubtedly complex, he refused an office as director of the provisioning of Paris; yet that he wanted office of some sort is undeniable. Among the papers of the Comte Beugnot there has long survived a police report on Henri Beyle, dating from this period. It is an indulgent, intimate, and understanding document which has often been reprinted by the biographers; it indicates M. Beyle's weakness for books, actresses, and operas, but generally speaking gives him a clean bill of political health. Recent research has established that it is written throughout in the hand of Henri Beyle.*

After his departure for Italy, Beyle's attitude toward Restoration France solidified; the spectacle of France, he said (and it has been much repeated), disgusted and disheartened him. During the Hundred Days he did not budge physically, mentally, or morally, either to help or hinder Bonaparte. And at the end of *Rome, Naples, and Florence* (1817) he renounced explicitly, though not formally, his French citizenship; his phrase is an illusion to "the author, who since 1814 has no longer been a Frenchman." (True, he was writing under a German pseudonym; but the remark about being "no longer a Frenchman" does not strengthen, rather it undercuts and exposes his pseudonym. If he is no longer a Frenchman, what was his name when he was one?) At least five and perhaps fifteen years would have to pass before he began sketching epitaphs in which he designated himself a "Milanese" † (it was an act which still ruffles French patriotism, still provokes passionate declarations). But the point of view was already crystallizing. And henceforth, indeed, his attitude toward French internal politics is that of a detached and disinterested observer, not merely from another nation but from another planet. He took no part whatever in the barricade-battles of 1830, though he was, appropriately, at the Comédie Française, where the bullets flew thickest; he observed, with the same sceptical, indulgent interest as Byron, the conspiratorial machinations of the Italian carbonari. But he took no part in political activities as such, and used what insight he had into French political life only for sardonic, destructive commentary on the intellectual fads of the

---

* François Michel, *Etudes stendhaliennes* (Paris, 1958), 17 ff., "Le policier qui espionna M. de Beyle?"
† The first of these epitaphs is a marginal note on a *Dialogo di Ermès Visconti*, published in 1819; unfortunately, the date of the note cannot be established exactly. See Vittorio del Litto, "Sur un volume annoté par Stendhal," in Yves Du Parc, *Dans le sillage de Stendhal*, p. 150.

day,* and to maintain a snug harbor for himself in the administration and on the pension-rolls. His conduct has thus been arraigned as opportunism of the most degraded sort, and hailed as the most implacable and determined patriotism—a veritable model of the underground resistance man, surrounded and cut off but intrenched in his own unyielding convictions. Maurice Bardèche in a sly volume has even represented Beyle's political spirit as paralleling that of a sturdy and devoted fascist after 1945—a patriot of the *vichyssoise* persuasion, surrounded by oceans of servile and flabby liberalism. It is jesuitry of a high order which not only acts in a way capable of three distinct interpretations, but makes each of these interpretations seem to those who hold it exclusively correct.

But Beyle's biographical jesuitry and the overt political equivocation of the novels are only the opening aspects of an attitude which cuts into the texture and structure of Stendhal's fiction from beginning to end. We are struck, to begin with, by the "honest" hypocrisy of the Stendhal heroes. They cultivate hypocrisy as the best weapon available to them in the war against society, and find it amusing to be as dishonest as possible. It is just a matter of learning to say stupid, acceptable things with a straight face, and since we all have to do a good deal of this, Stendhal is not hard-pressed to make it seem sympathetic and acceptable behavior. Among themselves, the happy few are frank and funny about their dishonesty; and since society is shown as both stupid and ruthless in its demands for conformity, all expedients are clearly justified. But on occasion the bargain which they drive with life is made to seem almost unpleasantly sharp for the Stendhal heroes. When Julien Sorel

---

* *D'un nouveau complot contre les industriels* (1825) is typical of his cavalry tactics in journalism. It is a slashing, ten-page foray against Saint-Simonian utilitarianism, an attempt to recapture the word "industriel" from the manufacturers. Stendhal, that arch-materialist, points out that the real *workers* of any age are its artists and thinkers.

promises the Abbé Chélan that he will leave Verrières immediately, without seeing anyone, we are not greatly upset to find
that this vow does not prevent his coming back to visit Mme. de
Rênal after he has gone a mile out of town. On the other hand,
Clélia Conti's oath never to see Fabrizio again, which turns out
not to preclude rendezvous in the dark, has a somewhat different effect. It is a joke, but a blasphemous joke; and its effect
upon pious people gives a dark and gloomy coloring to the
whole concluding episode of the novel. Finally, in an incident
of thoroughly questionable taste, the Duchessa Sanseverina's
submission to Ernesto-Ranuccio V (the final consequence of a
suggestion by Conte Mosca), comes perilously close to standing
the whole *Chartreuse* on its head. If these are the straits into
which close steering and skillful equivocation lead, perhaps one
had better begin and end with open defiance.

Such, at least are some of the reflections to which the passages give rise. They lead to another aspect of Beyle's ambiguity
which the reader cannot help feeling with regard to the Stendhal
heroes themselves. Are they spoilt and petulant puppies, or profound social critics; diseased minds or noble ones? Are they ambitious little hypocrites or heroic adversaries of social hypocrisy;
honest men with noble souls or vulgar opportunists? They tread
a narrow line, and so does the author, who, when he dedicated
his novels "To the Happy Few," showed how much he felt he
was demanding of his audience in sympathy and understanding.
This ambiguity goes very deep in Beyle's psychology; it is not
even an ambiguity of moral or esthetic ideas, but an ambiguity
between them, so that values which are dramatically admirable
may sometimes be sensed as socially evil, and *vice versa*. "You
can have bicameral legislation in North America, but there's no
opera, and you would die of boredom,"—the antinomy is left
wide open, with nothing but a shrug of the shoulders to fill it.

Thus, from one point of view, Julien Sorel's career is exactly
that described in the letter written by Madame de Rênal; he is

a man who tries to rise in households through his connections with women. This is only part of the truth, though it is the "republican" part, and some true aspects of his character are in flat contradiction of this aspect. But this aspect is true too, and to appreciate the novel properly, one must be willing to hold these elements in indefinite suspension. Fabrizio is a handsome young Italian à la mode, with a horse, a mistress, a position in the church, and family connections which underwrite everything. He is also, somehow, a dreamer supremely indifferent to the mundane considerations which in fact make up the texture of his life. . . . These are logical contradictions into which we must not look too closely, at least while we are experiencing the full impact of the novels.

Finally, there is a sort of indefiniteness about elements in the fiction which are sketched in but not given any definite weight or function. There is, for example, the Priore Blanès and his phophecy about Fabrizio's future; or the incident of the little tree which symbolizes Fabrizio's well-being in the *Chartreuse*, or the bit of newspaper which Julien Sorel finds in the crimson light of the church at Verrières, which prophesies in the form of an anagram his future and warns of his ending. But these elements are only thrown in as hints. They are the "Montesino's Cave" of Stendhal; and it is the same with Mathilde's representing "love of the head" and her passion for men who have the energy to get themselves beheaded; there is no knowing what these puns, images, and prophetic hints mean, if anything, or how seriously they are to be taken. The most exquisite bits of dissimulation in the novels are those passages where an unrecognized passion struggles toward the light and is repelled with horror the minute it becomes recognizable. This is best seen in Gina's anguish over her passion for Fabrizio and Conte Mosca's turmoil over his own jealousy.

It is true that we are getting, here, beyond the bounds of jesuitry properly so called. Not every subtle analyst of the human heart is a jesuit or need be supposed indebted to the jesuits for his insights. But it is also true that an interest in casuistry, tergiversation, equivocation, and the act of mental reservation springs readily from a preoccupation with jesuits, and shades easily into an analysis of the dark shadows and unturned corners of the human mind. The jesuits were famous for their skill in putting and resolving "cases of conscience"; and delicate, almost sickly, cases of divided conscience (no less than of consciousness and unconsciousness) were precisely the center of Stendhal's novelistic focus.

In a sense, then, it is possible to say that Stendhal hated the jesuits, or made the jesuits a symbol of what he hated, partly because they were not jesuitical enough for him.* He represents them as mechanical and arbitrary in their repressions; but as neither afflicted by nor perceptive of an ordinary sincere con science. It is by taking away their understanding of the conscience that he makes such ogres of the jesuits; it is by giving a conscience of one sort or another to Julien, Fabrizio, the Abbé Chélan, the Abbé Pirard, and the jansenists, that he makes them human to us. But the conscience which he gave them all was strikingly jesuitical; the Abbé Pirard can wipe out a seduction and betrayal with a marriage as easily as Fabrizio can forget about simony, or Julien overlook a promise made to the Abbé Chélan, his ghostly father. A conscience of this ductile character is in many ways closer to what we consider a distinctively jesuit trait than the ruthless power-politics which is common to condottieri, communists, and capitalists as well as the followers of Ignatius Loyola.

---

* His whole attitude toward jesuitry and jesuitical tactics, needless to say, depends on a distinction between inner and outer life, between the dream and its enemies. His proceedings are jesuitical only when they are defensive. Nobody is less prone to dissimulate than Beyle, when he feels free. But the new Anglo-Saxon school of irony-reductionists makes nothing of this distinction—and so makes something very simple-minded indeed of *notre Henri.*

Did Stendhal ever have, in fact, a long-term perspective, such as would render him a "sincere" jesuit—a total intellectual commitment, to which he oriented all his other thoughts and appearances? Or did he, on the other hand, merely copy jesuit manners for the pleasure of seeming sinister? The truth, as usual, is probably somewhere in the middle, but it bends toward the latter alternative. Though he was much occupied with posterity, and confident that it would do him justice in his quarrel with the nineteenth century, Beyle does not seem to have had a very distinct notion of what it would or should be like. His idea of posterity was chiefly that it should not have certain of the follies which afflicted Restoration France. But neither his jesuitry nor that of his heroes was devoted to bringing about any social or intellectual change of significance; it shows itself more in hypocrisy as a spectacle, for the sake of personal convenience, or for purposes of personal protection. Even in his addiction to jesuitry, he avoided the substance of it, and emphasized chiefly the manners—he made, in other words, a personal virtue out of what even true jesuits affect to think only a social necessity.

There is an oblique relation to ideas and principles here, which reminds one of Stendhal's dealings with personality. He likes to attenuate the center and accentuate the periphery; to hold onto ideas and make use of them by their edges and implications. An intellectual method so markedly indirect and, in the stolid middle-class sense, so irresponsible, suggests a kind of political bad conscience which is not hard to recognize in Stendhal. The fantasy of Danton, all blood, fire, and virtue, haunts his imagination. With such a leader, Beyle would be a republican. But, lacking such a leader, and a band of sublimely devoted followers to make the cause practical (one had almost said, "easy"), he amuses himself with cynicisms. There is an analogue here with Julien, who could be religious if Fénelon's God

were somehow made available to him.* Such haggling with the
terms of life does not ordinarily strike us as graceful. Yet it is
just the conditional mood of the Machiavelli-maneuver, which
salves acceptance of political realities with the proviso that they
be used for a noble purpose. If Beyle could find a noble purpose, he would shrink from nothing; perhaps it is a feeling that
he is merely looking for an excuse, a pretext, to shrink from
nothing that has given him a slightly ugly name.

But in point of fact, Stendhal relates to those literary toughs,
Machiavelli and Nietzsche, only in a thoroughly indistinct way.
Nietzsche praised him as a European figure who dared to be
himself; and Beyle read Machiavelli with relish. But both were
men of rarely catholic tastes, and the passages in Stendhal which
actually suggest a distinct intellectual affinity with Nietzsche or
Machiavelli are few. As to Nietzsche, they are (as I see it)
the exact minimum necessary to make a plural verb. Outside
the *Rouge*, II, 9, I do not think there is in the works of Stendhal
a passage which would naturally suggest to an unsuspicious
reader the philosopher of the *Uebermensch*. No doubt the
passages in question are striking. In conversation with Count
Altamira, Julien learns that the Count's conspiracy was crushed
because of his failure to cut off three heads; we should call it
liberal chickenheartedness. Julien is no less severe, remarking
abruptly that the ends justify the means, and that he would
hang three men any time to save the lives of four. Next day,
still brooding on this problem, he meets Mlle. de la Mole in
the library, and when she questions him about his revery, advances on her, asking " 'Was Danton justified in stealing?' and
then, with an air that grew more and more savage, 'The Revolutionaries of Piedmont, of Spain, ought they to have compro-

---

* The ironies of the idea were doubtless apparent to Stendhal himself.
Cf. his passing comment in a totally different context, "la religion de
Fénelon n'était q'un égoisme tendre." *Histoire de la Peinture*, II, 241.

mised the people by crimes? To have given away, even to men
without merit, all the commands in the army, all the Crosses?
Would not the men who wore those Crosses have had reason
to fear a Restoration of their King? Ought they to have let the
Treasury in Turin be pillaged? In a word, Mademoiselle,' he
said as he came towards her with a terrible air, 'ought the man
who seeks to banish ignorance and crime from the earth to
pass like a whirlwind and do evil as though blindly?' "

This sounds, in interrogative form, very much like the philosophy of *The Prince* and *Beyond Good and Evil*; particularly as
it conceals a lurking fondness for the Higher Good, from which
neither Nietzsche nor Machiavelli could ever quite get disen-
tangled. But the parallels are less significant than they seem.
Stendhal's situation is thoroughly dramatic; Julien's attraction
for Mathilde is that of a potential Danton, a man who has the
energy to get his own head cut off, as well as to cut off the heads
of others. Once set in this track, Stendhal has only one direction in which to move his hero, toward a potential bloodthirsti-
ness which makes him sound like a *Realpolitiker* or even an
Uebermensch: but which is explicable as a product of his own
moody, difficile temper, and which functions in the novel to
make apparent Mathilde's penchant for dangerous passions.
The ordinary tenor of Julien's thought and feeling, no less than
that of Beyle himself, has little room for the hardminded, realistic analysis of power, and even less for the apocalyptic visions
of a transfigured authoritarian Antichrist.

The Conte Mosca is a figure who recalls Machiavelli rather
more distinctly; his easy cynicism, perfect pliability, and readiness to sacrifice lives, not for a noble cause but for an ignoble
necessity, are qualities too marked to require emphasis. But he
is only one chord in the complex symphony of the *Chartreuse*;
and Machiavellianism is only one element of his character. Shy
at La Scala, jealous of Fabrizio, and magnificently devoted to

his Gina, the Conte owes as much to Beyle's psychological veracity and to Castiglione's archetype, as to Machiavelli.

In the end, it remains a nice question whether a man whose imagination is ruthless, unprincipled, and corrupt is not more disturbing than one who calmly advocates ruthless, unprincipled, and corrupt behavior as a means to a practical end. *The Prince* is perhaps a work of fiction, quite as much as the *Chartreuse*; but its tone, its function save it from seeming vindictive. Stendhal has a permanent bad conscience which, when he is at his best, forbids him to salve the situation with a pious hope. Evil is done, not that good may come of it, but because evil, just as much as, or even more than, good, can express the real nature of man. "I love force," Beyle once wrote, "and of the force I love, an ant can display as much as an elephant." Martineau's characterization of this force as "moral" seems a gratuitous act of piety, in which the author himself could scarcely have believed. Actually, the interests of the will (force) are like a magnetic field running N-S through another (the interests of morality) aligned E-W. Congruent, mutually interfering, and forever, yet not directly, opposed, the demands of the self and of social morality are for Stendhal reducible to no single standard of law. His refusal of the pious hope in the *Chartreuse*, it seems to me, raises this novel stylistically one stage beyond the *Rouge*. Julien's outpouring in prison is a fine piece of rhetoric, in which the soul's yearning for something better than the dark prison of this world is expressed with all Chateaubriand's florid eloquence, or Jeremy Taylor's. But finer than this, to a sensitive imagination, are the little touches of retribution-expectation and blighting, unexplained melancholy, which darken the ending of the *Chartreuse*. In these shadings Stendhal shows us what it is to live in permanent anxiety, with a revolting rat forever gnawing in one's pocket, bowed by an indefeasible guilt which is entirely beyond or beneath the reach of reason.

6

Octave and Emma:

or the Promiscuous Impotent

Fatigué des clartés confuses
Qui m'ont égaré bien souvent,
J'allais bannir amours et muses;
J'allais vouloir être savant.
Mais quoi! pour une âme incertaine
La science est d'un vain secours.
Gardons Lisette et La Fontaine:
Muses, restez; restez, Amours.

"*Les Sciences,*" *Béranger*

"With that audacity which never failed to distinguish him, the Baron Stendhal drove, in his first fiction, upon an impossible topic, and shattered the resources of his gallant cavalry against an impregnable position." Reports from the foothills of Parnassus rarely fail to speak in some such mournful metaphors as these of Stendhal's first skirmish with the art of the novel; and they are right, it is hard to present *Armance* as a triumphant

encounter. The plain fact is that so long as one sees it under
the aspect of a story about physical incapacity—impotence, in
a word—it must necessarily appear grotesque. *Babilans** have,
no doubt, their problems, which the Good Society will some day
do something about; but the responsibility for doing it will have
to be divided between Dr. VanDeVelde and the Firestone-
Goodyear combine. As Stendhal found out, fiction cannot
safely have any traffic with matters so mechanical. Faced with
the necessity of confessing his incapacity to his mistress (and
so, perforce, to the patiently inquisitive reader), the hero of
Armance blushes and blunders like a bashful school-boy; he
resorts to desperate expedients, heroic evasions; writes short
notes which he tears up without revealing what is in them; hints
and blurts and retracts; confesses, but inaudibly; and so, fairly
gagged on his own humiliation, finally removes himself from
this mortal sphere, still unspeaking—leaving to poor Henri
Martineau the ungrateful task of explaining what it has all been
about.

Editors can do anything; and M. Martineau, drawing upon
the correspondence of Beyle, the textbooks of clinical psychology, and physiological researches of impeccable authority, has
spared us little. Numerous diagnoses of Octave de Malivert have
been indicated; various practical alternatives to suicide have
been suggested, some extremely ingenious, all giving a fine impression of French resourcefulness, aplomb, and finesse under
awkward circumstances. Biographers and psycholiterary commentators, loth to overlook the rich implications of the topic,
have hastened to explore the life of Henri Beyle for appropriate
castration-fantasies, inversion-indices, and subnormal regressive
anal-erotic libido fixations. Needless to say, they have found
what they were looking for.

But if we put aside these juicy topics, for a moment anyhow;

---

* On the derivation and usage of this elegant term, see P. P. Trompeo,
Nell' Italia Romantica, Chapter X.

if we forget temporarily that Octave is impotent and that this fact has delicious implications in all conceivable directions, what have we left? Very much what the subtitle of *Armance* describes: "Quelques scènes d'un salon de Paris en 1827." This is not by any means a contemptible theme for a novel; indeed, the detailed satiric study of social manners furnishes at least half the materials which make up the *Rouge* and the *Chartreuse*. It may well be argued that in *Armance* this groundwork is pricked out with even more precision, point, and subtlety than in the later works. Every Stendhal novel is a concerto for passionate soloist and social orchestra; the solo violin part in *Armance* is quite unplayable, but the orchestral score is almost a model of virile, satiric delicacy.

Paris in 1827—Stendhal is meticulous in indicating the precise stage in the development of hypocrisy and selfishness which his specimen-society has attained. (By 1830, when Julien Sorel traces his quick, brilliant orbit through the upper salons of Paris, their tone will have changed considerably. They will be darker, duller, more dogmatic, more in the hands of jesuits and fanatical legitimists. On the other hand, in 1834 and 1835, the period of *Lucien Leuwen*, society is once more in the hands of the dead-center, and fanatical royalist circles in dreary little provincial towns like Nancy are taking on a vaguely nostalgic, pseudo-chivalric set of snob values.) And the novel, without ever moving far outside its indicated theater of the salon, does in fact present a remarkable parade of social psychopaths, unsparingly rendered with a clinical objectivity which has reminded some commentators of Proust. There is Madame d'Aumale, featherheaded by a kind of sublime principle—so frantic in her avoidance of boredom that she never knows from minute to minute what she will do next. There is M. de Soubirane, the Commander, a hangover from 1789, bold, bluff, and stupid, in whom the fatuity of argument has simply replaced the affectation of youth. There are the Duchesse d'Ancre and her friend

Madame de la Ronze, in whom malicious jealousy is forever frozen. There is the Chevalier de Bonnivet, a jesuit in the new style, malicious, ambitious, and reactionary, who at a moment's notice can interrupt the pleasures of a flirtation in order to read a moral lecture to the servants. There is Madame de Bonnivet herself, with an architect at her country estate who understands so intuitively when promotions to the Order of the Holy Spirit are to be announced, that his clients are always in the politic place at the politic moment. Madame de Bonnivet it is who is so infatuated with the new German metaphysics that to find a *rebellious nature* in need of reclamation is, for her, sheer ecstasy. She is, says Stendhal, like that "celebrated Doctor of the last century, [who], summoned to the bedside of a great nobleman, his friend, after examining the symptoms of the disease slowly and in silence, exclaimed in a sudden transport of joy: 'Ah! Monsieur le Marquis, it is a disease that has been lost for centuries! Vitreous phlegm! A superb disease, absolutely fatal. Ah! I have discovered it, I have discovered it!' Such was the joy of Madame de Bonnivet; it was in a sense the joy of an artist."

There is the apex of all French snobbery, a Duke with a gift for divining things or people that are going to become the fashion; a weekend invitation to his estate puts one automatically in line for a peerage. There is the half-pay lieutenant, M. Dolier, a firm and honorable man, who once served Napoleon and therefore has no hope of making any headway whatever in the new society of 1827. And finally, in the background behind these people, are the serried rows of new snobs and new arrivals, jealous of their petty distinctions and quite indistinguishable. There is the Napoleonic nobility, coarse, common, and invincibly complacent; there are the surly manufacturers, whose essential way of life is rude, clumsy, and competitive; there are the stupid manufacturers, who probably mean no harm, as they mean no good, but simply don't know how to behave. All are equally rich, equally unmannered. There are the obsequious deputies, who make awkward allusions in drawing-rooms to the money they are going to vote the people of quality; there are galaxies of mothers with daughters to dispose of; there are aunts with nieces to sell, and of course there are the innumerable, anonymous envious. *Armance* sets before us the whole range and run of a snob society invaded by vulgarians; it has some trouble putting these people in motion, but they are magnificently present; and from this aspect the novel is, indeed, something of a triumph.

Appearing as he does among all these mannered grotesques, it would be tempting to explain Octave de Malivert in terms appropriate to the creation of a modern novelist, writing with "The Waste Land," *The Sun Also Rises, Ulysses,* and *Lady Chatterley's Lover* in his immediate background. Clearly, then, Octave would symbolize the sterility of the culture which surrounds him. Unfortunately, there is not the slightest ground for supposing that anything like this notion ever crossed Beyle's mind, though various eager critics have undertaken to make it cross the reader's. Quite unjustifiably; for Octave is far from a languid, effete, or spiritless young man. On the contrary, he is in rebellion against the languor of his own class; he has just left the Ecole Polytechnique, he reads the utilitarian philosophers, and dallies with the idea of taking the name of Martin or Lenoir and getting a job as a chemical engineer or a valet. Various circumstances suggest that he has interesting difficulties in expressing his antipathy for the society in which accident has placed him, and placed him very well. He tends to cultivate with unnatural assiduity the society of people whom he is known to despise; he is perfectly obedient towards his mother and father, and painfully respectful of social opinion; after reading a liberal paper or book, he immediately and mechanically reads one of the opposite complexion. Yet alongside this almost parodic meekness flourish fits of unpredictable and uncontrollable rage. Irked at the vulgarity of a countess, he rushes out into the street and picks a sabre-fight with a couple of common soldiers; in the midst of a cheerful game of charades, he turns furiously on a footman and throws him out the window. These are known as the "migraines" of the young Vicomte de Malivert; and they have interesting social as well as psychological overtones. Boredom breeds violence; the frustration of feeling useless culminates in an aimless act of smashing. But that this charming and very modern syndrome has any bearing on his hero's impotence, Stendhal will not tell us.

It is not simply that he will not spell out the impact of helpless ambivalence on a sensitive organism; he appears to have in mind a different set of motivations altogether. Octave's difficulties apparently derive from, or are attributed to, an excess of sensibility, not an impasse. In the bread-and-butter terms of the everyday world, there is absolutely no reason why he cannot marry Mademoiselle Armance de Zohiloff, or live fraternally in her society, or reach any arrangement he wants to with her. His mother conspires to throw Armance at him; his father is willing; the young lady herself is, in a sublime way, agreeable. Society will accept anything—but loftiness of sentiment is carried to such extremes, on both sides, that all undertakings become quite impossible. Armance thinks that people will consider her a fortune-hunter if she likes Octave; Octave imagines people, especially Armance, will think him purse-proud if he continues to exist; and, in short, purity of motives is so much mooted by these very impurely motivated people, that one would welcome a breath of satire. Though it is liberally diffused elsewhere, there is none for the hero or his lady.

Chapter Nine introduces a theme which gives promise of producing some elementary illumination. Armance hotly accuses her lover of frequenting what can only be, though they are not overtly anything, houses of ill fame. He admits the charges are true, he offers no excuses or explanations, he merely promises never to appear in such places again. The subject is dropped, and disappears forever from the novel. All this is clearly noble as the dickens, but it gives us not the faintest idea of what our impotent is up to in these interesting circumstances. Does he go to the brothels merely to utter witticisms? To test his manhood or confirm his lack of it? If he goes out of boredom, does he find brothels more amusing than salons? Is it conceivable that he is not as impotent there as he is with Mademoiselle Armance? These are delightful questions with which to while away the weary hours, but Stendhal's novel, alas, gives no grounds for answering them. His correspondence suggests answers to a couple of them, but this circumstance merely underlines the incompleteness of the fiction.

All these considerations point toward the conclusion that the characters of *Armance* are under-activated and over-motivated; faults which coincide nicely with the general tendency of the writing itself to be over-emphatic. The fact that Octave is not impressed by coming into a fortune, the fact that Armance is indifferent to worldly pelf, the fact that maman de Malivert loves her son beyond all else in life—these points are made and remade and overmade, till they become impossibly intrusive. And meanwhile the narrative languishes. All very well to say that Stendhal's narrative technique is essentially episodic; but to introduce the Chevalier de Bonnivet, upon whom the novel's action is to hinge, at the beginning of Chapter 25, out of 31, is to abuse the privileges of authorship. And, broadly speaking, one of the great faults of *Armance* is a failure to dramatize. The book is discursive, not narrative; with the exception of several purely lyrical passages celebrating the airy, intimate delights of two perfectly attuned souls, its emotional and intellectual abstractions are not adequately embodied in metaphors of action. Instead of once acting out Octave's contempt for the nineteenth century, and being done with it, the author pounds it on the reader's nerves till they ache.

How to find an adequate vehicle for expressing and disposing of the hero's irritating hauteur? It is a problem in itself, a very adequate problem for a man writing his first novel at age 43, even without the additional embarrassments of the impotence-theme. One is disposed to dismiss the whole idea of the Babilan-hero as a regrettable error, into which Beyle was drawn by Hyacinthe de la Touche, his own scabrous imagination, and the circumstances under which *Armance* was conceived. But there is an oddity about the ending which provides a far-fetched yet amusing alternative to this rather severe conclusion.

Having been tricked by circumstances into marrying Mlle. de Zohiloff without telling her of his condition, Octave makes an impressive, compensatory testament, and then embarks for the war of Greek independence with the firm intention of not returning. On the way to Greece he feigns illness in order to allay later suspicions, and then, on the last night out, consumes a mixture of opium and digitalis which wafts him on his way with a peaceful, heroic smile on his lips. Now a novel published in 1827 which wound up on this key could scarcely avoid re-minding the contemporary reader of Lord Byron, who had perished quite as heroically and almost as uselessly, in the swamps of Missilonghi just three years before. The reminiscence is reinforced by a pair of epigraphs from *Don Juan;* and in point of fact, there is a good deal of peripheral similarity between Octave and Byron. They are both handsome, witty, brave, noble, rich, and young; both mysteriously melancholy, derisive of middle-class manners, bored and violent, capable of immense worldly success, but scorning it with lordly hauteur.

This is an interesting list of parallel characteristics; but surely it must founder completely when we juxtapose the impotence of Octave with the immense, priapic vigor of the English lord. But perhaps the sexual contrast merely modulates the parallel into a new key. If Beyle had meant to imply that at the heart of Byron's personal and literary promiscuity there was an essential sterility, he would not have been the first to feel this. Byron himself sensed and expressed it. His immense comic epic, *Don Juan*, was planned to parade its Jack-in-the-bed hero throughout Europe, from boudoir to boudoir and boredom to boredom, till his sins achieved their final and fitting punishment. He must be sent to hell, i.e., to England, and there frozen to death with respectability and cant. Octave de Malivert, to be sure, is not a blasé bankrupt like the Byron hero, whose essential attitude was finely expressed by Scott Fitzgerald under the metaphor of a man who was given a fixed sum of capital (a limited capacity for sensation) and spent it all by the age of thirty. So far as his impotence is given any distinct motivation at all, Octave seems to be suffering, as I have said, from an excess of sensibility. On the other hand, an excess and a deficiency of sensibility are not always at opposite ends of the spectrum; Octave's passion makes him incapable of love, Don Juan's immense talents and pro-longed practice in love finally make him incapable of passion. The promiscuous figure is emotionally sterile; that is, ultimately, the reason for his promiscuity. The impotent figure is emotion-ally too deep and responsive; that is the indicated reason for his impotence.

Whether Beyle had all these paradoxes in mind when he produced *Armance* may be debated; within the novel itself he is not even explicit about the causes of Octave's impotence, though the motivations indicated within the novel mostly run this way, and Beyle's references to the topic outside the novel fully confirm it. The celebrated chapter on fiascos in *De l'Amour* deals only with this particular variety; and Beyle's own misadventure with Mlle. Alexandrine (*Souvenirs of Egotism*, Chapter 3) was of the same sort. He failed this handsome young harlot completely (much to her surprise) simply because he happened to think inappropriately of the divine Métilde. The Byron-parallel may be one of those gratuitous critical contribu-tions of which we are, nowadays, properly suspicious. Had it been fortified only a little, it might have helped relate the social satire of the novel to the hero's peculiar psychological problems, and given the reader welcome grounds for deciding where, in Octave de Malivert, the healthy protest leaves off and the morbid reactions begin.

It seems likely that Beyle learned something of interesting failures in love, such as Octave exemplifies, from reading Jean-Jacques Rousseau. Love *à la* Rousseau, which is tender, sublime, heroic, and expressive of a man's whole soul, obviously runs various perils from which more sordid and practical attachments are exempt. But, looking forward in the modern direction, the dichotomies which Beyle was groping to express, between sex and love on the one hand, love and passion on the other, have an immense future in nineteenth- and twentieth-century writing. Emma Bovary, along with all her hundreds of town and country cousins, is instinct with these erotic incompatibilities; pale, esthetic, autobiographical young men like Stephen Dedalus will delight in the difficult contrasts made possible by Eros and Agapé; the miseries of sacred and the consolations of profane love are nowadays the stock-in-trade of every anxious novelist, poet, or playwright who attempts to unknot his characters' neurotic-erotic fixations. Perhaps it is just as well that Beyle, by trying a Babilan-novel which was too much for him, found himself shunted off into other, and more active themes.

For nothing in *Armance* prepares us to think that the next fiction its author attempts will be a masterpiece, or even the particular sort of novel that the *Rouge* is—leaving aside the question of its merits. *Armance* is slow, strained, and choked; the *Rouge* is swift, confident, and full-throated. Octave is sometimes an amusing satiric talker but most often a pathetic sufferer; Julien unhesitatingly acts. Armance de Zohiloff is nothing more than highmindedness, personified but never animated; Madame de Rênal and Mathilde de la Mole are women, heroic and complete.

Authors are often known to undergo breakthroughs, transformations as startling as they are absolute; and Stendhal, whose art was in large measure an art of improvisation, was particularly dependent on the unpredictable fluctuations of his subconscious. But once he had broken through, the *Rouge* by no means placed him in the clear. Sharp outline and wiry bounding narrative line are as remote from *Lucien Leuwen* (1833-35) and *Lamiel* (1839-40), as they are from *Armance*; the active hero or heroine is still muddled by over-motivation, assertion and analysis are still asked to do duty for action, and clinical investigation still shades vaguely into satiric exposé. Above all, the sense of unpredictable and mysterious danger, which fills the two great novels with light and passionate energy, is replaced in *Lucien* and *Lamiel* by a sense of predictability and passivity in which the two protagonists repeat the weakest characteristic of Octave de Malivert.

Of all Stendhal's novels, *Lucien Leuwen* is undoubtedly the most nineteenth-century. The steam-engine, the telegraph, and the forms and formalities of public opinion have now combined to produce a new, dull, and narrow world within which Lucien, equipped with nothing but money and republican scorn, is asked to survive. Salons exist in this world but only on the fringe of that enormous, anonymous machinery which, whether one regards the way in which it really works or merely the way in which it is supposed to work, is greased only by the universal unction of human *bassesse*. Within this world, Napoleon is gone and forgotten, or all but forgotten; his memory lingers as a vague nostalgia among the veterans gone cynical and corrupt in the service of the Restoration; or as an ideal, still living but hopeless, in the hearts of one or two firm and honorable men, set to do the dirtiest chores of the new regime and cynical of any reward. The provinces are populated by uneasy grotesques, timid, greedy, gauche, and cynical; the capital is inhabited by ruthless and cynical manipulators. Of all careers conceivable within this cosmos, young Lucien Leuwen is presented with the trade of a garrison soldier; and in a moment of depression he very accurately foretells the future which this position offers him.

> I shall make war only on cigars; I shall become a pillar of the military café in the gloomy garrison of an ill-paved little town; for my evening's pleasures I shall have billiards and bottles of beer, and occasionally, in the morning, war with cabbage-stumps, against filthy workers dying of hunger. . . . At best, I shall be killed like Pyrrhus, by a chamber-pot thrown from a fifth-floor window by a toothless crone! What glory! (25)

Stagnation is unforeseen, and stagnation occurs; in its first volume, at least, *Lucien Leuwen* is almost an epic of stagnation, in which the tepid, scummy pond of provincial life is endlessly poked and prodded by an idle young man who has neither the envious energy to make war on society like Julien, nor any need to take unscrupulous advantage of it, like Fabrizio. As soon as he sees Nancy, Lucien despises it; 300 pages later, he is still despising it. His great question in life is, What must one do to respect oneself? and in looking for the answer in the 27th Lancers, garrisoned at Nancy, he is clearly beside all the possible points. Only the incident of his falling in love with Mme. de Chasteller has caused the 300 pages of the first volume to move in any particular direction. Here, indeed, the sensitivity of Lucien, which in the world of practical affairs freezes him into a permanent posture of *mépris*, finds its proper element. In the entire canon, there is nothing in its own way quite so fine as Lucien's love for Mme. de Chasteller. Julien's love affairs are perhaps rather embittered by his role as outsider; his hypocrisy makes for several little comedies of misunderstanding and imperception, but it also casts a shadow over the moments of tenderness which punctuate the social struggle. Fabrizio in his passion for Clélia, on the other hand, is almost

purely heroic. But Lucien is both comic and heroic at once, both
sublime and ridiculous; his love is simultaneously airy and intimate; and the whole delineation of his passion has that quality, which Beyle admired so much in the *Matrimonio segreto,*
of tenderness mingled with gaiety. The affection of François
Leuwen for his son, which finds expression in a fine vein of
disillusioned drollery, suggests something of the warm comic
feeling which Lucien generates in this most inward and self-
absorbed of love affairs. He is a fine, spirited young animal;
but his political ambitions are stunted from the beginning by
the crass dead-centrism of Louis Philippe's bourgeois monarchy
and his own exquisite scruples. When the satire on provincial
society has begun to languish for lack of fresh material, and the
threads of Lucien's love affairs are finely snarled between his
own prickly conscience and that of Mme. de Chasteller, one
begins to wonder if the novel will ever get off the ground.

There are in *Lucien,* as in *Armance,* patches of brilliant social
satire and subtle psychological analysis; there are devastating
situations implicit in the relations between silly liberals,
panicky ultras, and "dead-centers" whom everyone despises.
There are special glints and avenues of satire in the hero's
being himself a dead-center, for lack of anything more significant to be. But in a garrison regiment, Second Lieutenant
Leuwen is almost as much stunted in his possibilities of change
and development as Octave the impotent. He has nowhere
to go. It was Stendhal's first fault, in that miserable, abbre-
viated "Romance of Métilde" which he began in 1819; it was
one of which he never quite cured himself. He tended to start
his characters at the end of a rope, and hope for inspiration to
get them moving.

Some of the most disappointing things about *Lucien* are the
fragments of fascinating social flotsam with which Stendhal
evidently attempted to prime his pump. Milord Link, a mysterious English homosexual, turns up late in the first volume, and

looks like a promising storm-center, but he drifts out of sight without getting himself involved in an action. Dr. du Poirier, who is an ultra in Nancy and gets his principles altered to those of a liberal in Paris, arrives on the scene as late as the Chevalier de Bonnivet in an action which he is to influence decisively; he is clearly a fascinating fellow, but his motivations are utterly indefinite, and having shown himself a liberal and a coward in Chapter 57, he quietly fades away. There is a lancer in the regiment, formerly a book-binder, actor, fencing-master, deserter, and almost a galley-slave; but Ménuel, after regaling us with his life-history for a few pages at the beginning of Chapter 8, also disappears for good. All the novels of Stendhal contain characters who turn up for a short stretch of time and then drop into the background; when the narrative stream is bearing strongly along, these passing encounters, which may or may not turn out to be significant later, give an immense sense of richness and hidden potentiality. But when the narrative is anemic, it is irritating to see potential sources of energy go to waste.

The best elements of *Lucien Leuwen* are found, undeniably, in the second volume. Lucien is transformed here into the secretary of a minister; in this capacity he must ensure that a poor devil of a government spy, shot in the exercise of his function, expires without talking; and he must go to Caen, to arrange the political defeat of an overwhelmingly popular liberal candidate. Both these episodes are fictional arrangements of actual incidents; Lucien's spy Kortis is an actual government spy, Corteys, and the campaign to defeat M. Mairobert is a composite of episodes and incidents nicely sketched out by Bardèche (pp. 254-55) plus a M. Desrobert briefly indicated in one of Stendhal's marginal notes. The satire cuts deeply and truly into French political life; the hero's self-disgust counterpoints enchantingly his genuine pride at playing a man's role in the actual, dirty world of men. He is a perfectly delightful sinner, only less so than his father. For meanwhile, M. Leuwen, taking the rules of democratic government at the foot of the letter, has organized a burlesque political party of obedient nonentities, "the legion of the *midi*," whipped them into shape with promises, stupidities, and self-importance, and made himself a vigorous figure in the administration.

These are elegant and rollicking themes; as a maker of ministers and a Machiavellian ironist of government, the banker Leuwen is altogether peerless. His amorous and social advice to his son is a veritable model of French fatherly concern tempered with total sophistication; indeed, he is in a fair way toward running off with the novel entirely. But the picaresque adventures of these rich rascals, the Leuwens father and son, lead us ever farther from the strange, half-chivalric world inhabited by Bathilde de Chasteller. Lucien at least can only profit by having some of the sentimental bloom rubbed off him. In Chapter 67 we find him holding the swooning Madame Grandet in his arms and thinking about party politics—and in this role he is, momentarily at least, a worthy successor to Julien Sorel. But though Stendhal had at least one perfectly elegant denouement in mind for his novel, he seems to have hesitated about working it out, and left the story unfinished from sheer indecision. Lucien's affair with Madame Grandet was to have been the keystone in a vast political stratagem of his father's; at the height of this plot, he was to desert Mme. Grandet, and find true understanding with Mme. de Chasteller at Nancy, or, perhaps after some further intrigues, at Rome. In a plot like this, Lucien's love, by triumphing over his own sardonic and his father's serious ambition, might take on a touch of the heroic. But, caught between this ending and several other possible ones, with a sense of weariness at the necessity for new characters, and a distaste for a hero who seemed to be nothing more than "a nail exposed to the blows of the hammer of fate" (II, 324), Stendhal gave up on his story entirely.

Despite fine touches, then, *Lucien Leuwen*, which was written after the *Rouge* suffers from some of the same deficiencies as *Armance*, which was written before; and yet the *Rouge* itself is quite free from them. There seems to be no simpler way of accounting for this pattern than by Stendhal's need for a pre-existing narrative framework. Fine as it is in spots, *Lucien* as a whole runs the constant risk of "turning out soggy" because there are not enough scenes involving "change of attitude." They were his own phrases, jotted on the MS as he went along or looked over what he had already written; and in another moment of misgiving, he wrote, "If this is worthless, one of the prime reasons will have been having to think of a plot." The fact is, that for a novelist who considered that "the business of a novel is to narrate," Stendhal had little capacity for devising extended and coherent actions. He sometimes tried to rationalize this deficiency into a merit, saying that it helped his invention, in writing, not to know from day to day or even from page to page what was going to happen next. "One never goes so far," in the words of an ancient proverb, "as when one does not know where one is going" (note on *Lucien Leuwen*, I, 316). It is clear that very often this is indeed the character of his best writing, where the dialogue seems to spring from the immediate needs of the situation, and the action is directed as much by the whims, schemes, mistakes, and preconceptions of the characters themselves as by any intent of the author's. It is clear too that his first drafts were usually too voluminous by far; that he relied upon the last revisions to chasten his language, simplify his style, and give nerve to his prose. *Lucien*, never having undergone this process, cannot fairly be compared in point of economy with the corrected novels.

But for all these limitations and rationalizations, the fact remains that a novelist who does not know where he is going does not know what effects he is building toward, and is in no position to pick and choose among the economies and extravagances available to him. Lucien Leuwen is, if anything, too one-sided emotionally to be a successful protagonist; the only deep passion of his life is Madame de Chasteller, and if his father were one-tenth the Machiavellian he is made to seem, he would see that Lucien can only be led securely by this one cord. But the other characters in the fiction are wide-open possibilities. Dr. du Poirier is a rascal, clear enough, but a totally unpredictable rascal; we get one fix on him, deceiving Lucien about Mme. de Chasteller's "bastard"; we get another when he apostasizes to "liberalism"; still a third when he turns out to be a physical coward; but, were we ever to see him again, one cannot doubt that he would be miles away, on the track of another snipe altogether. So too with Milord Link, or Mme. Grandet, or Louis-Philippe himself; any of these characters might be unexpectedly converted to serve any conceivable purpose in the novel. It is precisely because the bit players in the drama are too indefinite to give it a steady direction (in the words of M. Bardèche, they "never make up a system of forces on which the destiny of the hero will depend") that young Leuwen himself has to be tied down so tightly. And tying him down tightly almost forces him to be more pathetic than comic; deprives him of a field of maneuver, and reduces him, regrettably, to the stock sad young man of nineteenth-century fiction. Gide, who rather overestimated lack of impetus in a novel (surely it is excessive to hope that each chapter will seem like a fresh beginning to a story) thought *Armance* and *Lucien Leuwen* the finest of Stendhal's novels; but, as the world runs, this judgment tells us more of Gide than of Stendhal.

Of all the various ills which flesh and the mind are heir to, those involving love seem to involve most intimately the tone of the whimper. Sensitive, pathetic young people held helpless by large amorous problems are almost a stock in trade of the psychological novel; the mechanism often has a kind of deadly fascination for the sufferer, which it is not hard to feel he enjoys and by which he certainly profits. Stendhal was not altogether exempt from these sordid and now familiar little gambits; but he indulged them in his fiction only when he felt uncertain about the total system of forces in his novel, and needed a specially strong set of individual motivations to keep the action on a track. But he did not indulge the pathetic very much, and it does not represent his most fortunate manner. On the whole, he was harder than we are likely to give him credit for being. One way to sense this is to note specifically some themes which he does not exploit, even though circumstances might have seemed to invite his indulgence. For example, his heroes are all outsiders, and solitude was very much a part of his life. Aside from the isolation imposed by circumstance, there was one of temperament; he was a man who instinctively lived from affair to affair and furnished room to furnished room, who despised his family and mistrusted his friends. Yet he makes very little use of pathetic solitude as a theme, and does not sing the "poor-misunderstood-me" song at all. He does not think of art as a refuge from life, he is not hermetic, and he does not stand guard, with self-conscious Stoic heroism, over his bleeding heart.

In fact, he had a perfectly modern mistrust of self-pity; and if he said nothing of his loneliness, or very little, one reason may well be that he did not think it a particularly interesting condition. It is the natural consequence of being without a certain sort of woman, who is a rare and fugitive bird; one has moments of wanting to blow one's brains out, but, after a while, one recovers. As an essential lady's man, Stendhal had only a certain sort of masculine friend; he described Lolot, Mareste, Mérimée, and the Paris cronies to the life when he said they would have paid twenty francs apiece to see a pot of dirty water emptied over him whenever he wore a new suit. Yet they were his friends; he told them nothing of his passionate love-affairs, but he did not think of himself as a much-misunderstood man.

As a matter of fact, because he had some trouble understanding himself, he seems to have thought society did about as well by him as could reasonably be expected; even the melancholy moods of Lucien Leuwen and Octave de Malivert are lighted by glints of humor, and on the whole, for an early-nineteenth-century novelist, he handles the pathetic moods with model restraint.

Perhaps because the obvious principles of narrative structure are so scandalously neglected in these secondary novels of Stendhal's, considerable emphasis has been laid lately on the structural values of what the untutored eye is bound to view as secondary elements of the fiction. Such are, for example, the psychological patterns based on the interplay of seeing and being seen. Here there is no doubt a certain substance at the root of the observation. Frequently, in the world of Stendhal, to see others without being seen by them is to gain a kind of advantage. To be immured in towers may thus be an open door to revenge on one's jailers; to make love in the dark, invisibly, may be the only way of avoiding an intrusion, a judgment repugnant to instinctive *pudeur*. Mme. de Chasteller's glance at Lucien, tumbled by his fractious horse in the mud of Nancy, provokes his anxious promenades past her door, his almost compulsive efforts to see her again. Spies are always peeping at people, in Stendhal's novels; and people are always peeping over their shoulders or under their beds for spies. Glances convey unanswerable judgments; standing well in someone's eyes is an essential social occupation, and revery is an act of inward, uninterrupted vision, which takes place best on a physical height. Clearly so strong a reliance on the imagery of vision contributes greatly to the character of Stendhal's world, to its airy, mobile, and sometimes furtive quality. But to make of this interplay of seeing and being seen the primary tissue of the novels is to entangle them beyond hope of extrication.

The Abbé Castanède comes to peek at Julien as he pretends to be asleep; this is an offensive and perilous intrusion, no doubt. But if one must see in it a symbol of the moral rape which is confession, one is well on the way to making the *Rouge* and the *Chartreuse* into romances of Peeping Toms. What does it mean when Julien sees the young bishop of Agde practicing his benediction? Or when Mme. de Rênal, visiting Julien at the Valenod's, announces herself by covering Julien's eyes with her hands?

No doubt ingenuity can find allegorical significance for these or any other acts of vision which one strains out of the novels—Fabrizio's looking at himself in a mirror immediately after the fight with Giletti, for example, or Mme. de Bonnivet finding *rebellion* in the eyes of Octave. After this, nothing remains but to explore Stendhal's auditory allegory; loud talkers are always bad, soft voices are good, and echoes are fascinating. This sort of web-work is jolly fun, and it may not be to any particular point that Stendhal never expressed the slightest consciousness of these considerations, or referred to this sort of matter in discussing his (or anyone else's) compositions, or made any particular adjustment in these matters when he revised. But the real point against such cat's-whiskers is that they contribute no clear pattern to the novel and lead to no special insight. Rather than grant them any structural significance, it seems enough to point out that Stendhal was extraordinarily touchy on the issue of personal identity; that, as *Noli me tangere* might be considered the motto behind his peculiar use of pseudonyms, *Noli me videre* was the principle of that *pudeur* which is instinctive in all his noble characters. Always afraid of being tied down, his characters hedge as he himself hedged, seeking always to be as inexplicit, as ambiguous, as they can. Gestures and glances are the silent, auxiliary weapons used by intelligence in its underground guerilla warfare with authority. But to rewrite the novels in these terms, from the ground up, is to augment their camouflage and innuendo to the point where no other effects are possible.

Indeed, the sort of consideration which came to Stendhal's mind when he reflected in general terms on the art of fiction, was far from Byzantine; it was concerned, in a straightforward, almost a primitive, way, with the different techniques of telling a story. In one of the most interesting of his notes on the novel, Stendhal differentiates his own fictional method from that of *Tom Jones*. The difference is that "Fielding describes the feelings and actions of *several* characters *simultaneously*, and Dominique of *only one*." About this difference Stendhal himself had the gravest misgivings. "Where does Dominique's method lead? I don't know. Is it an improvement? Is it a return to the childhood of art, or rather is it a drop into the frigid genre of the philosophic character?" Sidestepping these rather extravagant alternatives, we may perhaps say that the method of Dominique imposes grave limitations on the novelist. If his central character is not more than open to the possibility of radical change, if he is not actually threatened with such change under the urgent impulse of overwhelming forces (as in *Don Quixote*) then the total amount of narration is beside the point, and the lack of dramatic potential must inevitably make itself felt.

The change with which Don Quixote is threatened so closely and at such length is probably the richest and most complex in fiction. He is pursued, in a hundred ingenious ways, by the forces of social sanity, which offer to make him not only safe and sane but dull, which by rendering him good will prevent him from being holy, which by solving his spiritual warfare will end the book and our entertainment. The heroes of Stendhal balance over less profound abysses; but at their best, they balance, they teeter. Julien, as we have seen, is either a vulgar, ambitious little rascal, a Tartufe and perhaps even a madman, or a prophet denouncing society from his own private wilderness; he repeats in enlarged form the unresolved antinomy of Molière's *Misanthrope*. Perhaps it all depends on the angle from which we see him; perhaps it depends on the person in whose company he happens to fall; perhaps it depends on sheer accident, what sort of character he will turn out to have. His existence has been cast into a battle, which is not even consistently a battle; and in the wild kaleidoscope of whirling events, every possibility of his nature is thrown up. The roulette wheel is not by any means an extravagant or irrelevant implication of Stendhal's title. . . . Fabrizio del Dongo also represents a fabulous and deliberate tissue of instabilities; he is either a prisoner or a prelate, a scoundrel or a saint, depending on the play of emotional light which surrounds him, or the operation of very trivial circumstances and apparently unrelated incidents. But whether Lucien gets his Bathilde or simply continues to play with papa the cynical, successful games of money and politics, seems to matter very little to his identity. He will be the same nice, unhappy young man, whatever happens.

On the evidence, Stendhal was perfectly mistaken about himself; he never went so far as when he knew exactly where he was going and did not have to give a thought about the problems of getting there. As a novelist, he was properly unconcerned with the shortest distance between two points, but when he was given a narrative string, stretched loosely from one end of his novel to the other, he could cover it with crystals.* He talks a good deal about narration as the essential concern of the novelist, but his own narrative technique has a good deal in common with the cinema; it is a sequence of rhythmically

* See the MS note to "A Social Position," fragment of a romance, cited by Bardèche, p. 242: "Inventing facts and noting their developments, two *contrary* actions in the mind of Dominique. He invents in September, in January he has forgotten, and can draw the details as if he were stealing the story from some old manuscript." But sometimes he forgot too much and too completely.

connected still shots which the eye and empathy of the viewer translate into motion. One of the chief charms of his fiction is the variations in tempo, rhythm, and emotional coloring of which this impressionistic narrative mode is capable.

Tom Jones and *Don Quixote*, which recur so frequently in discussions of Stendhal's fiction, point up the constant presence in his works of the picaresque tradition. A rascal who has seen society from the bottom up is obviously well suited to see it, cynically, from the inside out; and a rascal involved in a sequence of loosely related episodes is a fine vehicle for the free and lawless energy which our author is supposed to admire so much. Yet in fact the freedom of the *picaro* is radically limited, in Stendhal's best novels, by the hero's sensibility and circumstances. Both the physical *picaro*, a coarse rascal like Roderick Random, and the purely spiritual *picaro*, like Goethe's Faust, suffer from fitting too well into their milieu. One knows pretty securely that they will never get out of it, and what they do within it can only have the cumulative effect of many comparable units of narration (episodes, physical or spiritual) piled together. Aside from the ambiguities of his best heroes, already noted, Stendhal gains a special tension by putting them at odds with their milieu, and, in effect, with their own destiny. Fabrizio, born for love, is a churchman; Julien, born to wield power, is a peasant. The pattern of their circumstances, and sometimes of their character, is quite out of synchronization with the episodes of their story. The result is a tension for them, a drawing out of their characters in odd and unanticipated directions. It represents also a kind of tension for the author, something which Henri Martineau has very nicely described by saying that the *donnée* of a novel like *Lamiel* is for Stendhal the moral equivalent of a bet. Given a bizarre, an unnatural situation, what dialogue, what episodes, what psychological impulses can he invent to make it credible and effective? A "bet" of this sort is of absorbing interest to the reader and a real wager for the novelist only so long as there is a chance he may lose it; the "failures," like *Armance, Lucien Leuwen,* and *Lamiel,* are so many proofs, as it were, of the achievement of the great novels. The perils those books skirt are not imaginary; Stendhal did not know beforehand how to get around them; when he fell, he fell hard, he fell awkwardly, he fell irretrievably.

If the point needed further making, *Lamiel* would suffice to show both the audacity of Stendahl's "circumstantial" imagination and the hesitant course of his narrative instinct when unguided by a pre-formed plot. The raw materials of the novel represent a fantastic challenge. A hunchbacked sadistic doctor who fancies himself a Don Juan, and a handsome young girl, impatient of her sex yet resolved to trade upon it and ambitious for the supreme experiences of life—these are startling characters with whom to start a story. That they are capable of fine comic effects the story itself, as far as Stendhal carried it, brilliantly demonstrates.* Bold, naïve, inquisitive, and unpredictable, Lamiel embarks on her travels with all the energy she is supposed to be seeking; infinite possibilities lie before her, including the wry one that she will discover energy in others only when she no longer has it herself. But over none of his novels did Stendhal ever hesitate more confusingly than over this one. There are several different notions of the central action; there are varying lists of subordinate characters; there are dozens of different time-schemes. Two or three versions of the opening passage

---

* Mme. de Beauvoir thinks Stendhal's projection of himself into the character of Lamiel a fine tribute to woman's ability to be as free as man. But the domination of Sansfin over Lamiel is not freedom, it is shown as an act of intellectual rape; and in fact the young lady, once intellectually deflowered by Sansfin, has nowhere to go but the oldest of professions, and only the most futile and self-destructive of protests to voice. That the novel is unfinished suggests a deficiency of invention within the social frame; the Wagnerian love-death sketched for a conclusion shows that men and women are in the same boat, but as the boat is sinking, it is neither freedom nor a tribute to have a place in it.

were written; a number of different endings were contemplated. It is odd to find the man who had just written off the *Chartreuse* in one brilliant, uninterrupted surge of six weeks' work, paltering and hesitating over *Lamiel* like the most unpracticed of novices. And yet what could one expect? At the core of each of his other novels there is a solid bit of fact borrowed from someone else; for the *Rouge* it is the Berthet trial, Métilde, Alberthe, and Méry de Neuville; for the *Chartreuse*, that 16th-century pamphlet on the origins of the Farnese family, and episodes from the life of Pierre Bonaparte; for *Lucien*, a MS called *The Lieutenant*, by Mme. Jules Gaulthier; for *Armance*, the joke of La Touche. Only *Lamiel* is almost without a grain of sand for the pearl to grow around. There was to have been a brigand in open warfare with society, with whom Lamiel was to have fallen in love; and for him at least, Jean Prévost discovered a number of real-life originals. But a good deal of the novel as Stendhal first sketched it was original creation; like all his original work, it was curiously formless; and he never did decide how much of it would or would not be useful to him in carving out the ultimate intrigue.

Much more interesting than the obvious episodic deficiencies of a MS which, as it exists, was very likely nothing more than preliminary work for a story which never got written, is the extraordinary character of Dr. Sansfin. A brilliant and unscrupulous mind hidden in an ugly body, he dreams, like Beyle himself, of letting his spirit take possession of a handsome corpse. Finding Lamiel dying of boredom, he undertakes to seduce her by being entertaining; and he manages, single-handed, to make out of this frank and energetic Norman peasant-girl an accomplished Parisian hypocrite. His fate is one familiar to Pygmalions; having given Lamiel the spirit of a cold and deliberate adventurer in evil, he sees her seduce, or be seduced by, a good-looking simpleton. And in one of the many fragments which clutter up the MS, Dr. Sansfin falls furiously on this young fellow with a dagger, and acts out his destruction in a fine symbolic way.

It may well be that in the dualism of hideous cynical Sansfin and lovely innocent Lamiel are represented two aspects of Henri Beyle, the coldly experienced and the naïvely ardent. If this were so, and one were set to seek evidences of the same contrast elsewhere in the novels of Stendhal, it would not be hard to fix on the division between Conte Mosca and Fabrizio in the *Chartreuse*, between Leuwen *père* and Leuwen *fils* in *Lucien*, and perhaps between M. de la Mole and Julien in the *Rouge*. Earlier than the *Rouge*, one is probably wandering among shadows; there is no one person who plays for Octave the role which, with steadily darkening overtones, M. de la Mole, François Leuwen, Mosca, and Dr. Sansfin play for their respective innocents. But the repetition of a dualism which sets black so distinctively against white—which is pregnant, as it were with Dr. Jekyll and Mr. Hyde as well as the two faces of Dorian Gray, Lafcadio and Fleurissoire, William Wilson and his double, and a whole string of schizophrenic romantic protagonists,—throws into relief the entire problem of Stendhal's pre-Freudian insights, as the biographers have delighted to call them. These can be usefully divided into complex analyses of psychic causation, which are good; and simple delineations of psychic pattern considered as a final effect, which are bad.

The trouble with Dr. Sansfin, squat like a toad by the ear of Lamiel, inoculating her with the first principles of Beylism, is that it brings us too quickly to the end of Sansfin; and the end of Sansfin imposes a whole fresh beginning on Lamiel, which is hard to avoid depicting as a regression, and over which, in fact, Stendhal consistently faltered. For the Stendhal hero (and heroine, too, be it understood) is a flexible and unpredictable creation precisely as he combines the passionate freshness of youth with the cynical experience of age. Any tendency to sort out these two elements, and embody them in separate *personae* leads at once to the stiffness of allegory and the embarrassment of confessional writing. Stendhal was by no means exempt from this fault of the two-dimensional, analytically-motivated character; but it afflicted him chiefly where he was most conscious of the oddity of his basic premise and desirous of throwing its consequences into high relief. The first two or three chapters of *Armance* recite, almost in textbook fashion, various clinical symptoms of the Vicomte de Malivert. Interesting as they are, in fact, just because they have a special clinical interest of their own, these symptoms remain unassimilated in the novel. Having been mentioned once, they never appear again; the author feels no obligation to make use of them. And so it is with Lamiel and Dr. Sansfin; his work in introducing her to the realities of life is mechanically performed; one may feel either grateful at having it out of the way, or irritated at having it so gracelessly in the foreground; but at best it merely postpones and complicates the evil hour when Lamiel must test on her own pulses, and prove through her own experience, the falsity of social convention, the reality of passion and energy. Prologue or epilogue, footnote or commentary, whatever one wants to call it, Beylism personified is outside a true Stendhal novel.

But in any event, it is not clear that Stendhal's special gift lay in the discussion and analysis of cases of so-called "abnormal" psychology. There is a certain sort of nightmare fiction, such as that of Dostoyevsky, which takes place entirely within the theater of a fevered brain, and which gains much of its power from these twisted perspectives. Stendhal is too dry and clear a writer to exploit this technique. (He wrote, in 1804, a brief note on his experience with Mélanie, called "The House with Two Doors," which has reminded Jean Prévost of Dostoyevsky; and if *Lamiel* had been seen through the eyes of Dr. Sansfin, it might have had something of the Dostoyevsky quality; but essentially Stendhal's mind included too large a strain of geometry and ideology to have major affinities with the turgid, tortured Russian.) When he writes of love, his best effects come from perceiving the many complex elements which ordinarily enter into the passion, not from anything bizarre about the passion itself. The progression in oddity of subject is essentially dull and obvious. A man in love with several women at once, with the ideal of a woman, with his sister or mother, with another man, with a peri, fairy or goddess, with a snake, lioness, or beast of some sort—these are the various alternatives, all fairly tedious by now as set themes for literary exercise. Stendhal's acuteness showed itself most brilliantly in the analysis of recognizable but infinitely interiorized sexual passion; above all in psychological circumstances where the romantic conventions of his day decreed that the emotions must flow freely and the undifferentiated sublime must prevail. The complexities of the act of sexual conquest are a favorite set theme for Stendhal, to which he rarely fails of doing full justice. The calculated coldness, the anxiety, and vanity-considerations which enter into that situation are sketched with such acuteness in the *Rouge*, that one will not see the like of it in fiction for another hundred years.

Even finer are insights which are allowed to loom up in the background of the reader's, as of the characters' consciousness. The fantasies, cherished by both Fabrizio and Julien, of a hated father who is not really one's father, but an illegitimate who has crept into the father's place, a bastard-father,—these fantasies are brilliantly managed precisely because they remain a little more than fantasies, a little less than substantial realities. The motherly sentiments of Mme. de Rênal and the Duchessa Sanseverina in their relations to the young heroes are seen only through the uneasy, half-transparent veil of their own rationalizations. Whatever subtle emotional changes are to be rung on the ideas of prisons and towers and glances are allowed to have free play in the novels, without the obtrusion of precise definitions and logical consistencies. The Luini portrait of Herod's daughter and the luminous melody of Cimarosa's *Matrimonio segreto* rise recurrently from the layers of Stendhal's half-conscious feeling like charming and mysterious fantasies. Redolent for Stendhal with private associations, they come in time to mean just as much for the practiced reader; like Proustian leitmotifs, they summarize and concretize a whole complex of moods. These are the triumphs of Stendhalian psychology; and, in proportion as they are indirect, remote, and untied by the deadly cords of mechanism to the consciousness of readers or characters, they seem to enrich without stiffening the fabric of his fiction.

From the mechanical operations of the psyche certain comic effects very often derive; but these generally fall under the heading of mannerisms; and as such they are compatible only with the satiric half of Stendhal's outlook. That is, they are a form of pseudo-psychology used to defeat or manipulate genuine understanding. The woman who is courted as a way of provoking jealousy in her rival is a common figure in the novels. Julien uses Mme. de Fervaques against Mathilde, Octave uses Mme. d'Aumale against Armance, Fabrizio uses Anetta Marini against Clélia—and, where the aim is not wholly satiric, a distinct monotony ensues, as of emotional billiards cleverly played. It is really the awkward attempt to combine psychological inwardness with psychological mechanism that produces Stendhal's most unfortunate effects. Lamiel's bargain with the young peasant who is supposed to teach her about love is of this character; it falls, like Gina's capitulation to Ernesto-Ranuccio V, halfway between the sordid and the funny. And yet, if there were not this danger, and Stendhal were not willing to skirt it, would one have the same perilous sense of Mathilde de la Mole's fine balance between compulsion and audacity?

His prevailing success in keeping the psychological patterns of his characters bold but ambivalent and unmechanical—voluntary, in a word—contrasts curiously with the one major unbalance in Stendhal's color-patterning. He has so much scorn for money that his entire image of the nineteenth century is thrown off-key simply because he cannot imagine people taking the dirty stuff seriously.* Anyone who has taken lessons in the first principles of bribing a public official knows that a rather dainty protocol surrounds the whole affair. Certainly you do not march into your official's odious little office and fling him a bag of sequins like a grand seigneur bribing a slavish Oriental gatekeeper. Ordinarily the money which is to oil an official must itself be rendered slippery by personal unction. At least the first time, there must be some talk of service, sincerity, mutual appreciation, a little diffidence on both sides, an atmosphere rather genial than business-like, in which *you,* for example, make a point of accepting a cigarette from *him*—and only then does the money change hands, in small bills and a plain envelope. But of all this Stendhal knows nothing. All his life long, he was a chevalier where money was concerned; dropping purses disdainfully from horses was his style, and he could imagine no other. A miser might conceivably have been within his range, but never a banker. Just one glance at François Leuwen, and one sees he is not a banker at all; he is an oriental potentate, a Haroun-al-Raschid, with a Dutch genie at his disposal. His partner does the banking. M. Leuwen, with his opera girls and his parliamentary "legion" merely dips his hand from time to time into the till. He is gloriously entertaining in the meanwhile, but he is no more a working partner in a banking house than M. Rothschild could pass for a character out of *Scheherazade.* If Stendhal's treatment of love were of a piece with his treatment of money, his novels would be no better as a guide to human

* The principle of despising lucre was of course "Spanish" in origin; Beyle's correspondence declines even to contaminate the French tongue by mentioning money. When he has to discuss payment for journalistic work, he speaks of it, in English, as so many "fish." Cf. the current Marseilles argot for money, "le grimsby."

nature than the essays of Emerson. Happily, there is a difference; such a difference as makes of love neither a schematic chart nor a *terra incognita*, but the enchanted ground of perpetually fresh discovery.

7

The Dandy,
The Roman, and Domenico Cimarosa

Mais le calme héros, courbé sur sa rapière,
Regardait le sillage, et ne daignait rien voir.

Baudelaire, "Don Juan aux Enfers"

All the Italian writings of Stendhal would make, if collected together, a sizable volume; but though the foundation-works are extensive, only one finished structure of original fiction was actually built on them. It is a masterpiece, disproportionate only in bulk to the amount of preparatory spade-work which went into its making; indeed, it was doubtless just because that spade-work was so prolonged and thorough that the *Chartreuse* rose like an exhalation, glittering and complete, between 4 November and 26 December, 1839.* And what is the *Char-*

---

* Beyle's letter to Romain Colomb, dated from Palermo, 27 August, 1832, probably represents the first seed of the *Chartreuse*; thus, at least seven years went into its germination, unless the date of this letter is as fraudulent as its place of origin. Stendhal was never at Palermo.

treuse itself but an Italian chronicle, half-translated out of its period and extended to miraculous lengths by a series of fascinating improvisations? With the pace and hard outline of a short story, it combines depths and complexities appropriate to a novel; and so accomplishes for the Italian scene what even the greatest of the Italian novelists could never do. *I promessi sposi* is fine fiction; but there are moments when it smells of Mrs. Radcliffe, and its conversion-scene is simple, brutal sentimentality.

It is an old paradox among visitors to Italy that the land is artistically too rich for successful creation. The forms are too strong, the colors too vivid; they glut the eye. The qualities of the people are too marked, they will not stand still long enough —they are too much the real thing, in their own right, to adapt gracefully to the needs of art. Stendhal illustrated the conventional artistic perversity before the raw materials of his fiction. While alone at Civitavecchia he wrote the gray-toned *Lucien Leuwen*, set in Nancy, Paris, and Caen, full of French wit and overflowing with superfluous but charming French conversations. (Though he pruned them from his MS, they are perfectly legible, are said to be completely delightful, and constitute still another volume of Stendhalian writing, as yet unpublished, which may someday be added to the seventy-nine already available.) While at Rouen and Le Havre, French provincial towns *par excellence*, he conceived the *Chartreuse*, and he wrote it off in Paris, 8 rue Caumartin, on the fourth floor.

Italy laid claim to more than half his imagination; for him it was the country of pure passion, of natural behavior, of pleasure, fancy, and the arts. Above all, it was anti-France. France was the land of vanity and selfishness; Paris was its capital. Yet all the greatest of his fiction was produced at Paris; and in the aggregate, Italy inspired him to a good deal more commentary, criticism, editorial work, and translation than original fiction. Perhaps he confronted art too directly there; like a crab's, his best gait was ever sidewise, and it seems clear that to produce the *Chartreuse* a certain complex cross-fertilization had to go on among the Italian chronicler of the Farnese family, memories of Métilde and Angela, memories of an awkward, ardent young jacobin who had worshipped Napoleon, and certain cynical political conclusions drawn from the history of the Directoire, the Empire, the Restoration, and Louis-Philippe "dead-centrism." A work which fuses so many different elements is almost obliged to be slow, indirect of genesis, and remote from the raw materials which are, if only technically, its "sources."

Thus the reader who approaches the *Italian Chronicles* fresh from the symphonic *Chartreuse* and anticipating more of the same, must necessarily find himself disappointed. Dry, abrupt, and external, the *Chronicles* have sometimes the quality of extended coroners' reports. A beady-eyed Latin exactness informs them, and they relate the most atrocious crimes of violence with a perfect impassive composure and sang-froid which evidently enchanted Beyle, for he steadily enhanced this quality of his original, wherever necessary. But to a modern reader the style can only appear limited. Its character is simply to understate.

When Stendhal thought about his addiction to the plain, understated manner of writing, it was almost always in opposition to more popular writers of his day—George Sand, Chateaubriand, Victor Hugo—who employed a more emphatic style, garnished with what French criticism drily calls "*enflure*." He was often quite emphatic about what he was not emphasizing. On Sunday, the sixth of April, 1834, a young girl was stabbed in the streets of Rome, close to where Beyle was strolling. He noted in the margin of one of his books that as she lay in the middle of the street, there was a little puddle of blood near her head, about a foot across; and added that for Victor Hugo, this would amount to "being bathed in one's own blood."

The hard, matter-of-fact style of which Stendhal was so conscious, and which he cultivated as a deliberate antidote to the literary vices of his day, is particularly evident in the *Rouge* and the *Italian Chronicles*; yet these are also, according to his conception, tales of true passion, of such sublime and profound energy as one never sees at Paris, and rarely in the nineteenth century, even in Italy. Especially the *Italian Chronicles* deal with people totally absorbed in the passions of the moment; this was the special character which Stendhal attributed to Italians generally and Renaissance Italians particularly. As he put the matter with brilliant succinctness in *Rome, Naples, and Florence*, "the Italian feels and believes that one is made happy in this world by satisfying his passions and in the next world by performing certain rites" (I, 264). Yet it is just where the passions are most grotesque and extravagant that Stendhal's style grows most sharp, distinct, and impassive. The *Italian Chronicles* differ from the *Rouge* in dealing with Gothic crimes, such as sacrilege, incest, patricide, and vendetta; they differ also in recording these horrific episodes after the fashion of a documentary movie—from the outside, literally, with all the distinctness in the world and none of the inwardness. For ulterior reasons, probably having something to do with his perpetual fear of political reprisals, Stendhal always claimed that he had translated his originals literally and exactly; but this is far from true. His original was often prolix, repetitious, and confused; he abridged it ruthlessly, cutting out commentary he did not like and adding observations of his own, augmenting the narrative pace and compressing the descriptive details. But almost all his changes are in the direction of, or at least are not incompatible with, an ideal of literary chastity which sometimes verges on literary barrenness.

Nothing could show up the peculiarity of Stendhal's astringent literary method better than the quite accidental circumstance that two of his Italian tales had already established an English reputation. "Vittoria Accoramboni" is of course familiar as *The Duchess of Malfi*; and Shelley's *Cenci* (1819) is a dramatic rephrasing of the same story told by Stendhal. But Webster gives full play to the horror and grisly dangers implicit in his situation; none of his characters is afflicted with French *sang-froid*. Even the villains are astonished by their consummate villainy. All this makes for a black and devilish atmosphere, very powerful in the theater. Shelley is rather more interested in innocence; but as it is innocence in the toils, he has drawn from its helpless struggles the material of a fine melodrama. Stendhal's interest in the *Cenci* story is divided between Francisco Cenci, whom the lengthy preface describes as a Don Juan; and the details of the execution-ceremonies, which take up a full third of the story proper. The art of the story is to describe horror impersonally and unemotionally; in doing so, Stendhal tones down most of the highlights and dark shadows which provide the fable with its *raison d'être*.

Even a story which, though it is customarily included with the *Italian Chronicles*, is actually original with Stendhal, shows the same marks of externality and emotional barrenness. "Vanina Vanini" has gained some critical attention as representing an original sketch for the *Rouge*, Volume II. But the resemblances to Mathilde de la Mole are purely superficial. Vanina falls in love with a carbonaro, betrays his political activities out of jealousy, and then tries unsuccessfully to avert the fatal consequences of her betrayal. This is not by any means the fascinating Parisian princess who wants her lover's head on a platter; nor is the story of Vanina told with any of the inwardness which marks Stendhal's best descriptions of passionate love. There is restraint aplenty in the *Italian Chronicles*; there are the bare bones of passion. But of the actual, authentic voice of passion itself, there is less than the devoted and hardened Beyliste is accustomed to.

The *Italian Chronicles* are not typical Stendhal; but it is impossible to deny that they represent one aspect of Stendhal's development, a development which included so many contrasting tendencies that it can, perhaps, best be described as the separating-out of diverse elements. One might note, for instance, a gradual softening of Stendhal's imagination as the career progresses. There is more gentleness in the *Chartreuse* than in *Leuwen*; more in *Leuwen* than in the *Rouge*; and more in the *Rouge* than in *Armance*. On the other hand, the *Italian Chronicles* and *Lamiel* stand flat against this trend; and this tendency to separate out the hard and impersonal factors of his writing culminates in a short, unpublished story dating from the very last years of Stendhal's life. *Don Pardo* is a vivid, colloquial sketch of a Civitavecchia slum-boy, done in a strict, cold manner which has reminded M. Bardèche of a sketch by Goya; it points, in the modern direction, toward some of the bitter little genre-tales of Alberto Moravia. The whole Stendhalian personality, apparatus, and mystique disappear from this story, as if the author were exercising momentarily a *privilège*. The little *lazzarone* it describes is, at nine, a thief, a beggar, a smuggler, and an agent in the hands of anyone who wants to make use of him; his best patrons are priests. The details of his life are seen with cruel, impersonal clarity, and with a thickness of detailed observation which will not recur till the professed "realists" of the late-nineteenth century.

The *Italian Chronicles* have a biographical interest, then, as they represent a major stage in the separating-out of those elements which in combination are called "Beylism." In addition, they provided raw social materials for Beyle's imagination; they offered him a model of the severe, unemphatic, external style which corresponds to one half of his sensibility; and they described an archaic simplicity and energy of action which delighted him. On all these scores, the side of Beyle to which they appealed was that which he shared with his young friend Prosper Mérimée, the side which we can for the moment distinguish as the dandy.

The image of the artist as dandy is too indefinite to have become, as yet, the subject of elaborate study;* in fact the very concept is less familiar to English-speaking peoples than on the continent. England, America, and Germany, the countries of naïve inwardness and sentimentality, had on the whole less interest in the dandy than France; though each of them shows traces of the character, Poe, Byron, and Heine were alien to the prevailing cultural climate in their native lands almost in the measure that they did so. But in Beyle, Mérimée, Delacroix, and their circle, dandyism found an expression which occasionally rose to the articulate level, and which invites a moment's analysis.

The dandy is a curious, momentary complex of elements peripheral and essential. In its original meaning, with its original envious-contemptuous connotations, the word referred simply to the wearer of a particular costume of English origin. Immensely uncomfortable and supremely elegant, it combined the loose and lavish with the painfully compressing in a way which almost entitles Mr. George Brummel to pass as one of our great symbolic jokers. The skin-tight trousers, silk stockings, and narrow waistcoat tightly cinched, were topped by a vast frilled shirt, an enormous cravat, and a splendid coat in a drape shape, giving the lucky wearer of these garments rather the air of a topheavy pouter-pigeon.

> *Above* so loose, below so *braced*
> In chest exuberant, and in waist
> Just like an hour-glass. . . .
> H. Luttrell, *Advice to Julia*

* John C. Prévost, *Le dandysme en France 1817-1839* (Geneva, 1957) is prosaically factual in its treatment of the subject, and its cut-off date is sacred, so that there is nothing about the theory of the dandy as developed later in the century by writers like Barbey D'Aurevilly. Mr. Prévost promises to fill out these deficiencies in a later volume. Early studies are largely bundles of character-sketches and anecdotes.

But sartorial elegance of this splendid, elaborate mode was only the first element of true dandyism. There is a dandy-character, a dandy-attitude, which may even, as a last resort, express itself in sartorial negligence. The dandy is by definition conscious of himself; he is out to make an impression, such an impression as is compatible with the impression that he is supremely indifferent to impressions. Thus he never dresses sensationally, but simply and with staggering good taste.* He never mingles; he never prolongs the moment of his impact on society; he stands distinct, aloof, and impassive, just long enough to be appreciated. He is an unmoved mover; he is just there.

He is idle; he is indifferent to the inward thoughts of people; he does not think their private lives are very interesting, nor is his own. With typical irony and negligence he sometimes puts off his own identity entirely and assumes someone else's. His activities are horsemanship, gambling, boredom, sexual conquest, and self-adornment. He has money and despises it because everyone worth knowing has it. By and large he is not homosexual nor even frigidly Narcissistic. On the contrary, he is often aggressively buckish, despising women with all the force of his cold, contemptuous masculinity but seeing in them also a proving ground for his carefully cultivated self-control. They are an alternative to, or simply another form of gambling; as gambling itself is simply a way of testing oneself against the universe, a miniature warfare, a duel against bankruptcy and the undiscipline of the features.

The dandy is an aristocrat, genuine or artificial, it does not matter; he has a code, to which he may or may not live up, but which in itself sets him apart from the bourgeoisie. He is supremely careless of everything; he does supremely well whatever he undertakes, and undertakes nothing but what he can

---

* It may be worth recording that during his bourgeois days at Paris, Stendhal inventoried his wardrobe, and found, among other things, 18 vests and 15 shirts without jabot, 27 with.

do carelessly and supremely well. "A magnificent performer of life's commonplaces"—it is an extravagance of style, squandered on matters of no importance whatever, that distinguishes him. A first principle of his life is Castiglione's "sprezzatura"; he acts in everything with supreme confidence and in accordance with those gentlemanly instincts which subsume and substitute for "human nature" on the one side and the prosaic, plebian rules of art on the other. He is the courtier personified, with one difference, that he no longer has a social function or tries to be socially useful in any way. He is a dandy and not a gentleman simply because his appearance is now called upon to substitute for his function. Religion, as an inward and spiritual conviction, is a matter of no interest to the dandy, one way or the other; but as it assimilates him to vulgar people or invites him to assume a posture of contrition, it is dangerous to his dandyism. By and large, his best adjustment to the problem of religion is either to have none or to be a damned soul—proud, ironic, and disdainful.

Early commentators on the dandy customarily had in mind only one of these varied characteristics at any one time; and they rarely agreed as to which was most truly distinguishing. The most obvious handle to grasp was extravagance of dress or style, such as Romain Colomb thought characteristic of prose in his day, and which he opposed to the simplicity and naturalness of the Président de Brosses (Preface to *L'Italie il y a Cent Ans*, p. xi). On the other hand, Stendhal thought the affectation of superiority, the emotional immobility of the dandy, was his distinguishing feature ("La Duchesse de Palliano," Preface); and so contrasted him with the fiery and passionate Italian of the sixteenth century. It is not till fairly late in the history of the type that these various elements come to be synthesized into a semi-systematic attitude by a man like Wilde; and by his time, the dandy has started to slip into the larger current of the esthetic movement as a whole. He has become effete, not energetic; one who rejects society rather than claiming to fulfill it; an intellectual intent on explaining himself rather than a natural and instinctive actor. Beau Brummel was an ideal dandy, not because he was stupid, but because he was inarticulate; because he was motivated by caprice which gave rise, as a by-product, to principles which lesser men imitated—not by principles to which he tried to give the appearance of caprice.

Indeed, the extraordinary literary ramifications of the dandy-character are beyond tracing here. With a thousand different shadings, in a thousand different stages of completeness, he turns up throughout the nineteenth and twentieth centuries; so profusely and variously, indeed, as to suggest to susceptible minds an archetypal influence. But there is no need for any such presumption. Antiquity knew no such figure, the middle ages are without dandies, the Renaissance divided the type between fops and gentlemen, but never made dandyism a career in itself. It was precisely the Regency in England, the Restoration in France—the phenomenon of a freshly unemployed aristocracy faced with an aggressive, distasteful bourgeoisie—that produced the dandy (see Baudelaire, *Salon de 1846*, Sect. XVIII, "De l'héroïsme de la vie moderne"). And for current purposes, it suffices to note that there are a literary style and a literary subject-matter specially appropriate to dandyism. Strict form and classical, or more than classical, severity of outline are asked to combine with romantic barrenness, desolation, violence, ugliness, horror. The inner life of the dandy is not only boring and common, it has streaks of terror, visions of ghastly malaise, against which the dandy, like a self-appointed sentinel, maintains the severe vigil of his artist's discipline. Form is not an expression of content, or a substitute for it, but a weapon against it.

This special quality of the dandy-style, the quality which aligns Stendhal most intimately with Mérimée, is pre-eminent in the plainly written but horrifying *Italian Chronicles*. Their concern for the lawless figure who violates the law partly from sheer impulse and partly from perversity creates a series of vigorous, vivid outlines, set sharply against a neutral or non-existent background. Mérimée and Baudelaire are evidence of an essential affinity which the dandy-character had for such figures of total energy, existing in strict isolation, and outlined in sharp and nervous strokes by means of writing which is classically precise. For Stendhal, as for Mérimée, the style was a vehicle for conveying the essential truth of a violent situation which rhetoric could only smudge.

So far as rhetoric is concerned, one can hardly fail to agree; but the dandy-style itself tends to define its situations in fairly limited and conventional terms, terms made familiar by the development of Stoic thought. In fact, these are grounds on which one is obliged to deprecate some even of the finest achievements of the manner. It creates almost a stock-situation and a stock-response—eight notes on the piano, as Stendhal said, in a devastating comment on Mérimée (*Mélanges intimes,* II, 102-03). The "testing" action, for example, which occurs in "The Taking of the Redoubt" and *Colomba* is hardly different at all from that which recurs in *The Sun Also Rises* and "The Short Happy Life of Francis Macomber." When an adumbration of dandyism turns up in Stendhal's *Italian Chronicles,* we recognize it as an artificial mask, not because it is particularly artificial—in its own right, it is real as real—but because it is only half-adjusted to the man who wears it. The mask by which the true man is known, the full Stendhalian paraphernalia, was, if anything, just as artificial as the dandy-mask; but it was far more complex, far more individual. It was something which he assembled, out of the accidents of his life, and composed by deliberate effort into an artistic disposition. One of the examples of the self as artistic creation which lay before him was the dandy, phosphorescent corpse of the courtier. Another was the artificial heroic spirit of ancient Rome, as exemplified in the Romans of Livy, Plutarch and Shakespeare. These noble characters, who speak of themselves so easily and naturally in the third person, exerted a tremendous, indirect appeal on Beyle's imagination. That civic, republican virtue which he believed in the more, the less he saw it exemplified in his contemporaries, had really existed, as a transfiguring force, among the Romans. It enabled a man to erect himself above himself; to become, for a moment, the actual embodiment of a spirit which was sometimes defined as Rome itself, sometimes only in his personal name. Livy tells how the ideal of behaving in a manner worthy of the name of Fabius inspired the Fabii to tremendous exertions; and Shakespeare's Romans are particularly eloquent on the subject. Antony will do nothing unworthy of Antony; Caesar must live up to a public idea of Caesar which he has himself created. Perhaps it was this notion, that a man owes a duty to his own definition of himself, which furnished to Stendhal the seed for his concept of Beylism; a "philosophy" which actually provides not only obligations and guidance but immunities and liberty, based upon one's consciously defined relation to a self one is in effect creating.

There is, then, a touch of the moral dandy in the Roman who talks of himself in the third person; there is a touch of the Roman element as well as of dandyism in Beyle; but the truly distinctive quality of Stendhal is the combination of Brutus, personifying the republican ideal and the motivation of duty, with the Count Almaviva personifying aristocracy, pleasure, and the light touch.

In the field of literature, one is likely to look far for a man who might have exemplified to Stendhal this enchanting and slippery combination. Republicans are likely to be serious, moralistic fellows, impatient of literary whipped cream; dandies are not earnest republicans or earnest about anything else. But in a musician whom Stendhal venerated, he might have found the combination of qualities which were to be his own literary hallmark. Domenico Cimarosa haunted the life of Beyle (who, when he gave himself the pet-name of "Dominique," may have been glancing at an identification); he haunts the writings of Stendhal. He was a composer of light, social, yet (for Stendhal) infinitely voluptuous music; and he died, in exile from his native Naples, while under the grievous accusation of harboring republican sentiments and conspiring in the short-lived Republica Parthenopea, which Nelson and his mistress betrayed to Bourbon vengeance in 1798-99.

Recent research has succeeded in demolishing many edifying legends about Cimarosa the republican. There is now no greater evidence for republican sentiments than the fact that he composed music (which no longer exists) for an ode to republican words. The sin itself was grievous enough, not lightly to be mitigated; and it remains true that for this misplaced enthusiasm Cimarosa spent four months in jail. But he was not liberated by the generous enthusiasm of Russian auxiliaries in the Bourbon service; he was just let out. And the permanence as well as the profundity of his republican feeling is shadowed by the existence of certain "ultra" compositions, positively lyrical in their adoration of the great Fernando IV and their scorn of the hateful French. These pieces date from the period of the reaction, after Cimarosa's release from prison, but before his exile to Venice.

Cimarosa, then, was not a hardened radical, as the "Parthenopean Republic" was not a hard-headed political venture, worthy of a Danton. But it was a heroic and generous venture, rising out of a national history black with despair; it involved the noblest minds of a lively intellectual tradition; it began, not with blood and ill-feeling but with acts of forgiveness and brotherhood; and it deserved a better fate than the blind vengeance exacted by a stupid and fearful king supported by bandits and Englishmen. Cimarosa supported it with childish enthusiasm, for the first political act of his career; and he betrayed it with childish readiness when he found out a little of what it involved. One thing is sure; had the cause of the Republic been twice as black as it now seems noble, the allegiance which Cimarosa gave to it would have been very adequately punished with an ironic smile and a pointed remark. He was a man of impulsive sympathies; he had friends among the insurgents; and song-writing was his trade. But it is doubtful, and perhaps unimportant, how much of all this Stendhal understood; the tears which he describes Cardinal Consalvi as shedding for the memory of Cimarosa are tears not for a political renegade or a political martyr, but for a generous and noble soul, ill-treated by the uncomprehending world.

What Stendhal found in Cimarosa was a soul in classical balance. The underlying tenor of Cimarosa's feeling, as of Stendhal's, was melancholy; not a Mozartean melancholy, but a gentle, even reflectiveness, often veiled and never despondent. It is set off by a ready recourse to wit and the comic, which has nothing in common with the sharp satiric gift of Rossini. There is no sense of strain or effort; all is smooth, effortless, natural; the comic gives way to the sentimental without either quality diminishing the flow of naturalness, or sparkle of delight. The "classicità" of which the critics speak in connection with Cimarosa rises from this natural combination of emotions fully realized but never out of balance. It was implemented by a vocal and dramatic tradition which it is absurd to describe as either popular or learned, so universally was it practiced in the musical seed-bed which was eighteenth-century Naples. And this tradition flowered in the *buffa* style which is indigenous to Italy and adaptable to no other national style in the world.

Of Cimarosa's masterpiece the critic can say nothing better than that he composed *The Secret Marriage* in a state of grace [Tibaldi Chiesa, *Cimarosa ed il suo tempo* (Milano, 1939), p. 253]. It is a playful domestic comedy of circumstance on a text originally English. Rich in comic and pathetic pieces, tender, reflective, satiric, perfectly informal and unpretentious, it answers to the *beau idéal* of Stendhal's art. It appealed particularly to that side of Stendhal, the existence of which one is apt to overlook, the good and happy little boy who rejoices in the play of domestic circumstance.* The essential goodness of human nature is not an idea which associates itself naturally with Stendhal; no doubt in certain moods he thought of it as a foolish delusion; but Cimarosa could create other moods, in which the bright potential of civilized man glowed with all the allure of an ideal republic—and to this mood Stendhal was also deeply susceptible. It was not by any means a mood of unrelieved austerity; indeed, though Stendhal regularly equates the republicanism of America with the death of the arts, the word "republicanism" had for him a much larger application than any individual example suggests. He sometimes spoke of the medieval Italian city-states as good examples of "republicanism"; he had an intense awareness of the danger that the rule of law may degenerate into a rule of the supine. And his republican ideal included an almost Shavian perception of the need for strenuous individual effort—not only to realize the ideal, but to prevent the ideal from over-realizing itself to the detriment of the essential human materials.

The prototype which Stendhal found in Cimarosa, the republican whose joy of life expresses itself spontaneously through art and sentiment as through a generous politics, he might also have found in the figure of the Romanized voluptuary. That strange episode in taste, the artifice of the natural which is represented by the paintings of Ingres and David, the Made-

---

* Stendhal is so fully armed in exterior sophistication that the equal extravagance of his naïveté is easy to overlook. After receiving Balzac's article on the *Chartreuse*, he confided, secretly, to the margin of a volume in his library, the note "Jam Gre at." It has been deciphered recently, "I am great." He was, indeed—yet how boyish are both the act and the sentiment!

leine, and dresses *à la* Madame Récamier—Directoire Classicism, in two words—had its impact on Beyle, as on everyone who lived through it. Republican strictness was oddly combined, under the First Consul, with moral standards as loose as, or a little looser than, the French norm. But so far as it was no more than a fashionable veneer, the vogue of ancient Rome could have little permanent effect on Stendhal or any other creative figure. In any event, his attitudes are more extreme in both directions; his Roman tastes and republican sympathies amount to a bit more than a style; while, at the same time, the ramifications of his sensibility go a good deal beyond the simple search for pleasure. His taste for clarity, simplicity, hardness of outline, and truth stripped of all rhetoric, is more than Roman, more than Napoleonic; it is geometrical, even cynical. His sensitivity is more than that of a voluptuary (which, in itself, contradicts, but just barely, the previous character) it is that of a romantic, a sentimentalist, who gloried in excesses of private emotion and preferred to be the dupe of his illusions rather than a worn-out and cynical realist.

There is a logical contradiction here, which with mere discursive logic we shall never get to the bottom of. Just for this reason, perhaps, one might well look for the inspiration of it among the non-discursive arts; in music, particularly, because Beyle was from the beginning of his imaginative life particularly sensitive to music; and in Cimarosa still more exactly, because this was the most peculiar and pronounced musical taste of Stendhal. And, pointing the parallel the other way, it may help us to feel the full impact of the *Chartreuse* if we consider it a musical composition which plays with its given "facts" from two points of view which are logically contradictory but musically complementary.

The influence of music on the great novels is especially likely if we recall that the sort of criticism which Stendhal found most agreeable to his temperament was that which is now called "impressionistic." He put no stock at all in absolute standards or formal esthetic systems; as he emphasized the freedom of the artist to respond to his environment, he felt free also to cultivate his own critical temperament. His scepticism of cultural absolutes culminates in a perception much like that to which modern criticism has attached a lumpy phrase out of Keats. "A true talent," he wrote in the *History of Painting*, "like the Vismara, an Indian butterfly, takes the color of the plant on which it lives." This is negative capability, expressed with charm and hokum instead of polysyllables.* And he loved to make fun of those Koenigsberg disciples (we ought to call them, today, "esthetic metaphysicians," but it is distressingly easy to say simply "critics" and be done with it) who had to put themselves through a two-hour course of logical gymnastics to know whether or not they should approve of a picture, a statue, or a musical composition.

Whether he is drawing parallels between Guercino and Shakespeare, or simply describing the effect produced by the interior of St. Peter's, Stendhal has few hesitations about trying to describe verbally the effects of non-verbal arts. He gives his impressions of an opera, a painting, a building; ordinary guide-books, to which he refers the reader cavalierly, can tell about the mechanical details of the work of art. Without being wilful or eccentric about it, he is interested in what the work of art conveys to him, because he thinks this is about what it ought to convey to any intelligent and open-minded man. Such a reader can profit by knowing what the work of art conveyed

* Need one point out that Vismara is the name of Stendhal's liberal lawyer friend at Milan, that there is no Indian butterfly of this name, and, in fact, that no known butterfly is endowed with the properties of the chameleon? The passage clearly invites a revaluation of P. P. Trompeo's judgment (*Nell' Italia Romantica*, pp. 74-75, note 9) that Beyle first knew Vismara in 1818; since Vismara was a free-mason, the earlier and easier their acquaintance, the more significant it would seem to be. The phrase is from *L'Histoire de la Peinture*, I, 319.

to Stendhal, even if in the end he decides that it means something different to him. Criticism so modestly phrased and so
casually unpretentious can scarcely fail to give pleasure; especially when, to the pleasure of discussion and analysis, is added
that of discovery. Stendhal was a delightful travelling companion, a magnificent guide to the sights of the city. One can
really gain a better notion of his esthetic preoccupations from
books of travel, like *Rome, Naples and Florence* or *Promenades
dans Rome* than from a more or less formal critical treatise like
Racine et Shakespeare.

In effect, Stendhal the critic, like Stendhal the practicing
novelist, had one taste for the plain truth in the chaste style.
In literature this is his chronicle-taste; with notable exceptions
for Cervantes, Ariosto, and Shakespeare, he tends to apply it to
almost any piece of writing that is old. For example, he explains
his fondness for Massinger and Ford, the Elizabethan drama-
tists, on the grounds that they represent reality exactly; the
memoirs of Cardinal de Retz, of Duclos, and Saint-Simon also
satisfied the chronicle taste. In art this taste finds expression in
a tolerance of Masaccio, Ghirlandaio, Mantegna, and even
Giotto, a tolerance (to use no warmer word) which is well in
advance of European appreciation as a whole. In music there
is simply no equivalent for chronicle-taste. On the other hand,
Stendhal has a second taste, which exists right alongside the
first one, and apparently without jostling it; this is his taste for
the "beau-idéal." Shakespeare represents a supreme genius in
the genre of the "beau-idéal"; and in post-Raphaelite painting,
as in music of all eras, the "beau-idéal" constitutes an almost
unchallenged standard. The first standard may decline into vulgarity—a sort of "housemaid's realism" which consists of enu-
merating the dreary details of everyday life. The second standard
may rise to a kind of abstract and unindividual "general nature";
it may diffuse itself completely in the lazy universals of Pla-
tonism. But, though Stendhal does not say so, it is evident that

each standard helps balance and correct the other. In opposite directions, too, both extend a little beyond the classical bounds of gentlemanly "good taste." Chronicle-taste is colder, more outward, and perhaps more vulgar, and the "beau-idéal" is more inward and personal than classical standards of taste altogether allow.

Yet even though he permitted himself ample theoretical ground for eccentricity, Stendhal's taste was firm, fair, and consistent.* He was carried away by very little which was second-rate; against the popular opinion of his day, he endorsed a great deal in which modern taste would tend to justify him. Piranesi, in whom one would expect him to have delighted, he overlooked woefully; but he wrote more than generously of Caravaggio (including, specifically, the "Decollation of John Baptist" which was the sensation of the *Seicento Europeo* exhibit at Rome in 1956-57) and of Bernini, that "brilliant hérésiarque." † He failed, no doubt, to give Beethoven his due; but he knew that Mozart, Haydn, and Rossini were among the greats. For political reasons, he thought Béranger a fine poet; he applauded Werner's *Luther*, but only to make a point against French tragedy, he never took Werner for an author of stature. His appreciation of Cimarosa was colored by a warmth of personal experience which made him, if anything, over-enthusiastic. In fact, he was at his best in the generous art of appreciation. However limited his theoretical machinery, and sometimes, one suspects, just because it was limited, he customarily gave all his attention to the work he was writing about. His criticism was never self-aggrandizement, it was sympathetic and civilized

---

* Only his own saline impudence about solemn criticism prevents one from saying more; see, for example, a delightful phrase in a letter to Mareste of 24 February, 1831, "Actuellement, j'ai bon goût, c'est-à-dire une *difficulté de sentir.*"
† Yet his appreciation of the Caravaggio is suspect, since he never visited Malta where it hung during his lifetime. Probably he got his very intelligent opinion of it from Lanzi, *Storia pittorica* (Firenze, 1834), II, 139.

comment. Without trying to "explain" the work of art in terms of its circumstances, he tended to offer such background information as he thought would be useful, borrowing it, when necessary, from the sources where it was to be had. Without trying to legislate for Parnassus or arrange elaborate hierarchies, he offered evaluative judgments on the scope and intensity of the works under discussion. When he put forward personal judgments, he called them personal judgments, not universal truths. He rarely sneered; he never tried to mystify; he was not afflicted with the myth of his own omniscience. In other words, his critical deportment was admirably modest and humane. His reward was one which good critics can dream of—the spirit of the works which he most admired descended on him, and became a part of his own best writing.

One aspect of his character as literary commentator calls for special notice. Stendhal took with some seriousness the cosmopolitan role which he was specially fitted to play. The range of his literary reference is extraordinarily wide; he knows Pope and Goldoni, Alfieri and Goethe, Massinger and Buratti, the letters of Madame du Deffand, Lucan, Lucian, Propertius, and the satires of Ariosto. Europe has known many polyglots with a wider range of reading than Stendhal; still, there were not many critics of his day who made so conscious an effort to see each author as a product of his own individual temper, wrought upon by his own peculiar circumstances; and who, delighting in the differences between people, still endeavored to open the paths of sympathy among them. At 27 he was inditing the first of his 32 testaments, by which he left his (hypothetical) fortune to found an annual prize, to be contested alternately at London, Paris, Gottingen, Berlin, Naples, and Philadelphia, for the best essay on the nature of ambition, love, revenge, hatred, laughter, sorrow, or comedy. Though less directly and quixotically, his later work is still devoted to clarifying the international and interlingual understandings of men. He is particularly acute at seeing that words which "mean the same thing" in different culture do not often have the same connotations. Thus his comments on differences in manners often reveal, behind mere trifles of behavior, a major variance in the strategy of pursuing happiness. The deficiencies of Italian literature are related to a peculiar policeman's conception of the written word as a commitment; but the Italian author's relation to his public is shown to be, for just this reason, particularly warm and intimate. The exact quality of a *risqué* story, which causes it to be laughed at in France and to fall flat in Italy, is analyzed and discussed. The quality of French wit in Voltaire's time is distinguished from that of the present day. Perhaps the quality of any particular insight is less impressive than the fact that Stendhal was making such observations at all. The tourist who converses with anyone besides his waiter and his hotel-clerk usually sees a social situation in gross; eighteenth-century travellers were not as a rule interested in observing or interpreting the shades of social coloring, which are interesting precisely as they are subtle and evanescent. Stendhal has a deftness in the recording of international manners which gives us some confidence in his judgments of international literature; even his most patent blind spot, which is German literature and thought, may be understood and perhaps condoned by having recourse to his own principles. Profundity, amplitude, and systematic abstraction are simply not Stendhalian virtues; indeed, they are destructive of the virtues to which Stendhal was committed. His temper is stretched to the limit in admitting sympathies for Gallic, Latin, Hispanic, and Saxon authors; to add the Teutons would smack of vulgar eclecticism.

Sometimes Stendhal mars the fine finish of his cosmopolitanism by using it for snob purposes.—He has fifteen delicious anecdotes to illustrate a particular point, but Frenchmen could never understand them.—This sort of bland, superior affectation is a bothersome mannerism; it appeals to a kind of coterie-consciousness still afflicting the happy few, who frequently like to give the impression that they would be happier if fewer. By teasing they invite. But these are obvious mechanisms.

On the other side, and just as obvious, is a mechanism which arises almost as a hack issue whenever Stendhal's criticism is mentioned, the issue of plagiarism. There is no blinking the simple facts. The *Life of Haydn* was abridged from Carpani; Winckler and Cramer provided most of the material for the essay on Mozart, and Baretti was the original author of the commentary on Metastasio. The *History of Painting in Italy* was taken from Lanzi with some side-contributions from Bossi and Vasari. The stock excuses are these: that literary ethics were undefined in the early nineteenth century, that Stendhal added to and improved the works from which he adapted his books, that he may have transcribed notes without realizing how closely he was treading on the heels of the original. All these excuses are more or less specious. Only the plea of improving on the originals has any substance; and it exposes one to the obvious retort that a man with enough wit to improve on Carpani need not have plagiarized from him in the first place. This is perfectly true. Stendhal had no need to pillage Carpani or anyone else as blatantly as he did. Of course he had to get his facts somewhere, but a slight degree of paraphrase, a modest number of transpositions, a very few additions from other sources, and a frank acknowledgment of indebtedness would have transformed "plagiarism" into "scholarship." They have done so many times since.

None of these devices were beyond Stendhal, though he may have felt some of them beneath him. At any rate, his plagiarisms lie open for all to see; and they occur in such a way as to convict Stendhal of laziness, perhaps, and of naïveté, certainly, but not of mental insufficiency. What he took from other people is largely matter of fact; his interpretations are not all his own, but when he contributes something in his own person it is likely to be a new interpretation, a fresh perspective. He likes to draw analogies between the arts; in the *Vie de Rossini* this principle gives rise within a few pages to: an extended comparison of Rossini's intermingling of harmonies and arias with Sir Walter Scott's intermingling of description and narrative; a capsule description of Rossini as the Voltaire of music; a comparison of Rossini with Canova in their abandon of the classical ideal; and a notion of close correspondence between the timbre of the flute and certain ultramarine draperies found in the backgrounds of painters like Carlo Dolce [tr. R. N. Coe (New York, 1957), pp. 23, 51, 57, 58]. But this last is ridiculed as a German idea, profound only because confused.

Because he likes to remain aware of the concrete circumstances under which artistic work was produced, Stendhal's criticism is meticulous about setting the scene. A contrast between Mozart and Cimarosa becomes an occasion for discussing the German temperament, the German ideal of beauty, as opposed to the Italian. The introduction to Haydn offers a chance to say something about Vienna, the character of the city, and its influence on the composer's music. A glancing contrast, an analogy thrown out in passing, a phrase of commentary, have the effect of suddenly widening our horizon, and giving to provincial discussions a truly European character. Standing before the "Last Supper" of Leonardo with the book of Giuseppe Bossi in his hand, he notes with satisfaction that his own description of the picture is much less detailed than Bossi's.* This is not the reaction of a man who doubts the value of his own work.

---

* Actually, three separate volumes have been made out of the materials (mostly descriptive and biographical details) which Stendhal pruned from the *Histoire de la Peinture*. Edited by Henri Martineau, the *Ecoles italiennes* convey the extent and quality of Beyle's acquaintance with Italian art better than the volumes which he himself published. The *Histoire* is rather generously interrupted with airy 200-page ideological digressions. Incidentally, it is curious to note how many of Stendhal's books

Stylistically, these works of criticism are among the most interesting that Beyle ever wrote; for they show his distinctive manner in the process of development. Descriptions are made light and vivid by a continuous interplay between subject and object. The object is presented personally, as it is seen at first glance, in its unity; then, after this first dash at the object, its major associations are explored and elaborated; a broad description follows, and finally, in a few phrases which seem as if dropped in passing, its last emotional reverberations are followed out.* Transitions are wayward and unpredictable; abrupt but not brutal. There is no effort to gloss them over with elaborate connectives; on the contrary, widely different points of view are sometimes drawn together without mediation, for the clash of perspectives which can develop. The wit which is inseparable from any writing of Stendhal's is not set at the end of paragraphs, to cap or culminate a development; in fact it seems to avoid positions of prominence, and lurks in the center of longer passages, from which it radiates its concentrated rays. Anecdotes serve to change the pace of long, discursive passages; they are often an occasion for insinuating the leading ideas of the author, which in their own right require only the very briefest and most concentrated statement. Concealing and revealing are complexly interlaced; there is light and dark in all Stendhal's descriptions, and the play of personal mood is frankly mingled with the descriptive material. Above all, Stendhal tries to combine all these elements with a casual, unlabored tone,

---

are trailed, as it were, by shadow-volumes: the *Histoire de la Peinture* by *Ecoles italiennes*; the *Vie de Napoléon* by the *Mémoires sur Napoléon*; the *Journal* by the *Pensées*; *Rome, Naples, & Florence* by *Pages d'Italie*; the *Mémoires d'un touriste* by the *Voyage au midi de la France*.

* The persistent contamination of object with sentiment is perfectly deliberate, and probably derives from a philosophical conviction of long standing that *sensations* must be mingled with reflections to produce *perceptions*—which alone are memorable. See Jules Alciatore, *Stendhal et Maine de Biran*.

with the impulsiveness and delight of immediate responsiveness. A man who is working on stylistic problems as ambitious and delicate as these should not plagiarize any more than another. But if he does, there is more to be noted than the fact of plagiarism.

And truly Stendhal, even in stealing, had style. He looted the library as a dandy should, or took spoils of it as a Roman would—disdainfully, unashamedly, for the raw materials to which he clearly considered himself entitled. The sort of research he did not scorn was done in drawing-rooms, at puppet-shows, in concert-halls, or on coaches; and this he never skimped. But the bare bones of someone's biography—as well take them from Carpani as another. From somewhere or other they had to come; and the important thing was not where they came from or what they were, so much as what was done with them. In the musical *Lives* and the painterly *History* it is not altogether evident that Stendhal's is the biggest contribution; poor Carpani had a point when he raged against the wrong done his *Le Haydine*. He deserved at least a better answer than that provided by the character Stendhal invented to answer him— an imaginary brother of the imaginary Bombet. But the attitude of the thief, who boldly contaminated with his personal sentiments private as well as public property, is more important than the right-or-wrong of the property issue itself. To develop a sublime artist in flim-flam and transformation, we must first put up for a while with a clumsy one. The one thing we do not want, and fortunately do not find, is a shamefaced pirate, a half-hearted, conscience-stricken forger. If Stendhal is a shameless thief, he is also a conscientious craftsman. His main tool is his self, and to provide it with what it needs, he steals. Already he is learning to raid the strongbox of his own memory. But he never doubts that the things his talent can make are more valuable than the miserable morsels of fact with which he feeds it.

8

*

Mme. Roland, M. Daru,
and the Improvisatory Novelist

De là vient que sous la forme bipède de l'homme il n'y a aucune bête innocente ou malfaisante . . . que vous ne puissiez reconnaître: il y a l'homme loup, l'homme tigre, l'homme renard, l'homme taupe, l'homme pourceau, l'homme mouton; et celui-ci est le plus commun. Il y a l'homme anguille; serrez-le tant qu'il vous plaira, il vous échappera. L'homme brochet, qui dévore tout; l'homme serpent, qui se replie en cent façons diverses; l'homme ours, qui ne me déplaît pas; l'homme aigle, qui plane au haut des cieux; l'homme corbeau, l'homme épervier, l'homme et l'oiseau de proie. Rien de plus rare qu'un homme qui soit homme de toute pièce. . . .

Diderot, Satire 1

"My desire is to be read by a very few people, thirty or forty perhaps, friends like Mme. Roland, M. de Tracy himself, General Miollis, General Foy, Mme. de Barkoff, Philippine de Bulow, Béranger. . . ." The sentiment recurs many times in the writings of Beyle; but though the list of names varies a good deal, Mme. de Barkoff, who is simply Mélanie Louason under her married name, is usually there, and Mme. Roland always. This is odd only because Mme. Roland was not a friend of Beyle's, having died on the guillotine November 8, 1793, when her prospective admirer was a school-boy in Grenoble and barely ten years old. Yet she was closer and dearer to him than friends with whom he had been on intimate terms for years. He would never have thought of including Mareste, Lolot, or even the admirable Colomb in these little lists of precious spirits, but Mme. Roland, of the Gironde, is never missing. Describing Mélanie to his sister Pauline, he struck the highest note of which his vocabulary was capable when he said, "she is Mme. Roland, but more graceful" (2 August, 1805).

The lady is known to Anglo-Saxon posterity for a single eloquent remark, her last, delivered at the foot of the guillotine. "O Liberté! que de crimes on commet en ton nom"—it implies a lofty intimacy with the abstraction, tinged with regret at the intrusion of coarse outsiders. But Beyle saw in Mme. Roland a symbol of something more than political martyrdom, even in the name of a cause as nobly ineffectual as Girondist republicanism. For him, as for many other Frenchmen, Mme. Roland was hardly a political figure at all. Tender, noble, brave, generous, and witty, she was a soul's companion—one of whom M. Roland, that dry and elderly financier, proved himself worthy only by committing suicide the day he learned of her execution. And if there was an egotistical side to her noble stoicism, that scarcely diminished her enchanting appeal for one who was himself something of an egotist.

Even from one hundred and sixty years' distance, and with other political martyrs clamoring for attention in our foreground, it is not hard to sense what Mme. Roland meant to Stendhal, or to feel that she might mean it equally well to sensitive and poetic types today. Indeed, reading her *Memoirs*, it is hard to avoid the sensation that she was somehow fulfilling, fifty years before they began to be formulated, the requirements of a career in Beylism. It is not simply the pattern of events, but the form of her emotional reaction to them, which reminds us at every turn of the Stendhal hero, and his image of himself.

She was the offspring of a severe father and a sensitive mother; herself an imaginative, poetic child, easy to lead and impossible to drive. Offered medicine by her father, she suffered two beatings rather than take it, and was prepared to undergo a third; to save her mother grief, she finally took the medicine, but promptly threw it up, and got well in her own way, at her own pace. Such was the character of Mlle. Phlipon at the age of six; so it developed during her youth. Plutarch and Rousseau were the essential ingredients of her education; from the Roman characters described by the first of these reverberant names, she acquired the elements of a Stoicism which verged often on the self-conscious and sometimes on the artificial; but which, as she grew into it, developed into what can only be called courage in the grand style. During her life Mme. Roland evidently committed now this fault of taste and now that; she was a sententious little prude as a girl; she was not without moments of self-importance and artificial posturing as an adult; her role with poor M. Roland was often narrow and ungraceful. But in the last hours, when Stoicism was put to its ultimate test, she was perfectly natural, perfectly sublime.

The other half of Mme. Roland's education is represented by Rousseau. She had by nature, and through Rousseau she developed even further, a fine sensibility such as is not often found in French radical politicians. It showed itself in friendships and warm personal letters, in the glowing reveries of her *Memoirs*, in youthful experiences of religious ardor, in a striking sensitivity to flowers and natural scenery—and in one last romantic passion, which flourished under circumstances capable of touching every note in the sublime and sentimental imagination of Stendhal, throughout its entire register.

On the whole, fate and her own rather finicky disposition were not kind in providing Mlle. Phlipon with M. Roland de la Platière as a life-partner. Gray and reasonable at the time of their marriage, he was a strict and practical philosopher, a useful citizen, a competent *chef de bureau*, and, as the husband of a woman of spirit, intolerably dull. But she would not have a man who bullied her, nor one whom she could bully—displaying thus a very pretty unreasonableness as a young woman of intelligence and energy confronting her unpalatable destiny—and in the end, she went about as far in the affairs of this world with Roland as she would have gone with anyone.

But the land of the passions was quite outside M. Roland's orbit. Undoubtedly the experience which moved Stendhal most in his crystallization on Mme. Roland was her last passionate experience of life, in prison. Her whole life culminated in those few months; of her entire spiritual experience, one might say that only a tiny fraction belonged to her first thirty-five years. Half her life crowded into the next three years, and another major fraction in the last six months of her existence. For during the final frantic months of the Girondist struggle against that overwhelming Mountain of the left, Mme. Roland had fallen in love. She was nearly forty—a fine figure of a woman, hardened a little by the fires of incessant political warfare, and touched already with the bitterness of domestic and political disillusion, but with immense, untouched resources of tenderness and imaginative energy. She fell in love with the Girondist deputy Buzot, a brilliant, hectic young man, six years her junior. With the brutality of perfect honesty, she told her husband at once, not that she had been unfaithful to him, for she had not, but that she loved Buzot and he her. Just at that moment the Mountain fell on them all; Mme. Roland was jailed, Roland and Buzot went into hiding.

In jail Mme. Roland underwent, just as if she were anticipating the development of a Stendhal hero, an extraordinary spiritual flowering. She wrote furiously, an elaborate set of correspondences, a political justification, a memoir of her life, recollections, and opinions. Amid the squalor of the prison she carried out acts of charity, comfort, and gratuitous kindness, which, if she had not had the intelligence to be a deist, would have been called saintly. She conducted her own defence against a tribunal which was bound to convict her, declining the aid of a lawyer lest he render himself liable to suspicion. She prepared herself for death, and went to it with that flawless unconcern in which not only the will and mind but the whole nervous composition of the creature must conspire.

Above all, Mme. Roland experienced in jail a special Stendhalian exhilaration, a sudden, joyous concentration of mind, memory, and passion, which raised her far beyond the feeble creature she had hitherto been. The language of her last letters to Buzot is, it has rightly been said, as old as passion itself; but it conveys also the blind impersonality and terrible joy of a devotion which is beyond happiness, which exists in suffering, accepting the suffering, the passion, and the imminent end of both without the least question or hesitation. The death of Mme. Roland provides one of the great humanistic, which is to say, one of the great Stoic passages in history's great textbook on the art of dying well.

From one point of view, Stendhal's invocation of Mme. Roland and the happy few looks like nothing more than a critical hedge. A man who says he is writing only for Mme. Roland and her peers is fore-armed against detraction, for it is all too obvious that most of us are not on her level, and never can be. Could every author demand to be read only by specially sympathetic readers, we should soon have no grounds for distinguishing literary merit of any sort or any degree. One test at least of a book's value is its ability, taking readers as it finds them, to make them as it wants them to be—not necessarily to create Mme. Rolands out of the unfeeling many, but at least to evoke in them for the moment those responses which are the corollaries of being a sublime person.

Yet "evoke" is the word, not "create." The raw materials of elemental attitudes must probably be presumed in anyone who can read; but there is no doubt that some people are incapable of recognizing or responding to certain emotional reverberations, even as some people are tone-deaf and others color-blind. "A novel is like the bow of a violin," Stendhal says somewhere in *Henry Brulard*; "the sounding-box, which gives forth the tones of music, is the soul of the reader." In bespeaking an audience of Mme. Rolands, Stendhal bespoke nothing more than a certain sensitivity in his readers, a capacity for generous emotions. About this demand one cannot well say, without defining one's own self-image all too distinctly, that it is either excessive or reasonable. There are certainly no grounds for arguing that everyone should read and enjoy the novels of Stendhal; in fact there are a good many people who should not even make the effort. (One might make up an amusing list of tastes which are compatible and incompatible with a taste for Stendhal—but this is a matter for ironic, amused discussion by separate chapels of the Stendhal-Club [17 7/7 Ma. 19 9/9], not for public proclamation.) Wholesale recommendations are out of the question, then; but there are some grounds . for supposing Stendhal's commitment so special and his method so peculiar, that he offends or seems unbearably careless to readers whose expectations are conventional.

He composed his novels as improvisations and discoveries; they are written, that is, in the strict and difficult spirit of the amateur, and the last thing which he wished to have appear on the surface was any mark of the file. His technique was strictly proportioned to this peculiar method of creation. By a whole series of disciplines, both "natural" and "artificial," he prepared his self for the creation of a novel; then, giving himself a certain loose structure and a set of themes about which to group his memories and feelings, he allowed the book to write itself. Because the fable must never seem as if it were being "composed," because the story must give the air of telling itself, there must always be in the book something which the author did not do—of which, by preference, he seems incapable, and which requires an effort on the part of the reader. If the characters have it always within them to get away from the author, the reader must be more and more intimately involved with them; in effect, the book does not simply play on him as on a passive instrument, but involves his energies in its own completion.

Sometimes the method of Stendhal is perfectly careless of details and meticulous in its concentration on essentials; sometimes quite the contrary. But its first duty is to keep moving, to keep the reader a little off-balance, a little strained; and so to keep the unexpected always within striking distance. The style, then, must be nervous and unlabored, the note of the metronome must never be heard; and the touch must be infinitely variable. A plastic analogy suggests itself. There is a school of novelists who build their characters like a sculptor working in clay; the proceeding is slow, ordered, painstaking, and each little pinch of clay which is added is the product of infinite pains, endless trial and error, enormous consideration. The artist has taken it off, put it back, modified it, looked at it from all the angles; and the reader, at last, sees that it is exactly right. The effect is often magnificent, but it is prepared, and conscious; the author cannot really go wrong—at least, the reader's pleasure derives more from the sureness of his final judgment than from the flair of his original impression. Essentially it is a *built-up* effect.

But one simply cannot paint a water-color as one models a clay statue. There is no place for the second thought, the correction, the reworking. One gets the picture unhesitatingly right the first time, or one does not get it at all. Nothing is sillier than to tell a water-colorist that he must take infinite pains with his picture; there is no quicker way for him to botch it. His infinite pains must all be taken before he touches brush to paper; they lie in the preparation which makes possible his nervous, wiry line, his lucid, unmuddied colors. Once he is started, he cannot stop, correct, or go back; the thing must grow under his hand till it is filled out and finished (finished in the sense that the eye of the viewer finishes it for the painter), without spots which are weak or spots which are labored or spots which don't fit together; the artist must do his whole job and nothing more than his job, and then stop.

It is absurd to call the sculptor inferior because his work is methodically performed; absurd also to call the water-colorist careless because his painting is finished in half an hour. The techniques are simply different; the skills perhaps similar, but, because of the media, differently applied.

Stendhal works in the novel after the manner of a water-colorist, not a sculptor; after the manner of a musician improvising (to extend the analogy), and not after that of an architect. To suggest that he ought to be read carelessly is probably immoral, and "carelessly" is not really the right word. But he ought to be explored with *fougue* if not *emportement*—with an eye which is involved in the passion of the characters, not coldly fixed on the literal details of the story or the way it is being told. This is by no means the equivalent of reading him as one might read a mystery story, to "get to the end" or to "find out what happens." Indeed, it is not incompatible with a degree of comic suspension. Still, the point remains; Stendhal will not make any play for his readers' sympathy, or render that sympathy easy to localize, yet he expects it to be active, to be searching and soaring, subject always to ironical modifications. There is no denying it—Stendhal puts a heavy burden on his readers. They must love the lovable while never losing sight of the odious; they must bear with slovenly details, and no short list of them (see Appendix), while pursuing psychological extravagances of which the author often expresses himself as sceptical. They must avoid the literal state of mind, the pedestrian viewpoint, and understand almost intuitively the dramatic quality of observations which seem to be, and in a sense are, spoken literally. Even Mme. Roland might have been extended to the limit by certain passages in the *Chartreuse*.

Only a sensitive literary amateur can really lend himself to this complicated set of demands, while still retaining the freshness and directness of approach without which one might as well be reading Sir Walter Scott. The novels of Stendhal are not written to fill out certain patterns or achieve certain structural, textural, or verbal relations; they engage a special feeling of free and open possibility which is incompatible with the security of a fixed structure, as it is with the elaborate juxtaposition of ironic *topoi*. Reading the novels of Stendhal is like riding a surfboard—one is not exactly oblivious of the past or the future, but they do not help much to balance the perilous present. The longer one stays on top of the wave, the more exhilarating the triumph; and there is a special climactic thrill about getting all the way in a single unbroken sweep. Afterwards, looking back, there is much to remark about the course one has travelled; and it may even be that the detached and retrospective view is incompatible with the participant one. But "complementary" may be a more useful term and notion than "incompatible." Because many points of view are possible, we can know more things about literature than we can set in logical relations or arrange in a single system. Literary experience which does not fit into systems is "wrong" only if we are more interested in systems than in literature. Stendhal himself was deluded by no such systematic nonsense. "What is the good of writing a novel at all," he once demanded, "if it won't keep a pretty French marquise awake till two o'clock in the morning?" This does not mean that the most frivolous reader is always the best judge of literature; but that mobility and equilibrium are experiences at least as important to the total effect of a novel in the Stendhal vein as pattern and verbal structure. And these qualities are accessible, not to logical analysis, verbal dissection, and the armored machinery of criticism, but to the quick and fluid intuitions of educated feeling.

It seems all too evident that Stendhal did not expect his novels to be studied like theological texts; and while we, as readers, are not bound or limited by his conscious intentions, we are limited by the qualities of the literary work he produced. Because its "precepts" are indefinite and sometimes ambiguous, we may, if we are ruthless, impose almost any sort of reading on the fiction to which literary prejudices, moral principles, or philosophic systems seem to invite us. There is no doubt that by applying to the novels various special critical machineries, we may demonstrate within them various complex verbal or thematic arrangements. But that these are "structural principles" is true only in the very limited degree that they can be shown to contribute to the peculiar effect of the novel. The price of seeing them as primary is often a failure to recognize qualities which are truly distinctive; in the effort to see what is universal and therefore supposedly "basic," one overlooks what is individual.

Stendhal is a particularly challenging and troublesome novelist for the systematic critic because he is perverse. Nature for the physical scientist may be subtle, but she is not malicious; the literary mind is often, like Stendhal's, malicious without being particularly deep. Fluid, erratic, and defensive, his mind is influenced more by the impulse to achieve or avoid certain immediate effects than by a desire for meaning in depth or systematic consistency. His best achievements are miracles of mingled tact, wit, perception, impetus, and equilibrium, not of philosophic profundity or architectural stability. As he was fond of saying himself, we cannot all have the same virtues, nor even all have the same ones; the qualities of a trick-bicycle-rider are not exactly those of a weight-lifter.

How, then, to read Stendhal? First, with a relatively short and therefore highly focussed attention-span. A certain sort of large consistency may well exist within the individual novel, but we would do well to keep it on the edge of our attention, not in the center. There is no irresistible logic which conducts Julien Sorel to the scaffold or Fabrizio del Dongo to the charterhouse. This does not mean that the ending of either novel is illogical; simply that the two heroes are unstable and high-strung young men, placed in extremely fluid circumstances, so that their destiny includes, up to the last minute, numerous alternatives. The novelist does not want or try to make his ending seem inevitable, and his incidents are not tied intimately to the development of his hero's destiny. The fact that the tenor Geronimo turns up in Chapter 23 of Volume I and then in Chapter 23 of Volume II of the *Rouge* means precisely nothing, numerologically or otherwise. If his name makes one think of Saint Jerome or of an Apache chief, these connotations are wrong, and should be rejected equally and immediately. Geronimo does not symbolize anything consistent; he does not form part of any intricate machinery for maneuvering Julien to the scaffold. His two appearances are quite unrelated; they are in fact two episodes in a novel which is partly episodic in nature.

Stendhal's novels are not essentially social, they are strongly tinged with the tradition of the romance. The center of interest is the hero and the various difficulties he encounters in the course of his career. Society is either a proving-ground, on which his various faculties are displayed, or a series of monsters and labyrinths called into existence for the express purpose of baffling his intentions. Thus the reader is not called upon to judge the hero from the outside, in terms of social norms. One gets, from time to time, glances of the hero as society sees him, but ordinarily these are such gross and exterior caricatures that any rapprochement is inconceivable. A one-sided sympathy for the hero largely takes the place of that many-sided judgment which flows out of conversation, compromise, and the circumstances of social adjustment. The inner monologue thus becomes the channel of Stendhal's most important communications; and the reader who wished to penetrate to the novel's heart must pursue the hero's reflections with what can only be called a certain "inwardness." To follow a romance with any interest, one must care whether the hero achieves his quest or fails in it.

But the Stendhal hero is not really on a quest, though "quest" is the conventional terminology of romance, and Stendhal's novels, by their concentration on the adventures of a single hero, must be classified as "romances." Fabrizio and Julien do not really submit themselves to the discipline of an external quest. Even in love the gratifications they seek defy all settled and stable forms, all ultimate repose—their objectives are heroic, individual, and voluntary. In love, too, as in life, they know the pattern before they encounter it, and judge their experience as it lives up to a notion which is already formed, and which there is no question of changing. The Stendhal novel is unique in being a romance of manners, a quest without an ultimate. Certain vague and perhaps contradictory ideals of conduct there are—the sublime, the natural, the unduped, the contemplative —but no notion of a point of rest, a state of mind or body exempt from sudden change. Hence, however strongly the demands of an ideal may be stated, they are always to be understood as provisional.

Finally, under the indefinite heads of indulgence, conspiratorial inwardness, and energy, one touches on three qualities of Stendhal's ideal reader which will get him close to the heart of Beylism. The all-important heroes of the Stendhal novels are vigorous, high-tempered, wilful, and petulant; one feels frequently that they are a little bit spoilt. Perhaps the author feels so too; but he does not treat their fractiousness with any particular disapproval; indeed, their high temper and absurd chivalry shade off into a generally approved area of free energy and heroic decision. If one takes Beyle's heroes with undue solemnity, one misses the fresh impudence of their youthful caracolings and curvettings—the sheer comic delight of Julien's entry into the cafe at Besançon, or of Fabrizio's adventure with Fausta and the Conte M—. This sort of episode is not functional in any moral context; it is essentially a petty adventure in manners, to be viewed with indulgence for the charming little ferocities which the central young person displays. One brings to it some of those feelings which one has for a kitten trying out his claws on a leg the full extent of which he can hardly conceive. For almost everybody else in the novel, there is ethical rigor; settled institutions and people in authority are often attacked with all the crude unfairness of youth, but the heroes have a special advantage, which they scarcely seem to deserve. Like Falstaff, Beyle was much given to murmuring against those who oppress "us youth"; in the novels, he took his revenge, and imposed upon his reader a belief in the natural nobility of Fabrizio and Julien, a nobility so natural that it need not even be exemplified, much less emphasized. The upright reader, who feels himself insidiously led astray by this one-man conspiracy, so reminiscent of that involving the king's new clothes, may of course stand on his self-importance and resist. If he wishes to cry out that the Stendhal hero is a scamp and a scapegrace, the grounds for saying so are made painfully available to him—simply, the author is clearly in agreement with his happy few that something can be seen in Fabrizio and Julien which renders all these conventional moral judgments quite meaningless. The happy few are an invention for surrounding the reader, a sounding-board which makes the price of independent judgment nothing less than priggishness, a silent claque whose secret rapport with the author disarms the reader's doubts and relieves the author of the ugly need for emphasis and explanation. Stendhal's wonderful dry lightness and swiftness of touch is thus sustained by a masking, not of the novelist but of the audience. They must be seen through the image of Mme. Roland; and, being seen through that image, they may, if they want to, learn what it means to look back on life with the eyes of a heroine. The Stendhal audience is always implicitly feminine; there is always an assumption that it is, or can be if it wants, not only "natural" but "natural" in a special dimension, that is, "sublime."

The commitment is special, and is so intended. Old Count Pierre Daru, who had known Beyle well when he was an awkward young clerk in the war office and spelt "cela" with two l's, once had occasion, during the years of his retirement, to look among the booksellers for a volume by Stendhal, probably *Rome, Naples, and Florence*. He was horrified to find that, the edition being sold out and the book hard to come by, he would have to pay thirty francs for a copy.

"What, thirty francs!"

Yes, they told him, and if he did not wish the book at that price, they could easily sell it elsewhere for more. But the old gentleman merely lifted his eyes to the heavens, and repeated, "Thirty francs! Is it possible? That infant—ignorant as a carp!"

Ignorant as a carp; it is one of those absolute, mutual incomprehensions to which Stendhal was given. He tells the story himself, not without a certain pride, as it illustrates how this respectable member of an Academy was at the opposite end of the scale from himself; how they were quite incapable of understanding one another. (M. Daru had had himself elected to the Academy of Inscriptions; one recalls Julien's adversary, who, *though* he was a member of this Academy, knew some Latin.) In the same way Beyle was sure that the natural behavior of lovers in Italy would be perfectly incomprehensible in France, that land of vanity. It is a stock counter of Stendhal's mind; he used to end arguments, Mérimée tells us, by saying brusquely,

"You're a cat and I'm a rat." But more than this—it is quality which strikes us in the Gallic peoples as a whole. Their rationalism is so sharply tempered, so lucid, acute, and many-sided, that one is amazed to find them coming so quickly to the end of it. Their world is full of blank walls, incomprehensions so violent, complete, and sudden that when one comes up against them there is nothing to do but throw chairs, riot in the streets, duel—or shrug one's shoulders. Their rationality quite unmuddied by vulgar pragmatism, the French rest the house of reason on the airy darkness of a passionate mystery, and inhabit it with all the more gaiety because it is totally insecure. With Montaigne, Pascal, and Diderot in his background, with his own volatile, uneasy temperament always in the foreground, Beyle could scarcely fail to feel deeply the fragile, provisional quality of communication. Men do not communicate in order to agree, they must agree in order to communicate—it is a truth of which no novelist in English seems to have been aware down to the ends of his nerves; and it is a corollary of this truth which enables Stendhal to write such airy and assured fiction, to play with his reader so wilfully, and to reward his sympathy so richly.

The writings of Stendhal communicate either more or less fully than the writings of other men because they are more elusive, more demanding, and perhaps more limited. Contrasts with the well-known nineteenth-century novelists are not particularly illuminating here, for the gap is too extravagant. A thoroughly emphatic writer like Dickens is simply at the other end of the scale; his effects are simple but intense, they are emotional and involve extremes of emotional identification. Modern novels which pretend to literary stature are usually less frank about appealing to the backward twelve-year-old who used to be, and still is, the "typical" reader of novels. At their best many of them communicate with a grinding intensity which is visceral, not cerebral; both the urban-nightmare novelists who follow Dostoyevsky and the Southern Gothics who work in the tradition of Poe have profited in this respect by a heavy dosing of D. H. Lawrence. Enormous energy, then, is a hallmark of the modern novel; but it is largely blind energy, which beats (in Faulkner, for example) monotonously against the simple grammatical device of oxymoron or an inherent limitation of the seeing eye. In the novels of Stendhal rationality still plays a large part; their world is in part at least a daytime, a sunlit world, within which the piano music of Mozart can be imagined. From one aspect, this may seem a limiting and old-fashioned cosmos within which to create fiction. The search for special angles of vision has led lately among the fashionable novelists to the exploration of perverts, backward infants, mice, dogs, roaches, morons, idiots, and other planets; while the middle area of experience has been left contemptuously to middle-brow writers.

Stendhal lived in the days before this division was *de rigueur;* hence his commitment, which critics of his own day found so peculiar and special, may seem commonplace or dated today. The nineteenth century thought him hard and mechanical; the twentieth seems ready to condemn him as florid, Byronic, corny. And his orchestration accords with his outlook; it is prevailingly light, not grandiose, funereal, or percussive. He does not batter on the reader's nerves or strive after effects of great intensity. It is dancing prose, short in its rhythms and light on its toes; when Stendhal tries for grandiose effects, as in Julien's last revery, he lengthens the rhythms, relaxes the connectives, and falls back on—Chateaubriand. But we are bound to judge a novelist, above all a pioneering novelist, on his best and most original work. For his own days, his psychological accuracy was Stendhal's most important original contribution, and it is still impressive; without resembling in any particular the somber Germanic brand of depth-psychology, it takes us far into the interior of his characters, and it finds a mirror in the glittering, flexible prose which is dramatically valid just because it refuses ever to stand still. Finally, the quality of gaiety in the face of subjects which are still technically solemn seems to me a permanent source of value in our novelist, of which no defence is either possible or necessary. I am not endorsing here that old hack notion of romanticism, the "lovely illusion which alone makes life worth while," in any of its many variants; but the bubble of gaiety with which the mind delights to escape its own cages, the self-generating systole and diastole of its way with systems.

Men like Pierre Daru are not to be underestimated. His *History of the Venetian Republic* would be a splendid achievement if it were published tomorrow. For the year 1819 and as the work of a man whose primary vocation was action, it represents a heroic adventure in the use of archives and the painstaking collection of original documents. Even if temperament led him to the most stolid and clear-eyed of the Italian republics, M. Daru did a noble job of burrowing out and recording its prosaic and factual history. Yet what he exemplifies, in his writings as in his administrative career, is the professional spirit in its best and narrowest sense—a high degree of mechanical energy, an intense feeling for fact, a capacity for taking the synoptic view of vast social areas. Intellectually as politically, he was a conqueror, who owed his successes to the straightforward principles of hard work, solid, rational thought, and systematic planning.

Now Stendhal the novelist, who represents in this contrast the amateur spirit, clearly hated systems, worked by improvisation and inspiration, and habitually took the short view instead of the long one. His vision of life was truly oblique; it was also inconclusive, unspecialized, and inward. For anyone to whom the distinction seems useful, it might be added that the qualities Stendhal saw in Mme. Roland were distinctively feminine, those which he saw in M. Daru specifically masculine.

Stendhal himself felt that the two attitudes symbolized by Mme. Roland and M. Daru were utterly incompatible. I should not be surprised if this were so, nor at much of a loss as to the critical consequences of such a fact for the reading of the novels. The physicists do not seem to be much disturbed by the circumstance that they cannot observe simultaneously the momentum and the position of an electron. Theologians accept without many qualms the existence of contradictory structures built on the attributes of divine justice and divine love. So there is no cause for deep alarm if it seems necessary to predicate one sort of literary pleasure based on the fulfilling of a pattern and another, or others, based on its disruption, denial, or suspense. Complementarity is a handy notion whenever the available schemes seem on the point of strangling a sizable portion of the facts from which they spring.

But in point of fact, this whole notion places too portentous an estimate on the special qualities of the Stendhal outlook. Though remarkably coherent and fully worked out in him, it has remained almost too personal a commitment to provide any other author with a permanently inhabitable universe. The novel in Stendhal's vein continues to be written; nor is it simply the sort of pastiche which one sometimes suspects M. Jean Giono's *Horseman on the Roof,* and its various sequels, of being. But it is generally a single and more or less isolated undertaking in the career of an author who has other fish to fry. The hero of Camus' *L'Etranger* is as remote from society's comprehension, because of his stolidity and indifference, as Julien Sorel is because of his sensitivity. Like Julien, he murders for no clearly defined reason, and makes no effort to defend himself at his trial. But the larger issues of the two novels are not at all congruent, and the later work of Camus goes in quite a different direction.

Stendhal's influence on Gide was perhaps a little more permanent, no doubt because Gide himself was just as fluid and metamorphic a personality as Stendhal. In *Lafcadio's Adventures*, it is the style, hard, brilliant, poker-faced, and angular, which first suggests the influence; when Lafcadio punctures his thigh with a penknife to punish his own failure of dignity, we are merely confirmed in our memory of Julien, who for two months wore his arm in a sling, out of similar motives. Illegitimacy, indeterminacy, and a conspiracy of hard-minded realists are other common themes. But Gide is blacker and colder in his estimate of human nature than Beyle; and Lafcadio is more delicately and unstably balanced between more extreme alternatives than Julien Sorel. The killing of fat, foolish Fleurissoire is an act of deliberate, meaningless violence, of which only Octave (in Stendhal's fiction) would have been capable; and he would have acted in uncontrollable rage, not idly. In writing this sharp, indolent little Mediterranean burlesque, Gide was as careful as Stendhal to avoid the agglomerative, cumulative manner of story-telling. His observations and insights deliberately cut across the narrative flow at right angles; he is always stopping, fixing, particularizing. In *The Counterfeiters* he undertook to carry the method even further, by having every chapter seem to begin afresh. What one avoids by such a device is the rumble and impetus of a manner, something which epic poems deliberately cultivate. For a style which is nervous, spasmodic, incongruous—anything rather than mechanical—Stendhal seems to be one of the root inspirations. And if one key to this sort of novel seems to lie in the kind of question asked by Croce's criticism—well, even "discredited" critical ideas can sometimes help us to understand and enjoy works of art which were created with those ideas in mind. Whatever the price one pays for "authenticity," the novel in Stendhal's vein is eager to pay it. And on the abstract level, one can't ask a question which leads more directly to the heart of Stendhal's fiction than this, How does it achieve and maintain authenticity?

Particularly for the modern novelist, who often seems to be abjectly helpless between the raw materials of his fiction and the elaborate machinery of criticism, "Beylism" suggests a whole series of resilient resources. We hear much these days of art as a refuge from life, of the timeless, formal relations of the esthetic sphere, in which one finds an alternative to the whirling, aimless activity of history and the will. At the same time, we hear much of the intellectual and emotional bankruptcy of the writer. There is no way of saying that the one condition is responsible for the other; but if it were so, there would be nothing surprising about it. To deprive art of its roots in life, to set it in opposition to life, is to make of it the sort of safe sanctum which anything can become—a religion, a beloved person, *Tristan und Isolde*, or a yard of old flannel. But it is sharply to limit its human possibilities as art, both the quality of the audience's personal involvement with it, and the resources of the artist for variation and fresh discovery. And when the limits of the refuge are reached, then where to find a refuge from the refuge? If nothing better offers, the vindictive Byzantine attitude which makes art a refuge from life can always be had; but, like suicide, as a way of living it is limited. On some terms or other, life ought if it can to provide more for art than a big, blooming, blasting confusion from which paper poetry (like Eliot's) can escape, or in which pulpy prose (like Faulkner's) can wallow, to the sullen heart's content.

The usual palliative for the Schopenhauer view which underlies so much of the twentieth-century hard style, and the new criticism which complements it, is one of the flabbier forms of middle-class optimism. But there is a better alternative, which is simply to say, and to follow out the idea, that a part of life is an art just as much as art formally defined. The self is or can be an artificial creation, not a discovery but a creation, which man is capable of directing, controlling, and adapting to the ends he selects for himself. "Beylism" is the art of creating a man named Beyle, who shall in turn be capable of creating men named Julien Sorel and Fabrizio del Dongo. And the self thus created is not dead, formal, and static; it includes resources of experience, dramatic stratagems, and caves of memory. It includes, that is, processes for searching out fresh reality-forms, for structuring them, and for recovering and transforming them.

One result of such a view is an immediate conflict between the individual and society which is practically hopeless, but pathetic only if one accepts a practical standard of measurement. As against this depressing alternative, all the rich comic resources of the private fantasy are at our disposal, all the tricks and duplicities of the identity which we form after a shadow of ourselves, and follow without fully believing, all the magnificent affinities which accident and mutual wilful delusion put within our power. Verbal pattern and elaborate lapidary metaphorical structure, which in much modern fiction have usurped over character, incident, and all but the most attenuated or primitive forms of feeling, might, under such a dispensation, be reduced once more to a subordinate role. And the unexpected, the divine human unexpected, might find its way back into our fiction. I yield to no-one in my admiration for Mr. Faulkner; but a Snopes is a Snopes is a Snopes. The innumerable fictional offspring of *Madame Bovary* include some of our most memorable heroines—but grinding inexorability need grind no further. Perhaps the most enchanting byplay to which the comic improvised style invites is that connected with the problem of personal identity. To have an individual identity at all is a sort of achievement these days; to lose it, as can so easily happen, is a misfortune brilliantly iridescent with comic implications; and to make mistakes in the matter of one's own or someone else's identity is to open the way for all sorts of observations—tender, ironic, and satiric—on human conduct. It is a rare but wonderful fiction which can balance between the

systematic cruelty of society and the depth of instinct without
sounding the plaintive note—a fiction which, in the teeth of
opposed inevitabilities, somehow remains resilient and unfore-
seeable. As a formula, clearly this prescription is no more
valuable than formulas usually are; the sort of example set by
M. Roger Vailland's *La Loi* may lend it flesh and substance.
Fiction so dry of tone, so sharply angled, and so deeply involving is but one aspect of the Stendhalian heritage, though
its melodrama tinctured with irony is markedly and immediately
identifiable. But there are an infinity of different shadings to
the mystique of Beyle, each tolerant of as many transformations as Proteus himself could give it. Only the ceremonial
sequence of alienation, involvement, transformation, and conformity as ironic revenge mark a root-inspiration.

In the end, the acts of creating a self and imposing it on the
world (even in the artifice of fiction) rest on a passionate
mystery, a submergence of one set of givens in favor of another.
If the grain does not die, it can never live; this is not a glib
truism but a profound and active experience of the soul. We
are familiar with something like this experience from the exercise of extreme duty-motivations, when a man becomes transfigured by and identified with an abstract idea. We are familiar
with its happening as a deed of the total personality in great
acts of intellectual conversion. We have seen it as the finding
of a vocation, long sought and abruptly grasped; and it has been
seen in the sudden changes of style, subject, and emotional
polarization which enable us to talk of the "periods" of an
artist. But as a social and intellectual skill, consciously developed, setting a man at a distance from "himself" and the
accidents of his existence, and flowering finally into that supreme
artifice which has its own claim to truth, it has not often been
achieved since the Renaissance. Least of all has it been exploited in freedom from the mantic or shaman-personality,
dear to Yeats as to Milton, exploited for its comic or Stoic

possibilities. Yet if the French soul, that gallant tangle of contradictory clarities, has a contribution to make to Western life, surely it is more through the artificial tragic gaiety of Mme. Roland and the Baron Stendhal than through the genuine stolidity of M. Daru.

Even if we discover (perhaps want) no new Beyle, the old one is a permanent resource of the human spirit; we return to him to rejoice in a free, fine energy, uncompelled, intelligent, gay. His men and women can concentrate their energies in fierce, impulsive actions, expand their sensibilities in isolated revery, agonize over the oddities of their own disobedient hearts, and create, by the unerring impulses of their new-made selves, gigantic self-images for their own delight and guidance. Like delightful people anywhere, their companionship is its own reward. Even if we cannot be Madame Roland, to appreciate them fully, there must be someone between Saint Simeon Stylites and Benjamin Franklin to model ourselves on. If Stendhal has, in the end, nothing for us but nostalgia, so much the worse for us. Like his favorite Italians, he can afford to look on us and say, *"Je suis comme moi; tant mieux pour vous."*

9

*

Conclusion

La duchesse de la Ferté disait à Mme. de Staal: "Il faut l'avouer, ma chère amie, je ne trouve que moi qui aie toujours raison."

Histoire de la Peinture, I, 326

Love was his favorite theme; yet it was his fate to be thought, during his lifetime, an impenetrable man. What made him particularly liable to this misunderstanding was the experience of his friends; if Mérimée, a fairly threadbare article himself, treated Beyle as a buffoon and a Falstaff, how should an outsider suspect that pure and innocent spirit, that yearning for sympathy and chivalric impatience for heroism, which we now think typically Stendhal? Of course it was just because Mérimée was the man he was that he saw only the Stendhal he did.

The sardonic defender triumphed, then; and, all things considered, it was probably better so. For one special quality of the Stendhal theater is based on incomprehension and isolation. This is not only a quality of his characters; it lies at the root of many of his stylistic gyrations. The multi-directioned irony which comes ultimately to have a kind of lyrical, affirmative quality; the *tendresse* which is all the more moving because it is immured behind bristling walls of adolescent theory and pre-adolescent shyness—these are the qualities which intoxicate the fully committed Beyliste. The devotion of such a reader knows no limits because it finds or creates transparencies wherever they are necessary. One of Stendhal's typical devices is to provoke disagreement and dislike aggressively and on purpose; but the devotee knows that he does this only out of timidity, from fear of provoking disagreement and dislike in his own person, *naturally*.

His deepest impulse is to follow a private dream (*"chevaucher l'hippogriffe,"* in Martineau's fine phrase); that dream is unfailingly exalted, affectionate, sympathetic. Julien Sorel at his most provocative is an artificial Tartufe fallen into a world of instinctive Tartufes. In one sense, his sin is blacker than theirs, for he wilfully denies a light they cannot see. Yet the essence of his character is elevation. This is true of all the Stendhal heroes, as it was true of Beyle himself. Of young Fabrizio it is said that "everything is simple in his eyes because everything is seen from above." The action of the novel is to lower and complicate his vision. Yet though the central theme is initiation and its ultimate discovery vanity, this is the least despondent of fictions. Metaphorically, at least, the truncated, inconsequent ending is functional; Fabrizio simply modulates his primitive hauteur completely out of narrative range. It is instinctive hauteur which elevates the Stendhal manner above a burlesque or a vaudeville; it is the effect of seeing him on a plain level (of involving him in some system or other) to reduce him to a burlesque.

Fashionable machineries lately have been psychological and political. The sort of man who found Ibsen degenerate and

Dreiser immoral has made his appearance against Stendhal as well; but on the whole, Beyle has had more to suffer from well-intentioned friends than from overt enemies. Masochism and infantile regression are invoked to account for his timidity; compensatory sadistic fantasies take care of all the contrary evidences. The explanation might serve biographical purposes far better than it does without atoning for that dreadful rigidity and uni-directional symmetry which silently reduce an artist to a symptom. The Conte Mosca's jealous fit is as fine a set piece on jealousy as one will see till Swann is brought forth to suffer for Odette. But to label the whole imaginative episode "masochism" is to take it from a fluid pattern and freeze it in a fixed one; it is to impose on both Mosca and Stendhal a kind of clarity which both have done their best not to deserve.

In politics, there seems to be no category which corresponds to Stendhal's vagaries more accurately than that of the "spoilt radical." It is an irresponsible, inconsistent, eclectic position—aristocratic and popular, enthusiastic and cynical, contemptuous of privilege and of anti-privilege, the politics of a man who has wilfully constituted himself a party of one. He is conservative in his tastes, radical in his theories, and anarchist in his actions. His one unswerving principle is devotion to himself.

Like his characters, like his ideas, like his books, Stendhal is a penumbra of deliberate mystery shading off into a brilliance of contradictory clarities. At the heart of things there is always a darkness. In practical terms, his redeeming hauteur is as fraudulent as the barony he bestowed on himself. But in a world where all marks of distinction are on the market, the fake-aristocrat is often more genuine than the real. His hauteur has an artistic function, it gives him an outlook from which he can accomplish something better than snubbing parvenus. The genuine aristocrat is one whose ancestors have been associated with a piece of land for some centuries; the fake-aristocrat is a creature of air and impulse, who gives nobility to a spot chosen at random instead of accepting it meekly from the hands of others. The very name by which we know Stendhal is arbitrary, meaningless, and unexplained. "Stendhal" is a little town on the road from Hanover to Berlin; ancient capital of the old Margrave of Brandenburg, birthplace of Winckelmann the art-historian, and site of a minor skirmish won by General Michaud (1 April, 1809). But as the name of a novelist it is a perfect blank—all the more so in that there was a real Baron Stendhal, a Swede, living in London while Beyle usurped his name. Many of Stendhal's fictional names, like many of his pseudo-nyms, have a distinct meaning, or at least implication; many have a biographical context.* But the most important mask he ever assumed Stendhal made perfectly impervious. This quality he would doubtless have called "jesuit"; it is also perfectly *dandy*. His existence is that of a mirror, polished, impassive, per-ilous; lacking any of these qualities, would it have the dramatic interest it does? The soul of the Stendhal hero bears to his self the same relation that the Baron Stendhal bears to Beyle—they are aerial plants, fragile, predatory, exotic.

He spent his life contemplating no more than half-a-dozen basic ideas, and searching to the bottom of them. Yet he is impossible to catch in the nets of an easy consistency. The subtlest efforts yet made to analyze his double vision create at least as many consistencies as they discover, and ignore an equal number of inconsistencies. It is so patently silly to pin his heroes down to archetypal originals that no-one has even tried. Generally, the less elaborate one's theory of literary value, the

---

* There are, for instance, definite originals for the Abbé Chélan, Mme. Derville, and Gros the mathematician, of the *Rouge*; at a somewhat greater remove, Mocenigo, the name of a senatorial family in Venice, comes to stand in Stendhal's mind for a whole world of patrician pleasure and lux-ury; and finally, there are almost capricious transformations and transposi-tions over great spaces—e.g., Captain Burelvillers, who escorted young Beyle on his first journey across the Alps, turns up in *Lucien Leuwen* as the name of a forest near Nancy.

less abstract one's concept of psychological or social behavior, the better one's chances of adapting fully to the fiction. His books were not written to satisfy critical theories; they do not yield their full secrets to anyone armed with a single set of criteria. They are true primarily to a structure of sentiment and character which is always peculiar to him but sometimes analogous to us. Beyond this, they extend a frank yet challenging glance at the individual reader; at their best, they are not passive experiences, but a summons to self-definition.

There is something perverse, no doubt, in a critic who rejoices that "his" author has eluded critical categories—including his own. But the ground of this feeling is simply a limited, and rather old-fashioned, devotion to inclusiveness as a literary virtue in itself. There is more to life than can be captured in logical or even in literary structures; there is more to literature than can be captured in critical concepts. Literature is a series of slashing individual raids on the inarticulate; it is also a series of ordered structures for the thoughts and feelings of men. The Baron Stendhal was something of a housebuilder, but more of a hussar; one who ranged widely, slept rough, and watched late to bring back from the frontiers of feeling a *petit fait vrai*. His discoveries are sometimes disturbing, and disturbers of the public repose are not often thanked; but for those who have grown used to his wayward, irregular orbits, there is no equivalent to this complex and subtle spirit. He filled the opera house of his own personality with such melody that we shall never be done discussing him.

Appendix

Some of the major slips, inconsistencies, oversights, and verbal faults in Stendhal's two major novels are listed herewith:

THE RED AND THE BLACK

Within II, 1, Saint-Giraud changes his views, from having no politics to being a confirmed jacobin, and exchanges occupations with Falcoz the printer.

In I, 6, Julien is not yet 19; in II, 33, he says "I am 22"; even allowing him a year in the seminary and a year in Paris (II, 28), we are still short of the 36 months necessary to take him from an advanced 18 to a scant 22.

The ballet of *Manon Lescaut* (II, 28) was given for the first time on May 5, 1830; how can Julien exchange a dozen or more letters with Madame de Fervaques, be reconciled with Mathilde, get her pregnant, confess to M. de la Mole, report to his regiment, commit his crime, spend time (as much as two months) in prison, and be executed before the July revolution takes place?

"Nonante-cinq" in I, 23 is a word peculiar to 1830, in allusion to M. de Merindol, a Marseilles magistrate, who used the expression and was ridiculed for it; and I, 22 calls itself "Ways of Behaving in 1830." How can Julien be at Valenod's in 1830, at the age of 19, and then—after spending at least a year in a seminary and a year or more in Paris, so that he can be 22 years old in II, 33—find that the year is still 1830, *Hernani* is still being discussed, and *Manon Lescaut* has just been given as a ballet?

Norbert is said to be 19 in II, 1; in II, 3, 8, and 10, Mathilde is 19.

In II, 1, the execution of Boniface de la Mole is dated 26 April, 1574; in II, 10, it is dated 30 April, 1574.

In successive paragraphs of II, 23, Julien delivers his message to a Duke and a Prince; for other inconsistencies in the "Note Secrète" chapters, see pp. 109-113 above.

On successive pages in II, 19, confession and suicide are said to be like an ice-cold drink of water in the middle of the desert.

Having told the Marquis de la Mole the story of Julien Sorel in I, 29, the Abbé Pirard is amazed that the Marquis knows Julien's name in I, 30.

Mme. de Rênal's cousin at Naples is M. le Chevalier de Beauvais or the Signor de Beauvaisis in I, 23; but in II, 6, M. Charles de Beauvoisis occurs to Julien as possibly being the same man.

THE CHARTERHOUSE OF PARMA

In the year 1815, Fabrizio is advised that he may read the novels of Sir Walter Scott, the first of which came out anonymously in

1814 (Chapter V). In the year 1822, the Duchessa Sanseverina has been reading the *History of Louis XIII* by M. Bazin, which was not published till 1837 (Chapter 24).

A road running southward from Parma cannot possibly lead to Sacca and the Po, which lie to the north.

In 1815, when he first meets Gina, Conte Mosca is 45 and she is 31; in 1821, when Fabrizio is arrested, she is an arithmetically correct 37, but he is an inexplicable 56 (Chapter 17).

In Chapter 12 and 13 Stendhal twice explains the term *bulo*.

In Chapter 15, Fabrizio thinks of General Conti as a "nice Jesuit" when he feigns indignation over the handcuffs; but nothing elsewhere in the book is consistent with this view of the Jesuits on Fabrizio's part; in fact, he is shown to be a perfect product of Jesuit education.

See above, p. 84, for the inexplicable appearance and disappearance of the first wife of Conte Mosca.